T0324987

Semantic Web-Based Information Systems:
State-of-the-Art Applications

Amit Sheth
University of Georgia, USA

Miltiadis Lytras
University of Patras, Greece

Cybertech Publishing
Hershey • London • Melbourne • Singapore

Acquisitions Editor:	Kristin Klinger
Development Editor:	Kristin Roth
Senior Managing Editor:	Jennifer Neidig
Managing Editor:	Sara Reed
Assistant Managing Editor:	Sharon Berger
Typesetter:	Jennifer Neidig
Cover Design:	Lisa Tosheff
Printed at:	Yurchak Printing Inc.

Published in the United States of America by
    CyberTech Publishing (an imprint of Idea Group Inc.)
    701 E. Chocolate Avenue
    Hershey PA 17033
    Tel: 717-533-8845
    Fax: 717-533-8661
    E-mail: cust@idea-group.com
    Web site: http://www.cybertech-pub.com

and in the United Kingdom by
    CyberTech Publishing (an imprint of Idea Group Inc.)
    3 Henrietta Street
    Covent Garden
    London WC2E 8LU
    Tel: 44 20 7240 0856
    Fax: 44 20 7379 0609
    Web site: http://www.eurospanonline.com

Library of Congress Cataloging-in-Publication Data

Semantic Web-based information systems : state-of-the-art applications / Amit Sheth and Miltiadis Lytras, editors.
    p. cm.
 Summary: "This book covers new semantic Web enabled tools for the citizen, learner, organization, and business. Real-world applications in development of the knowledge society and semantic Web issues, challenges and implications in each of the IS research streams are included as viable sources"--Provided by publisher.
 Includes bibliographical references and index.
 ISBN 1-59904-426-9 (hardcover) -- ISBN 1-59904-427-7 (softcover) -- ISBN 1-59904-428-5 (ebook)
 1. Semantic Web. 2. Online information services. I. Sheth, A. (Amit), 1959- II. Lytras, Miltiadis D., 1973-
QA76.55.S46 2007
025.04--dc22
                  2006031349

British Cataloguing in Publication Data
A Cataloguing in Publication record for this book is available from the British Library.

Semantic Web-Based Information Systems:
State-of-the-Art Applications

Table of Contents

Section II: Frameworks and Methodologies

Section III: Techniques and Tools

Preface

Importance of semantics has been recognized in different areas of data and information management, including better access, exchange, interoperability, integration and analysis of data. Semantics of data is about associating meaning to data, and understand what data represents, and improve the value of data. Early use of semantics in the context of data and information management occurred in the context of development of multidatabase or federated database systems, to be followed by mediator and information brokering architectures. As the Web started to take the shape as a global information system and as a way to connect distributed data repositories, usage of metadata and semantics correspondingly started in early 1990s and increased there after. The first use of the term "semantic information brokering" in 1993 conceived the use of semantics in the form of domain models and ontologies for heterogeneous data integration, and about the same time, ontology-based information integration was proposed in some mediator based projects. In the last two chapters of his book *Weaving the Web* (Harper, 1997), Tim Berners-Lee started to put forth a vision of the next phase of the Web in which semantics would play a critical role, and the term Semantic Web was coined. Research community, first supported by the DARPA's DAML program (for which Jim Handler was the program manager) quickly saw the new research opportunity. This book contributes to the revolutionary domain of Semantic Web and information systems in four following aspects, namely, vision, methodologies, tools and applications.

Section I: Vision

The first two chapters of the book present a vision, a provocative or an alternate view, and/or a counter-point.

The first chapter "Semantics for the Semantic Web: The Implicit, the Formal, and the Powerful," by Sheth, Ramakrishnan, and Thomas, takes the expansive view of the semantics in the Semantic Web. Considering the role of semantics in a number of research areas of computer science and beyond, this chapter explores the broad role of semantics and different types of semantics in various capabilities that would define and build the Semantic Web. The central message of this chapter is that building the Semantic Web purely on description logics (and to limit knowledge representation on ontology representation language to description logics) would artificially limit its potential. It argues that we will need to exploit well known techniques that support implicit semantics, as done in information retrieval and text analytics, and develop more powerful representation that can model probabilistic and fuzzy information needed to capture incomplete, inconsistent and uncertain nature of information and knowledge.

The second chapter "The Human Semantic Web: Shifting from Knowledge Push to Knowledge Pull," by Naeve, provides an interesting counterpoint to the usual emphasis on machine-understandable (usually formal) semantics in the Semantic Web. It discusses a conceptual interface, providing human-understandable semantics. Correspondingly, the human Semantic Web is described as a "space for interaction," with three levels of semantic interoperability: isolation, coexistence, and collaboration.

Section II: Frameworks and Methodologies

This section of the book deals with architectural frameworks and methodological issues in building the Semantic Web.

Chapter III titled "General Adaptation Framework: Enabling Interoperability for Industrial Web Resources" by Kaykova et al. focuses on interoperability of smart industrial resources. The objective of this work is to develop an architecture, where distributed human experts and learning Web-services are utilized by various devices for self-monitoring and self-diagnostics. One aspect of the technical approach is the resource state/condition description framework (RSCDF), which with contextual and temporal extensions to RDF, is argued to facilitate adoption of the Semantic Web technology industrial adoption.

The fourth chapter titled "A Survey on Ontology Creation Methodologies" by Cristani and Cuel is a survey presenting the state of the art of a rapidly evolving field. The key value-add of this survey is in the form of offering a systematic analysis of current approaches in developing domain ontologies that can be used to understand the inspiring motivation, the applicability context, and the structure of the approaches. The chapter also presents a classification identifying bottom-up and top-down methodologies that are claimed to be useful both from theoretical and deployment practice perspectives.

Section III: Techniques and Tools

In this section we introduce some of major techniques and tools developed in the domain of ontology building and analysis and Semantic Web.

Chapter V, "A Tool for Working with Web Ontologies," by Kalyanpur, Parsia, and Hendler, presents a tool (SWOOP) for building, modifying and searching ontologies. SWOOP is a stand alone application program to work with OWL ontologies. The authors discuss some insights into Web ontologies that were gained through the experience with SWOOP, including issues related to display, navigation, editing and collaborative annotation of OWL ontologies.

Chapter VI, "An Ontology-Based Multimedia Annotator for the Semantic Web of Language Engineering," by Chebotko, Deng, Lu, Fotouhi, and Aristar, present an ontology-bases linguistic multimedia annotation tool called OntoELAN. The tool features:

- The support for OWL ontologies
- The management of language profiles that allow the user to choose a subset of ontological term for annotation
- The management of ontological tires that can be annotated by language profile terms and therefore, corresponding ontological terms
- Storing OntoELAN annotation documents in XML format based on multimedia and domain ontologies

Chapter VII titled "A Layered Model for Building Ontology Translation Systems," authored by Corcho and Gómez-Pérez, presents a model for building ontology translation systems between ontology languages and/or ontology tools.

Although there is a growing literature on ontology translation (and significant earlier literature on related topics of schema mapping and translation), the broader perspective of this chapter comes from considering four different layers: lexical, syntax, semantic, and pragmatic. This issue also proposes a method that guides in the process of developing ontology translation systems based on four main activities: feasibility study, analysis of source and target formats, design, and implementation of the translation system, and recommends the techniques to be used inside each of them.

Chapter VIII, by Bry et al., is titled "Querying the Web Reconsidered: Design Principles for Versatile Web Query Languages." In this chapter the authors provide a milestone based on an experience with research, standardized query languages for the conventional Web, and the emerging query languages for the Semantic Web. They offer a reconsideration of design principles for Web and Semantic Web query languages. They present features of "versatile query languages that can cope up markups and representations used for traditional Web and Semantic Web. One key aspect they argue for is the support for incomplete data specifications ("incomplete queries") and incomplete data selections ("incomplete answers").

Section IV: Applications

This section of the book deal with applications of Semantic Web. Among the areas where we see more significant activities include health care, life sciences, and government. Consequently, majority of the chapters deal with health care.

Chapter IX and the first chapter in the application part of this book is by Singh, Iyer, and Salam, on "Semantic E-Business" which is defined as "an approach to managing knowledge for coordination of e-business processes through the systematic application of Semantic Web technologies." This chapter discusses the application of Semantic Web technologies to improve the current state of the art in the transparency of e-business processes. Applications discussed include supply chain management, e-marketplace, healthcare and e-government.

Chapter X titled "A Distributed Patient Identification Protocol Based on Control Numbers with Semantic Annotation" by Eichelberg, Aden, and Thoben describes a protocol that allows one to locate patient records for a given patient in a distributed environment without the need to keep a master patient index. The protocol combines cryptographic techniques with semantic annotation and mediation, and presents a simple, Web-Service-based access to clinical documents.

Chapter X by Shabo and Hughes addresses the "Family History Information Exchange Services Using HL7 Clinical Genomics Standard Specifications." The future vision of the article is the use of these services based on health standards over the Web such that various family history specialized applications will be able to use them to seamlessly exchange family history data.

Chapter XII, the final chapter titled "Archetype-Based Semantic Interoperability of Web Service Messages in the Health Care Domain" by Bicer, Kilic, Dogac, and Laleci, addresses how to semantically annotate Web service messages through archetypes in order to provide Web service-based semantic interoperability in the health care domain. For this purpose, the Web service messages are annotated with OWL representation of the archetypes, and by providing the ontology mapping between the archetypes through an OWL ontology mapping tool called OWLmt, the interoperability of the Web service message instances are achieved.

Section I

Vision

Chapter I

Semantics for the Semantic Web:
The Implicit, the Formal, and the Powerful

Amit Sheth, University of Georgia, USA

Cartic Ramakrishnan, University of Georgia, USA

Christopher Thomas, University of Georgia, USA

Abstract

Enabling applications that exploit heterogeneous data in the Semantic Web will require us to harness a broad variety of semantics. Considering the role of semantics in a number of research areas in computer science, we organize semantics in three forms — implicit, formal, and powerful — and explore their roles in enabling some of the key capabilities related to the Semantic Web. The central message of this article is that building the Semantic Web purely on description logics will artificially limit its potential, and that we will need to both exploit well-known techniques that support implicit semantics, and develop more powerful semantic techniques.

Introduction

Semantics has been a part of several scientific disciplines, both in the realm of computer science and outside of it. Research areas such as information retrieval (IR), information extraction (IE), computational linguistics (CL), knowledge representation (KR), artificial intelligence (AI), and data(base) management (DB) have all addressed issues pertaining to semantics in their own ways. Most of these areas have very different views of what "meaning" is, and these views are all built on some meta-theoretical and epistemological assumptions. These different views imply very different views of cognition, of concepts, and of meaning (Hjorland, 1998). In this chapter, we organize these different views to three forms of semantics: implicit, formal, and powerful (a.k.a. soft). We use these forms to explore the role of semantics that go beyond the narrower interpretation of the Semantic Web (that involve adherence to contemporary Semantic Web standards) and encompass those required for a broad variety of semantic applications. We advocate that for the Semantic Web (SW) to be realized, we must harness the power of a broad variety of semantics encompassing all three forms.

IR, IE, and CL techniques primarily draw upon analysis of unstructured texts in addition to document repositories that have a loosely defined and less formal structure. In these sorts of data sources, the semantics are implicit.

In the fields of KR, AI, and DB, however, the data representation takes a more formal and/or rigid form. Well-defined syntactic structures are used to represent information or knowledge where these structures have definite semantic interpretations associated with them. There are also definite rules of syntax that govern the ways in which syntactic structures can be combined to represent the meaning of complex syntactic structures. In other words, techniques used in these fields rely on formal semantics.

Usually, efforts related to formal semantics have involved limiting expressiveness to allow for acceptable computational characteristics. Since most KR mechanisms and the relational data model are based on set theory, the ability to represent and utilize knowledge that is imprecise, uncertain, partially true, and approximate is lacking, at least in the base/standard models. However, there have been several efforts to extend the base models (e.g., Barbara, Garcia-Molina, & Porter, 1992). Representing and utilizing these types of more powerful knowledge is, in our opinion, critical to the success of the Semantic Web. Soft computing has explored these types of powerful semantics. We deem these powerful (soft) semantics as distinguished, albeit not distinct from or orthogonal to formal and implicit semantics.

More recently, semantics has been driving the next generation of the Web as the Semantic Web, where the focus is on the role of semantics for automated approaches to exploiting Web resources. This involves two well-recognized, critical enabling capabilities — ontology generation (Maedche & Staab, 2001; Omelayenko, 2001) and automated resource annotation (Hammond, Sheth, & Kochut, 2002; Dill et al., 2003; Handschuh, Staab, & Ciravegna, 2002; Patil, Oundhakar, Sheth, & Verma, 2004), which should be complemented by an appropriate computational approach such as reasoning or query processing. We use a couple of such enabling capabilities to explore the role and importance of all three forms of semantics.

A majority of the attention in the Semantic Web has been centered on a logic-based approach, more specifically that of description logic. However, looking at past applications of semantics, it is very likely that more will be expected from the Semantic Web than what the careful compromise of expressiveness and computability represented by description logic and the W3C adopted ontology representation language OWL (even its three flavors) can support. Supporting expressiveness that meet requirements of practical applications and the techniques that support their development is crucial. It is not desirable to limit the Semantic Web to one type of representation where expressiveness has been compromised at the expense of computational property such as decidability.

This chapter is not the first to make this above observation. We specifically identify a few. Uschold (2003) has discussed a semantic continuum involving informal to formal and implicit to explicit, and Gruber (2003) has talked about informal, semi-formal, and formal ontologies. The way we use the term implicit semantics, however, is different compared to Uschold (2003) insofar as we see implicit semantics in all kinds of data sets, not only in language. We assume that machines can analyze implicit semantics with several, mostly statistical, techniques. Woods has written extensively regarding the limitations of first-order logics (FOLs) — and hence description logics, or DLs — in the context of natural language understanding, although limitations emanating from rigidness and limitation of expressive power, as well as limited value reasoning supported in DLs, can also be identified:

Over time, many people have responded to the need for increased rigor in knowledge representation by turning to first-order logic as a semantic criterion. This is distressing, since it is already clear that first-order logic is insufficient to deal with many semantic problems inherent in understanding natural language as well as the semantic requirements of a reasoning system for an intelligent agent using knowledge to interact with the world. (Woods, 2004)

We also recall Zadeh's long-standing work (such as Zadeh, 2002), in which he extensively discussed the need for what constitutes a key part of the "powerful semantics" here. In essence, we hope to provide an integrated and complementary view on the range of options. One may ask what the uses of each of these types of semantics are in the context of the Semantic Web. Here is a quick take.

- Implicit semantics is either largely present in most resources on the Web or can easily (quickly) be extracted. Hence mining and learning algorithms applied to these resources can be utilized to extract structured knowledge or enrich existing structured formal representations. Since formal semantics intrinsically does not exist, implicit semantics is useful in processing data sets or corpus to obtain or bootstrap semantics that can be then represented in formal languages, potentially with human involvement.

- Formal semantics in the form of ontologies is relatively scarce, but representation mechanisms with such semantics have definite semantic interpretations that make them more machine-processable. Representation mechanisms with formal semantics therefore afford applications the luxury of automated reasoning, making the applications more intelligent.

- Powerful (soft) semantics in the form of fuzzy or probabilistic KR mechanisms attempt to overcome the shortcomings of the rigid set-based interpretations associated with currently prevalent representation mechanisms by allowing for representation of degree of membership and degree of certainty. Some of the domain knowledge human experts possess is intrinsically complex, and may require these more expressive representations and associated computational techniques.

These uses are further exemplified later on using Semantic Web applications as driving examples. In the next section we define and describe implicit, formal and powerful (soft) semantics.

Types of Semantics

In this section we give an overview of the three types of semantics mentioned. It is rather informal in nature, as we only give a broad overview without getting in depth about the various formalisms or methods used. We assume that the reader is somewhat familiar with statistical methods on the one hand and description logics/OWL on the other. We present a view of these methods in order to lead towards the necessity of powerful (soft) semantics.

Implicit Semantics

This type of semantics refers to the kind that is implicit from the patterns in data and that is not represented explicitly in any strict machine processable syntax. Examples of this sort of semantics are the kind implied in the following scenarios:

- Co-occurrence of documents or terms in the same cluster after a clustering process based on some similarity measure is completed.

- A document linked to another document via a hyperlink, potentially associating semantic metadata describing the concepts that relate the two documents.

- The sort of semantics implied by two documents belonging to categories that are siblings of each other in a concept hierarchy.

- Automatic classification of a document to broadly indicate what a document is about with respect to a chosen taxonomy. Further, use the implied semantics to disambiguate (does the word "palm" in a document refer to a palm tree, the palm of your hand, or a palm-top computer?).

- Bioinformatics applications that exploit patterns like sequence alignment, secondary and tertiary protein structure analysis, and so forth.

One may argue that although there is no strict syntactic and explicit representation, the knowledge about patterns in data may yet be machine processable. For instance, it is possible to get a numeric similarity judgment between documents in a corpus. Although this is possible, this is the only sort of processing possible. It is not possible to look at documents and automatically infer the presence of a named relationship between concepts in the documents.

Even though the exploitation of implicit semantics draws upon well-known statistical techniques, the wording is not a mere euphemism, but meant to give a different perception of the problem.

Many tools and applications for implicit semantics have been developed for decades and are readily available. Basically all machine learning exploits implicit semantics, namely clustering, concept and rule learning, hidden Markov models, Artificial Neural Networks, and others. These techniques supporting implicit semantics are found in early steps towards the Semantic Web, such as clustering in the Vivisimo search engine, as well as in early Semantic Web products, such as metadata extraction on Web fountain technology (Dill et al., 2003), automatic classification, and automatic metadata extraction in Semagix Freedom (Sheth et al., 2002).

Formal Semantics

Humans communicate mostly through language. Natural language, however, is inherently ambiguous — semantically, but also syntactically. Computers lack the ability to disambiguate and understand complex natural language. For these reasons, it is infeasible to use natural language as a means for machines to communicate with other machines. As a first step, statements or facts need to be expressed in a way that computers can process them. Semantics that are represented in some well-formed syntactic form (governed by syntax rules) is referred to as formal semantics. There are some necessary and sufficient features that make a language formal and by association their semantics formal. These features include:

- **The notions of model and model theoretic semantics:** Expressions in a formal language are interpreted in models. The structure common to all models in which a given language is interpreted (the model structure for the model-theoretic interpretation of the given language) reflects certain basic presuppositions about the "structure of the world" that are implicit in the language.

- **The principle of compositionality:** The meaning of an expression is a function of the meanings of its parts and of the way they are syntactically combined. In other words, the semantics of an expression is computed using the semantics of its parts, obtained using an interpretation function.

From a less technical perspective, formal semantics means machine-processable semantics where the formal language representing the semantics has the above-mentioned features. Basically, the semantics of a statement are unambiguously expressed in the syntax of the statement in the formal language. A very limited subset of natural language is thus made available for computer processing. Examples of such semantics are:

- The semantics of subsumption in description logics, reflecting the human tendency of categorizing by means of broader or narrower descriptions.

- The semantics of partonomy, accounting for what is part of an object, not which category the object belongs to.

Description Logics

Recently, description logics have been the dominant formalisms for knowledge representation. Although DLs have gained substantial popularity, there are some fundamental properties of DLs that can be seen as drawbacks when viewed in the context of the Semantic Web and its future. The formal semantics of DLs is based on set theory. A concept in description logics is interpreted as a set of things that share one required common feature. Relationships between concepts or roles are interpreted as a subset of the cross-product of the domain of interpretation. This leaves no scope for the representation of degrees of concept membership or uncertainty associated with concept membership.

DL-based representation and reasoning for both schema and instance data is being applied in Network Inference's Cerebra product for such problems as data integration. This product uses a highly optimized tableaux algorithm to speed up ABox reasoning, which was the bane of description logics. Although a favorable trade-off between computational complexity and expressive power has been achieved, there is still the fundamental issue of the inability of DLs to allow for representation of fuzzy and probabilistic knowledge.

Powerful (Soft) Semantics

The statistical analysis of data allows the exploration of relationships that are not explicitly stated. Statistical techniques give us great insight into a corpus of documents or a large collection of data in general, when a program exists that can actually "pose the right questions to the data," that is, analyze the data according to our needs. All derived relationships are statistical in nature, and we only have an idea or a likelihood of their validity.

The above-mentioned formal knowledge representation techniques give us certainty that the derived knowledge is correct, provided the explicitly stated knowledge was correct in the first place. Deduction is truth preserving. Another positive aspect of a formal representation is its universal usability. Every system that adheres to a certain representation of knowledge will understand, and a well-founded formal semantics guarantees that the expressed statements are interpreted the same way on every system. The restriction of expressiveness to a subset of FOL also allows the system to verify the consistency of its knowledge.

But here also lies the crux of this approach. Even though it is desirable to have a consistent knowledge base, it becomes impractical as the size of the knowledge base increases or as knowledge from many sources is added. It is rare that human experts in most scientific domains have a full and complete agreement. In these cases it becomes more desirable that the system can deal with inconsistencies.

Sometimes it is useful to look at a knowledge base as a map. This map can be partitioned according to different criteria, for example, the source of the facts or their domain. While on such a map the knowledge is usually locally consistent, it is almost impossible and practically infeasible to maintain a global consistency. Experience in developing the Cyc ontology demonstrated this challenge. Hence, a system must be able to identify sources of inconsistency and deal with contradicting statements in such a way that it can still produce derivations that are reliable.

In the traditional bivalent-logic-based formalisms, we — that is, the users or the systems — have to make a decision. Once two contradictory statements are identified, one has to be chosen as the right one. While this is possible in domains that are axiomatized, fully explored, or in which statements are true by definition, it is not possible for most scientific domains. In the life sciences, for instance, hypotheses have to be evaluated, contradicting statements have promoting data, and so forth. Decisions have to be deferred until enough data is available that either verifies or falsifies the hypothesis. Nevertheless, it is desirable to express these hypotheses formally to have means to computationally evaluate them on the one hand and to exchange them between different systems on the other.

In order to allow the sort of reasoning that would allow this, the expressiveness of the formalism needs to be increased. It is known that increasing the expressive power of a KR language causes problems relating to computability. This has been the main reason for limiting the expressive power of KR languages. The real power behind human reasoning, however, is the ability to do so in the face of imprecision, uncertainty, inconsistencies, partial truth, and approximation. There have been attempts made in the past at building KR languages that allow such expressive power.

Major approaches to reasoning with imprecision are: (1) probabilistic reasoning, (2) possibilistic reasoning (Dubois, Lang, & Prade, 1994), and (3) fuzzy reasoning. Zadeh (2002) proposed a formalism that combines fuzzy logic with probabilistic reasoning to exploit the merits of both approaches. Other formalisms have focused on resolving local inconsistencies in knowledge bases, for instance the works of Blair, Kifer, Lukasiewicz, Subrahmanian, and others in annotated logic and paraconsistent logic (see Kifer & Subrahmanian, 1992; Blair & Subrahmanian, 1989). Lukasiewicz (2004) proposes a weak probabilistic logic and addresses the problem of inheritance. Cao (2000) proposed an annotated fuzzy logic approach that is able to handle inconsistencies and imprecision; Straccia (e.g., 1998, 2004) has done extensive work on fuzzy description logics. With P-CLASSIC, Koller, Levi, and Peffer (1997) presented an early approach to probabilistic description logics implemented in Bayesian networks. Other probabilistic description logics have been proposed by Heinsohn (1994) and Jaeger (1994). Early research on Bayesian-style inference on OWL was done by Ding and Peng (2004). In her formalism, OWL is augmented to represent prior probabilities. However, the problem of inconsistencies arising through inheritance of probability values (see Lukasiewicz, 2004) is not taken into account.

The combination of probabilistic and fuzzy knowledge under one representation mechanism proposed in Zadeh (2002) appears to be a very promising approach. Zadeh argues that fuzzy logics and probability theory are "complementary rather than competitive." Under the assumption that humans tend to linguistically categorize a continuous world into discrete classes, but in fact still perceive it as continuous, fuzzy set theory classifies objects into sets with fuzzy boundaries and gives objects degrees of set membership in different sets. Hence it is a way of dealing with a multitude of sets in a computationally tractable way that also follows the human perception of the world. Fuzzy logic allows us to blur artificially imposed boundaries between different sets. The other powerful tool in soft computing is probabilistic reasoning. Definitely in the absence of complete knowledge of a domain and probably even in its presence, there is a degree of uncertainty or randomness in the ways we see real-world entities interact. OWL as a description language is meant to explicitly represent knowledge and to deductively derive implicit knowledge. In order to use a similar formalism as a basis for tools that help in the derivation of new knowledge, we need to give this formalism the ability to be used in abductive or inductive reasoning. Bayesian-type reasoning is a way to do abduction in a logically feasible way by virtue of applying probabilities. In order to use these mechanisms, the chosen formalism needs to express probabilities in a meaningful way, that is, a reasoner must be able to meaningfully interpret the probabilistic relationships between classes and between instances. The same holds for the representation of fuzziness. The formalism must give a way of defining classes by their membership functions.

A major drawback of logics dealing with uncertainties is the required assignment of prior probabilities and/or fuzzy membership functions. Obviously, there are two ways of doing that — manual assignment by domain experts and automatic assignment using techniques such as machine learning. Manual assignments require the domain expert to assign these values to every class and every relationship. This assignment will be arbitrary, even if the expert has profound knowledge of the domain. Automatic assignments of prior values require a large and representative dataset of annotated instances, and finding or agreeing on what is a representative set is difficult or at times impossible. Annotating instances instead of categorizing them in a top-down approach is tedious and time consuming. Often, however, the probability values for relationships can be obtained from the dataset using statistical methods, thus we categorize these relationships as implicit semantics.

Another major problem here is that machine learning usually deals with flat categories rather than with hierarchical categorizations. Algorithms that take these hierarchies into account need to be developed. Such an algorithm needs to change the prior values of the superclasses according to the changes in the subclasses, when necessary. Most likely, the best way will be a combination of both, when the domain expert assigns prior values that have to be validated and refined using a testing set from the available data.

In the end, powerful semantics will combine the benefits of both worlds: hierarchical composition of knowledge and statistical analysis; reasoning on available information, but with the advantage over statistical methods that it can be formalized in a common language and that general purpose reasoners can utilize it, and with the advantage over traditional formal DL representation that it allows abduction as well as induction in addition to deduction.

It might be argued that more powerful formalisms are already under development, such as SWRL (Straccia, 1998), which works on top of OWL. These languages extend OWL by a function-free subset of first-order logics, allowing the definition of new rules in the form of Horn clauses. The paradigm is still that of bivalent FOLs, and the lack of function symbols makes it impossible to define functions that can compute probability values. Furthermore, SWRL is undecidable. We believe that abilities to express probabilities and fuzzy membership functions, as well as to cope with inconsistencies, are important. It is desirable (and some would say necessary) that the inference mechanism is sound and complete with respect to the semantics of the formalism and the language is decidable. Straccia (1998) proves this for a restricted fuzzy DL; Giugno and Lukasiewicz (2002) prove soundness and completeness for the probabilistic description logic formalism P-SHOQ(D).

So far, this powerful semantic and soft computing research has not been utilized in the context of developing the Semantic Web. In our opinion, for this vision to become a reality, it will be necessary to go beyond RDFS and OWL, and work towards standardized formalisms that support powerful semantics.

Correlating Semantic Capabilities with Types of Semantics

Building practical Semantic Web applications (e.g., see TopQuadrant, 2004; Sheth & Ramakrishnan, 2003; Kashyap & Shklar, 2002) require certain core capabilities. A quick look at these core capabilities reveals a sequence of steps towards building such an application. We group this sequence into two categories as shown in Table 1 and identify the type of semantics utilized by each.

Applications and Types of Semantics They Exploit

In this section we describe some research fields and some specific applications in each field. This list is by no means a comprehensive list, but rather samples of some research areas that attempt solve problems that are crucial to realizing the Semantic Web vision. We cover information integration, information extraction/retrieval, data mining, and analytical applications. We also discuss entity identification/disambiguation in some detail. We associate with each of the techniques in these research areas one or more of the types of semantics we identified earlier.

Information Integration

There is, now more than ever, a growing need for several information systems to interoperate in a seamless manner. This sort of interoperation requires that the syntactic, structural, and semantic heterogeneities (Hammer & McLeod, 1993; Kashyap & Sheth, 1996) between such information systems be resolved. Resolving such heterogeneities has been the focus of a lot of work in schema integration in the past. With the recent interest in the Semantic Web, there has been a renewed interest in resolving such heterogeneities. A survey of schema matching techniques (Rahm & Bernstein, 2001) identifies a wide variety of techniques that are deployed to solve this problem.

Schema Integration

A look at the leaf nodes and the level immediately above it, in the classification tree of schema matching techniques in Rahm and Bernstein (2001), reveals the combination of the technique used and the type of information about the schema used for matching schemas. Depending on whether the schema or the instances are used to determine the match, the type of information harnessed varies. Our aim is to associate one or more types of semantics (from our classification) with each of the bulleted entries at the leaf nodes of the tree shown. Table 1 does just that.

Table 1. Some key semantic capabilities and the type of semantics exploited

	Capabilities	Implicit Semantics	Formal Semantics	Possible Use of Powerful (Soft) Semantics
Bootstrapping Phase (building phase)	Building ontologies either automatically or semi-automatically	Analyzing word co-occurrence patterns in text to learn taxonomies/ontologies (Kashyap et al., 2003)		Using fuzzy or probabilistic clustering to learn taxonomic structures or ontologies
	Annotation of unstructured content *wrt.* these ontologies (resulting in semantic metadata)	Analyzing word occurrence patterns or hyperlink structures to associate concept names from and ontology with both resources and links between them (Naing, Lim, & Goh, 2002)		Using fuzzy or probabilistic clustering to learn taxonomic structures or ontologies OR Using fuzzy ontologies
	Entity disambiguation	Using clustering techniques or support vector machines (SVMs) for entity disambiguation (Han, Giles, Zha, Li, & Tsioutsiouliklis, 2004)	Using an ontology for entity disambiguation	Using fuzzy KR mechanisms to represent ontologies that may be used for disambiguation
	Semantic integration of different schemas and ontologies	Analyzing the extension of the ontologies to integrate them (Wang, Wen, Lochovsky, & Ma, 2004)	Schema-based integration techniques (Castano, Antonellis, & Vimercati, 2001)	
	Semantic metadata enrichment (further enriching the existing metadata)	Analyzing annotated resources in conjunction with an ontology to enhance semantic metadata (Hammond et al., 2002)		This enrichment could possibly mean annotating with fuzzy ontologies

Table 1. continued

	Capabilities	Implicit Semantics	Formal Semantics	Possible Use of Powerful (Soft) Semantics
Utilization Phase	Complex query processing		Hypothesis validation queries (Sheth, Thacker, & Patel, 2003) or path queries (Anyanwu & Sheth, 2002)	
	Question answering (QA) systems[1]	Word frequency and other CL techniques to analyze both the question and answer sources (Ramakrishnan, Chakrabarti, Paranjpe, & Bhattacharya, 2004)	Using *formal* ontologies for QA (Atzeni et al., 2004)	Providing confidence levels in answers based on fuzzy concepts or probabilistic
	Concept-based search[1]	Analyzing occurrence of words that are associated with a concept, in resources	Using hypernymy, partonomy, and hyponymy to improve search (Townley, 2000)	
	Connection and pattern explorer[1]	Analyzing semi-structured data stores to extract patters (technique in Kuramochi & Karypis, 2004, applied to RDF graphs)	Using ontologies to extract patterns that are meaningful (Aleman-Meza, Halaschek, & Sahoo, 2003)	
	Context-aware retriever[1]	Word frequency and other CL techniques to analyze resources that match the search phrase	Using formal ontologies to enhance retrieval	Using fuzzy KR mechanisms to represent context
Utilization Phase	Dynamic user interfaces[1]		Using ontologies to dynamically reconfigure user interfaces (Quan & Karger, 2004)	
	Interest-based content delivery[1]	Analyzing content to identify concept of content so as to match with interest profile	User profile will have ontology associated with it which contains concepts of interest	
	Navigational and research (Guha, McCool, & Miller, 2003) search	Navigational searches will need to analyze unstructured content	Discovery style queries (Anyanwu & Sheth, 2002) on semi-structured data which is a combination of implicit and formal semantics	Fuzzy matches for research search results

Table 2. Techniques used for schema integration and the type of semantics they exploit

	Type of Information Used	What Does it Mean?	Types of Semantics Exploited
Linguistic Techniques	Name Similarity	Using canonical name representations, synonymy, hypernymy, string edit distance, pronunciation, and N-gram-like techniques to match schemas' attribute and relation names	*Implicit Semantics* are exploited by string edit distance, pronunciation, and N-gram-like techniques. *Formal Semantics* are exploited by synonymy, etc.
	Description Similarity	Processing natural language descriptions associated with attributes and relations	*Implicit Semantics* are exploited by the NLP techniques deployed.
	Word Frequencies of Key Terms	Using relative frequencies of keywords and word combinations at the instance level	*Implicit Semantics*
Constraint Based Techniques	Type Similarity	Using information about data types of attributes as an indicator of a match between schemas	*Formal Semantics*
	Key Properties	Using foreign keys, part-of relationships, and other constraints	*Formal Semantics*
	Graph Matching	Treating the structure of schemas as graph algorithms to determine match degree; between graphs are used to match schemas.	Combination of *Implicit* and *Formal Semantics*
	Value Patterns and Ranges	Using ranges of attributes and patterns in the value of attributes as an indicator of similarity between the corresponding schemas	*Implicit Semantics*

Entity Identification/Disambiguation (EI/D)

A much harder, yet fundamental (and related) problem is that of entity identification/disambiguation. This is the problem of identifying that two entities are in fact either the same but treated as being different or that they are in fact two different entities that are being treated as one entity. Techniques used for identification/disambiguation vary widely depending on the nature of the data being used in the process. If the application uses unstructured text as a data source, then the techniques used for EI/D will rely on implicit semantics. On the other hand, if EI/D is being attempted on semi-structured data, the application can, for instance, disambiguate entities based on the properties they have. This implies harnessing the power of formal or semi-formal semantics. As listed in Table 1, the constraint-based techniques are ideally suited for use in EI/D when semi-structured data is being used. Dealing with unstructured data will require the use of the techniques listed under linguistic techniques.

Information Retrieval and Information Extraction

Let us consider information retrieval applications and the types of data they exploit. Given a request for information by the user, information retrieval applications have the task of processing unstructured (text corpus) or loosely connected documents (hyperlinked Web pages) to answer the "query." There are various flavors of such applications.

Search Engines

Search engines exploit both the content of Web documents and the structure implicit from the hyperlinks connecting one document to the other. Kleinberg (1998) defines the notions of hubs and authorities in a hyperlinked environment. These notions are crucial to the structural analysis and the eventual indexing of the Web. A modification of this approach aimed at achieving scalability is used by Google (Brin & Page, 1998). Google has fairly good precision and recall statistics. However, the demands that the Semantic Web places on search engine technology will mean that future search engines will have to deal with information requests that are far more demanding. Guha et al. (2003) identify two kinds of searches:

- **Navigational searches:** In this class of searches, the user provides the search engine with a phrase or combination of words which s/he expects to find in the documents. There is no straightforward, reasonable interpretation of these words as denoting a concept. In such cases, the user is using the search engine as a navigation tool to navigate to a particular intended document. Using the domain knowledge as specified in relevant domain ontology can enable an improved semantic search (Townley, 2000).

- **Research searches:** In many other cases, the user provides the search engine with a phrase that is intended to denote an object about which the user is trying to gather/research information. There is no particular document that the user knows about that s/he is trying to get to. Rather, the user is trying to locate a number of documents, which together will give her/him the information s/he is trying to find.

We believe that research searches will require a combination of implicit semantics, formal semantics, and what we refer to as powerful semantics.

Question Answering Systems

Question answering systems can be viewed as more advanced and more "intelligent" search engines. Current question-answering systems (Brin & Page, 1998; Etzioni et al., 2004; Ramakrishnan et al., 2004) use natural language processing (NLP) and pattern matching techniques to analyze both the question asked of the system and the potential sources of the answers. By comparing the results of these analyses, such systems attempt to match portions of the sources of the answer (for instance, Web pages) with the question, thereby answering them. Such systems therefore still use data like unstructured text and attempt to extract information from it. In other words the semantics are implicit in the text and are extracted from this text. To facilitate question answering, Zadeh (2003) proposes the use of an epistemic lexicon of world knowledge, which would be represented by a weighted graph of objects with uncertain attributes; in our terminology this is the equivalent of an ontology using powerful semantics.

Data Mining

The goal of data mining applications is to find non-trivial patterns in unstructured and structured data.

Clustering

Clustering is defined as the process of grouping similar entities or objects together in groups based on some notion of similarity. Clustering is considered a form of unsupervised learning. The applications of clustering use a given similarity metric and, as a result of the grouping of data points into clusters, attempt to use this information (implicit semantics) to learn something about the interactions between the clustered entities. The sort of information sought from the clustered data points may range from simple similarity judgments as in query-by-example (QBE) document retrieval systems or systems aimed at extracting more formal semantics from the underlying data, as is the aim of semi-automatic taxonomy generation.

Semi-Automatic Taxonomy Generation (ATG)

As described in Kashyap et al. (2003), the aim of automated taxonomy generation is to hierarchically cluster a document corpus and extract from the resulting hierarchy of clusters a sequence of clusters that best captures all the levels of specificity/generality in the corpus, where this sequence is ordered by the value of the specificity/generality measure. This is then followed by a node label extraction phase, where each cluster in the sequence is analyzed to extract from it a set of labels that best captures the topic its documents represent. These sets of labels are then pruned to reduce the number of potential labels for nodes in the final output hierarchy.

Association Rule Mining

An example of an association rule is given in Agrawal, Imielinski, and Swami (1993) and Agrawal and Srikant (1994) as follows: 90% of the transactions in a transaction database that involve the purchase of bread and butter together also have the purchase of milk involved. This is an example of an application where occurrence patterns of attribute values in a relational database (implicit semantics) are converted in association rules (formal semantics).

Analytical Applications

These come under the purview of applications that support complex query processing. It would be reasonable to hypothesize that search engines of the future will be required to answer analytical or discovery style queries (Guha et al., 2003; Anyanwu & Sheth, 2002). This is in sharp contrast to the kinds of information requests today's search engines have to deal with, where the focus is on retrieving resources from the Web that may contain information about the desired keyword. In this current scenario the user is left to sift through vast collections of documents and further analyze the returned results. In addition to querying data from the Web, future search engines will also have to query vast metadata repositories. We discuss one such technique in the following section.

Complex Relationship Discovery

As described in Anyanwu and Sheth (2002):

Semantic Associations capture complex relationships between entities involving sequences of predicates, and sets of predicate sequences that interact in complex ways. Since the predicates are semantic metadata extracted from heterogeneous multi-source documents, this is an attempt to discover complex relationships between objects described or mentioned in those documents. Detecting such associations is at the heart of many research and analytical activities that are crucial to applications in national security and business intelligence.

The datasets that semantic associations operate over are RDF/RDFS graphs. The semantics of an edge connecting two nodes in an RDF/RDFS graph are implicit, in the sense that there is no explicit interpretation of the semantics of the edge other than the fact that it is a predicate in a statement (except for rdfs:subPropertyOf or edges that represent data type properties — for which there is model-theoretic (formal) semantics). Hence the RDF/RDFS graph is composed of a combination of implicit and formal semantics. The objective of semantic associations is therefore to find all contextually relevant edge sequences that relate two entities. This is in effect an attempt to combine the implicit and formal semantics of the edges in the RDF/RDFS graph in conjunction with the context of the query to determine the multifaceted (multivalent) semantics of a set of "connections" between entities. We view this multivalent semantics as a form of powerful semantics. In the context of search, Semantic Associations can be thought of as a class of research searches or discovery-style searches.

Conclusion

We have identified three types of semantics and in the process assorted key capabilities required to build a practical semantic application involving Web resources. We have also qualified each of the listed capabilities with one or more types of semantics, as in Table 1. This table reveals some very basic problems that need to be solved for an application to be termed "semantic." It is clear from this table that entity disambiguation, question answering capability, context-based retrieval, and navigational and research (discovery) style query capability require the use of all three types of semantics. Therefore by focusing research efforts in representation mechanisms for powerful (soft) semantics in conjunction with fuzzy/probabilistic computational methods supporting techniques that use implicit and formal semantics, it might be possible to solve some of the difficult but practically important problems. In our opinion the current view taken by the Semantic Web community is heavily biased in favor of formal semantics. It is clear, however, that the focus of effort in pursuit of the Semantic Web vision needs to move towards an approach that encompasses all three types of semantics in representation, creation methods, and analysis of knowledge. If the capabilities that we identified do in fact turn out to be fundamental capabilities that make an application semantic, these capabilities could serve as a litmus test or a standard against which other applications may be measured to determine if they are "semantic applications."

References

Agrawal, R., Imielinski, T., & Swami, A. N. (1993). Mining association rules between sets of items in large databases. In P. Buneman & S. Jajodia (Eds.), *Proceedings of the 12th ACM SIGMOD International Conference on Management of Data* (pp. 207-216).

Agrawal, R., & Srikant, R. (1994). Fast algorithms for mining association rules. In *Proceedings of the 20th International Conference on Very Large Databases*, Santiago, Chile.

Aleman-Meza, B., Halaschek, C., & Sahoo, S. (2003, December). *Terrorist-related assessment using knowledge similarity* (LSDIS Lab Technical Report).

Anyanwu, K., & Sheth, A. P. (2002). The p operator: Discovering and ranking associations on the Semantic Web. *SIGMOD Record, 31*(4), 42-47.

Atzeni, P., Basili, R., Hansen, D. H., Missier, P., Paggio, P., Pazienza, M. T., et al. (2004, June). Ontology-based question answering in a federation of university sites: The MOSES case study. In *Proceedings of the 9th International Conference on Applications of Natural Language to Information Systems (NLDB '04)*, Manchester, UK.

Barbará, D., Garcia-Molina, H., & Porter, D. (1992). The management of probabilistic data. *IEEE Transactions on Knowledge and Data Engineering, 4*(5), 487-502.

Blair, H. A., & Subrahmanian, V. S. (1989). Paraconsistent logic programming. *Theoretical Computer Science, 68*, 135-154.

Brin, S., & Page, L. (1998). The anatomy of a large-scale hypertextual Web search engine. In *Proceedings of the 12th International World Wide Web Conference.* ACM Press.

Cao, T. H. (2000). Annotated fuzzy logic programs. *International Journal on Fuzzy Sets and Systems, 113*, 277-298.

Castano, S., Antonellis, V. D., & Vimercati, S. D. C. (2001). Global viewing of heterogeneous data sources. *IEEE Transactions on Knowledge and Data Engineering, 13*(2), 277-297.

Dill, S., Eiron, N., Gibson, D., Gruhl, D., Guha, R., Jhingran, A., et al. (2003). Semtag and seeker: Bootstrapping the Semantic Web via automated semantic annotation. In *Proceedings of the 12th International Conference on World Wide Web* (pp. 178-186). ACM Press.

Ding, Z., & Peng, Y. (2004, January 5-8). A probabilistic extension to ontology language OWL. In *Proceedings of the Hawaii International Conference on System Sciences*, Big Island, HI.

Dubois, D., Lang, J., & Prade, H. (1994). Possibilistic logic. In D. M. Gabbay et al. (Eds.), *Handbook of logic in artificial intelligence and logic programming* (Vol. 3, pp. 439-514). Oxford: Oxford University Press.

Etzioni, O., Cafarella, M., Downey, D., Kok, S., Popescu, A.-M., Shaked, T., et al. (2004). Web-scale information extraction in knowitall (preliminary results). *WWW*, 100-110.

Giugno, R., & Lukasiewicz, T. (2002). P-SHOQ(D): A probabilistic extension of SHOQ(D) for probabilistic ontologies in the Semantic Web. In *Proceedings of the European Conference on Logics in Artificial Intelligence.*

Gruber, T. (2003. March 26-27). *It is what it does: The pragmatics of ontology.* Invited talk at Sharing the Knowledge—International CIDOC CRM Symposium, Washington, DC. Retrieved from tomgruber.org/writing/cidoc-ontology.htm

Guha, R., McCool, R., & Miller, E. (2003, May). Semantic search. In *Proceedings of the 12ᵗʰ International World Wide Web Conference*, Budapest, Hungary.

Hammer, J., & McLeod, D. (1993). An approach to resolving semantic heterogeneity in a federation of autonomous, heterogeneous database systems. *Journal for Intelligent and Cooperative Information Systems.*

Hammond, B., Sheth, A., & Kochut, K. (2002). Semantic enhancement engine: A modular document enhancement platform for semantic applications over heterogeneous content. In V. Kashyap & L. Shklar (Eds.), *Real-world Semantic Web applications* (pp. 29-49). IOS Press.

Han, H., Giles, C. L., Zha, H., Li, C., & Tsioutsiouliklis, K. (2004). Two supervised learning approaches for name disambiguation in author citations. In *Proceedings of the ACM/IEEE Joint Conference on Digital Libraries (JCDL 2004)* (pp. 296-305).

Handschuh, S., Staab, S., & Ciravegna, F. (2002, October 1-4). S-CREAM — semi-automatic CREAtion of metadata. In *Proceedings of the European Conference on Knowledge Acquisition and Management (EKAW-2002)*, Madrid, Spain. Berlin: Springer-Verlag.

Heinsohn, J. (1994). *Probabilistic description logics* (pp. 311-318). UAI.

Hjorland, B. (1998). Information retrieval, text composition, and semantics. *Knowledge Organization, 25*(1/2), 16-31.

Jaeger, M. (1994). *Probabilistic reasoning in terminological logics* (pp. 305-316). KR.

Kashyap, V., Ramakrishnan, C., Thomas, C., Bassu, D., Rindflesch, T. C., & Sheth, A. (2003). *TaxaMiner: An experimentation framework for automated taxonomy bootstrapping* (Tech. Rep. No. UGA-CS-TR-04-005). Computer Science Department, University of Georgia, USA.

Kashyap, V., & Sheth, A. (1996). Semantic heterogeneity in global information systems: The role of metadata, context and ontologies. *Cooperative Information Systems.*

Kashyap, V., & Shklar, L. (Eds). (2002). *Real-world Semantic Web applications — Volume 92: Frontiers in artificial intelligence and applications.*

Kifer, M., & Subrahmanian, V. S. (1992). Theory of generalized annotated logic programming and its applications. *Journal of Logic Programming, 12*, 335-367.

Kleinberg, J. (1998). Authoritative sources in a hyperlinked environment. In *Proceedings of the ACM-SIAM Symposium on Discrete Algorithms.*

Koller, D., Levy, A., & Pfeffer, A. (1997). P-CLASSIC: A tractable probabilistic description logic. In *Proceedings of the 14th National Conference on Artificial Intelligence (AAAI-97)* (pp. 390-397).

Kuramochi, M., & Karypis, G. (2004). Finding frequent patterns in a large sparse graph. In *Proceedings of the SIAM International Conference on Data Mining (SDM-04).*

Lukasiewicz, T. (2004). *Weak nonmonotonic probabilistic logics, principles of knowledge representation and reasoning.* KR.

Maedche, A., & Staab, A. (2001). Ontology learning for the Semantic Web. *IEEE Intelligent Systems, 16*(2), 72-79.

Naing, M.-M., Lim, E.-P., & Goh, D. H.-L. (2002). Ontology-based Web annotation framework for hyperlink structures. In *Proceedings of WISE Workshops 2002* (pp. 184-193).

Omelayenko, B. (2001). Learning of ontologies for the Web: The analysis of existent approaches. In *Proceedings of the International Workshop on Web Dynamics.*

Patil, A., Oundhakar, S., Sheth, A., & Verma, K. (2004, May). METEOR-S Web service annotation framework. In *Proceedings of the World Wide Web Conference* (pp. 553-562). New York.

Quan, D., & Karger, D. R. (2004). *How to make a Semantic Web browser in WWW.*

Rahm, E., & Bernstein, P. A. (2001). A survey of approaches to automatic schema matching. *VLDB Journal, 10*, 4.

Ramakrishnan, G., Chakrabarti, S., Paranjpe, D., & Bhattacharya, P. (2004). Is question answering an acquired skill? In *Proceedings of the 13th International Conference on the World Wide Web 2004.*

Sheth, A., Bertram, C., Avant, D., Hammond, B., Kochut, K., & Warke, Y. (2002, July/August). Managing semantic content for the Web. *IEEE Internet Computing*, 80-87.

Sheth, A. P., Thacker, S., & Patel, S. (2003). Complex relationships and knowledge discovery support in the InfoQuilt system. *VLDB Journal, 12*(1), 2-27.

Sheth, A. P., & Ramakrishnan, C. (2003). Semantic (Web) technology in action: Ontology-driven information systems for search, integration and analysis. *IEEE Data Engineering Bulletin, 26*(4), 40-48.

Straccia, U. (2004). *Uncertainty and description logic programs: A proposal for expressing rules and uncertainty on top of ontologies* (Tech. Rep. No. 2004-TR-14).

Straccia, U. (1998). A fuzzy description logic. In *Proceedings of AAAI-98, 15th Conference of the American Association for Artificial Intelligence.*

Townley, J. (2000). *The streaming search engine that reads your mind.* Retrieved August 10, 2000, from smw.internet.com/gen/reviews/searchassociation/

Uschold, M. (2003, Fall). Where are the semantics in the Semantic Web? *Artificial Intelligence.*

Wang, J., Wen, J.-R., Lochovsky, F. H., & Ma, W.-Y. (2004). Instance-based schema matching for Web databases by domain-specific query probing. In *Proceedings of the 2004 Conference on VLDBs*

Woods, W. A. (2004, June 2-5). Meaning and links: A semantic odyssey. In *Principles of Knowledge Representation and Reasoning: Proceedings of the 9th International Conference (KR2004)* (pp. 740-742).

Yen, J. (1991). Generalizing term subsumption languages to fuzzy logic. *IJCAI,* 472-477.

Zadeh, L. A. (2002). Toward a perception-based theory of probabilistic reasoning with imprecise probabilities. *Journal of Statistical Planning and Inference, 105,* 233-264.

Zadeh, L. A. (2003). From search engines to question-answering systems — the need for new tools. In *Proceedings of the 1st Atlantic Web Intelligence Conference.*

Additional Online Resources

www.networkinference.com/Assets/Products/Cerebra_Server_Datasheet.pdf

www.topquadrant.com/documents/TQ04_Semantic_Technology_Briefing.PDF

The chapter was previously published in the International Journal on Semantic Web & Information Systems, 1(1), 1-18, January-March 2005.

Chapter II

The Human Semantic Web:
Shifting from Knowledge Push to Knowledge Pull

Ambjörn Naeve, The Knowledge Management Research Group,
Royal Institute of Technology, Sweden

Abstract

This chapter introduces the human Semantic Web (HSW) as a conceptual interface, providing human-understandable semantics in addition to the ordinary (machine) Semantic Web, which provides machine-processable semantics based on RDF. The HSW is structured in the form of a knowledge manifold and makes use of unified language modeling (based on the unified modeling language) combined with conceptual browsing to present its information to the user in a way that creates substantial benefits in terms of overview, clarity, and flexibility. The HSW browser Conzilla combines the semantics of RDF with the human-understandable semantics of UML in order to enable more powerful forms of human-computer interaction, such as querying the Semantic Web through Edutella and supporting the concept-in-context methodology. The Semantic Web is discussed in terms of three levels of semantic interoperability: isolation, coexistence, and collaboration. Collaboration, as the highest goal, can be achieved by conceptual calibration, which builds bridges between different ontologies in a bottom-up way, describing their similarities as well as their differences. An example is presented in Conzilla of conceptual calibra-

tion between systems for e-commerce. In the closing section, the Nonaka-Takeuchi theory of knowledge creation is discussed, and the HSW is described as a "space for interaction," where the SECI spiral of knowledge creation can be elevated to the global level. Three possible scenarios are presented: open research, enriching the economy by expanding the value ontology, and negotiating a sustainable future for all.

Introduction

The Globally Annotated Information Age

Recording, transmission, and annotation of information are three fundamentally important human activities that have exerted a strong influence on social and cultural development. The invention of persistent recordings (e.g., Cuneiform writing) initiated the recorded information age, and Gutenberg's invention of the printing press globalized the recording process and initiated the globally recorded information age. A few hundred years later, the emergence of electronic media globalized the transmission process and initiated the globally transmitted information age. Now, the emergence of the Semantic Web is globalizing the annotation process, thereby initiating the globally annotated information age.

New Demands on Management of Knowledge and Learning

Due to the rapidly increasing use of information and communications technology, the amount of information that we have to deal with in our everyday lives has become much greater than only a few years ago, a fact which has led to new ways of structuring information. Knowledge management is a rapidly growing field of research that studies these issues in order to create efficient methods and tools to help us filter the overwhelming flow of information and extract the parts that we need. Of course, the most complex information structure that we are dealing with today is the Internet with its linked anarchy, where anyone can connect anything with anything else. It is a well known fact that, unless these anarchical powers are balanced by careful design, they easily result in Web sites that are difficult to navigate and to conceptualize as a whole, which, in turn, makes it hard for the human recipient to organize and integrate the separate components of information that are presented into a coherent pattern of knowledge.

In Naeve et al. (2002) we[1] define (mental) knowledge as consisting of efficient fantasies[2] and describe (mental) learning as based on inspiring fantasies. Each

Figure 1. The globally recorded/transmitted/annotated information age

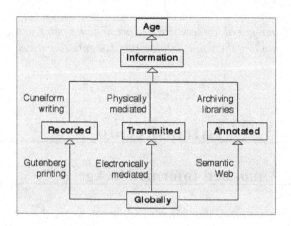

fantasy has a context, a purpose, and a target group, and it is only when we have described how we are going to measure the efficiency of our fantasies (within the given context, with the given purpose, and towards the given target group) that we can speak of knowledge in a way that can be validated.

With this definition, learning management is concerned with exposing the learner to inspiring fantasies and assisting in transforming them into efficient fantasies (Figure 2). Within a learning organization, this is complementary to knowledge management, which is concerned with creating, collecting, maintaining, and presenting knowledge in a way that makes it available within the organization wherever and whenever it is needed.

Lifelong, flexible, collaborative, personalized learning are words that are increasingly used in places where learning processes are discussed and designed. They express important wishes that put new demands on learning architectures with regard to pedagogy, organization, and technology. The traditional learning architectures are based on teacher-centric, curriculum-oriented, knowledge-push. The new demands are largely concerned with a shift along all of these dimensions in order to support more learner-centric, interest-oriented, knowledge-pulling types of learning architectures (Naeve, 1997; Grace & Butler, 2005). At the same time, within most organizations, new demands are being placed on effective knowledge management. Promoting the creation and sharing of knowledge in order to assure the right person with the right knowledge in the right place at the right time at the right cost is the overall aim of these demands.

Figure 2. The learning process modeled as a transformation from inspiring to efficient fantasies

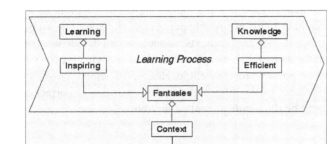

The (Machine) Semantic Web

On the Internet of today, the information is distributed and anyone can link anything to anything. After all, this is what has made the Web such a great success. However, the information about the information — the metadata — is still largely centralized and resides in databases that are hidden behind Web portals. These portals are advertised by their address with the underlying invitation: Come to our portal and search our database(s). This stage of Web development could be described as semantic isolation. It is characterized by the fact that you have to know where a database is located in order to be able to search in it. Also, the information on an ordinary HTML Web page is not represented in a way that is semantically interpretable by machines. For example, imagine that you want to find all the books written by Shakespeare. If you type the words book and Shakespeare into Google. com and hit search, you will get hits on Web pages that state things like "this book is not written by Shakespeare."

On the Semantic Web, the information about the information (the metadata) can be represented in such a way so that you can find the books written by Shakespeare.[3] This is most often done by the use of an ontology (Gruber, 2004), which consists of a set of formally defined terms with relations among them and (possibly) restrictions in the way that they are used. An ontology is a form of conceptual model, whose structure is similar to that of a thesaurus with its use of broader and narrower terms, part-of relationships, and so forth.

Moreover, on the Semantic Web, the information about the information can be as distributed as the information itself without losing track of what the information is referring to. Hence, anyone can state anything about anything in a way that is retrievable by machine.[4] This is possible because on the Semantic Web, even if our statements are made in different contexts, a machine can decide whether or not we are talking about the same thing, as opposed to deciding what we are talking about, which will never be possible for a machine. Hence, the semantics of the expression Semantic Web is rather misleading, and a more semantically correct label on this kind of Web would be the identity-resolvable Web.

Semantic Isolation, Coexistence, and Collaboration

Describing your information on the Semantic Web makes this metadata available for machine processing, and the things you describe become uniquely identifiable. Using semantic wrapping techniques,[5] a database can inform the Web about the kinds of questions to which it holds answers, making it possible to search the database without knowing in advance where it is located. This stage of Web development could be described as semantic coexistence.

However, there is still no way to know how your descriptions are related to those of others. In order to make this possible, you have to relate these descriptions to each other by creating some form of semantic mapping among them. For example, one repository might use the term author, while another might use the term creator to describe a person that has written a book. In order to search for books written by Shakespeare in both repositories using the same query, we must (in the case of books) connect the terms author and creator so that a machine can figure out that they refer to the same thing. In this way, when a set of description structures (ontologies) have been related by semantic mapping (ontological bridge), it is possible for a machine to relate them to each other, which is a prerequisite for achieving the much desired capability of semantic interoperability. This stage of Web development could be described as semantic collaboration.[6]

To summarize this discussion, we list some characteristics of the three different semantic stages outlined previously:[7]

Semantic isolation:

- XML (or other semantically free formats)
- Document-based descriptions
- Closed description spaces
- Fixed metadata set (tags and values)

- Databases with entry-portals
- No joint searching (intersearch)

Semantic coexistence:
- RDF(S)
- Graph-based descriptions
- Open description spaces
- Freely evolving metadata (tags and values)
- Databases with Edutella connections
- Joint searching (intersearch) with static queries
- Retrieval

Semantic collaboration:
- Ontology management systems
- Ontology mappings
- Contextualization
- Controlled evolution of metadata
- Joint searching (intersearch) with dynamic queries

The Knowledge Manifold

The research of the KMR group revolves around a structured information architecture called a knowledge manifold (KM) (Naeve, 1997, 1999, 2001b) which supports a number of different strategies for the suppression and presentation of information. A KM consists of a number of linked information landscapes (contexts), where one can navigate, search for, annotate, and present all kinds of electronically stored information. A KM is constructed by conceptual modeling of a specific knowledge domain in order to capture its underlying thought patterns in the form of context maps.

By defining a conceptual model (ontology), the concepts acquire an outside and an inside. In fact, a single concept acquires several outsides, since it can appear in several different contexts. In KM terms, we make the following:

Definition: *Let C denote a concept. An outside of C is called a context for C, and the inside of C is called the content of C.*

Hence, in a KM, the fundamental relationship among concept, context, and content can be summarized as:

content in context through concept.

The KM architecture can be used as a framework for the construction of interactive learning and knowledge management environments that enable a learner-centric, interest-oriented form of knowledge-pull that supports inquiry-based and personalized forms of networked learning (Naeve, Nilsson, Palmér, & Paulsson, (2005). An important design goal is to support the transformation of the teaching role — away from the traditional knowledge filter toward more of a knowledge coach (i.e., away from "teaching you what I know" and toward "helping you to find out more about the things that you are interested in").

The KM educational architecture is based on the following fundamental pedagogical assumptions (Naeve, 2001b):

- Nobody can teach you anything. A good teacher can inspire you to learn.
- Your motivation to learn is based on the experience of subject excitement and faith in your learning capacity from live teachers.
- Your learning quality is enhanced by taking control of your own learning process.
- No problematic questions can be answered in an automated way. In fact, it is precisely when your questions break the preprogrammed structure that the deeper part of your learning process begins.

A KM consists of a number of linked knowledge patches, each maintained by a custodian called a knowledge gardener. A knowledge patch, in turn, consists of a set of content components or resource objects[8] that are tied together with context maps that represent the corresponding conceptual model of the subject domain, and whose concepts (and concept-relations) can be filled with content[9]. Such context maps are preferably constructed using the ULM technique described in a subsequent section. A concept browser (Naeve, 2001a) lets the user navigate the context maps and view their content-filtered by a configurable set of context-dependent aspects (Pettersson, 2000).

When used for learning purposes, the KM architecture supports the following seven different knowledge roles (Naeve, 2001b):

- **Knowledge cartographer:** Constructs and maintains context maps.
- **Knowledge librarian:** Fills context maps with content components.
- **Knowledge composer:** Constructs customized learning modules.
- **Knowledge coach:** Cultivates questions.
- **Knowledge preacher:** Provides live answers.
- **Knowledge plumber:** Directs questions to appropriate preachers.
- **Knowledge mentor:** Provides a role model and supports self-reflection.

The KM architecture can be seen as a contribution toward the vision of a semantic learning Web, as stated in Nejdl et al. (2001): "a learning Web infrastructure, which will make it possible to exchange / author / annotate / organize and personalize / navigate / use / reuse modular learning objects that support a variety of courses, disciplines and organizations."

The Human Semantic Web

The stated goal of the Semantic Web initiative (n.d.) is to enable machine understanding of Web resources. However, it is not at all evident that such machine-processable semantic information will be clear and effective for human interpretation. The hyperlinked structure of the Web presents the user with a totally fluid and dynamic relationship between context and content, which makes it hard to get an overview of the context within which the information is presented. As soon as you click on a hyperlink, you are transferred to a new and often unfamiliar context. This results in the all too well known surfing-sickness, which could be summarized as "within what context am I viewing this, and how did I get here?" (Naeve, 2001a). The conclusion is that extracting usable meaning from Web pages is often as difficult for a human reader as it is for a machine. This strongly suggests that there is a need for a human-understandable semantics for Web resources as well.

Hence, in order to effectively harness the powers of the Semantic Web, it needs a conceptual interface that is more comprehensible for humans. We conceive this conceptual interface as a form of KM that we call the conceptual Web (Naeve, Nilsson, & Palmér, 2001) or the human Semantic Web (HSW). The HSW is a mixture of conceptual and pictorial information landscapes that are linked in the structure of a KM. It serves as a human-understandable front end that connects to the machine-understandable back end of the (machine) Semantic Web.

It is important to emphasize the following (often neglected) facts about metadata:[10]

- Metadata is not always objective; it must also allow subjective expressions.

- Metadata is not produced once and for all; it is the result of an ongoing annotation process that ideally should produce an ecosystem of annotations that highlight resources with high quality.

- Metadata is not a collection of documents but a global network of information.

- Metadata is not only for machines; we need conceptual metadata for people.

An important feature of the HSW is the ability to collect metadata from various sources into suitable contexts. These contexts can then be presented in various graphical user interfaces, such as adorned forms, through diagrammatic languages such as UML and so forth. Such contexts are also usable for the human management of evolving metadata (Nilsson, Palmér, & Naeve, 2002).

The different contexts of the HSW are described by context maps that are constructed by conceptual modeling and connected through the KM architecture. This provides a conceptual information atlas of connected context maps with human-understandable semantics for both abstract ideas and concrete resources. As discussed in a subsequent section, for the conceptual modeling, we make use of the ULM (unified language modeling) technique,[11] which is tailored to support the visualization of how we speak about things. UML (n.d.) provides a well proven, standardized modeling vocabulary with clearly defined visual semantics of the relationships between the occurring concepts.

Combining the human semantics of UML with the machine semantics of RDF (n.d.) enables more efficient and user-friendly forms of human-computer interaction. The HSW supports the mixture of human and machine semantics that is needed for efficient construction and use of modular and personalized learning and knowledge management environments based on retrieval and reuse of relevant knowledge resources.

In general, the HSW is designed to support the ongoing paradigm shift of social interaction patterns away from knowledge push and towards knowledge pull, such as the following shifts:

- from teacher-centric to learner-centric education;
- from doctor-centric to patient-centric health care;
- from bureaucrat-centric to citizen-centric administration;
- from government-centric to citizen-centric democracy; and
- from producer-centric to consumer-centric business models.

Conceptual Modeling

Wittgenstein has demonstrated that we cannot speak about things in their essence (Wittgenstein, 1953). In fact, we attach names to things in order not to have to talk about whatever lies behind these verbal interfaces to the unknown. Instead, we talk about the only things that we can talk about — the relations between the cognitive appearances of things. This fundamental fact forms the basis of the entire scientific project clearly stated by one of its most eminent proponents — Henri Poincaré (1905):

The aim of science is not things themselves — as the dogmatists in their simplicity imagine — but the relations between things. Outside those relations there is no reality knowable. (p. xxiv)

Hence, according to Poincaré, the conceptual relationships are fundamental to any linguistically based world model, because they represent the only things that we can talk about.

Introducing the Concept "Concept"

Concept formation helps us to disregard what is inessential by creating idealized structures that focus on what is essential. Efficient concepts disregard as much as possible in such a way that it is noticed as little as possible.[12] Classical examples of efficient concepts are point, line, and plane from the field of geometry.

There is a vast amount of literature on conceptual modeling. Here we will just give a brief summary of some important definitions related to the concept "concept" from the perspective of object-oriented modeling. For a more thorough discussion, the reader is referred to Odell and Martin (1998).

Definitions:
- A concept is a representation of something that we have experienced or that we can imagine, and which we can apply to the objects that we are aware of.
- A description of the most important concepts and their relations within a specific problem domain is called a conceptual model of the domain.
- The definition of a concept describes its intention (i.e., what qualities it aims to express and delimit with respect to its surroundings).
- The set of objects that exemplify a concept is called its extension.

- Each member element of the extension set is called an example = object = instance of the concept.

The concept, whose extension consists of a set of instances and whose intention describes their common structure, is called the type or the class of these examples.

To identify a concept by observing similarities and differences within a group of examples is called to classify the examples.

We say that a concept can be applied to a specific example, if this example fulfills the intention of the concept.[13]

Some Properties of the Concept "Concept"

- A concept must always be defined by making use of other concepts.
- A concept can be denoted by one or several names (= symbols).
- A concept is always idealized, because it contains simplifications that focus on some properties and disregards others.
- The definition of a concept always depends on the context within which it will be used. The aim is always to disregard the inessential and focus on what is essential within that context.

Unified Language Modeling Using UML

Unified modeling language (UML) (Rumbaugh, Jacobsson, & Booch, 1999; UML, n.d.) is a language for specifying, visualizing, and documenting conceptual models within many different knowledge domains. UML was developed from 1993 to 1997 within the object-oriented software community as an attempt to unify the more than 250 different modeling languages that were in use for software modeling by the mid-1990s. UML represents a collection of practically tested modeling techniques that have proven to be effective in the description of large and complex systems. Today, UML is a de facto industry standard for systems modeling.

Conceptual Weaknesses of Classical UML

Although it has many different uses, UML was created in order to model software systems, mostly to be implemented in strongly typed languages such as C++ or Java. This implies a sharp division between compile-time information (expressed in relationships between types, and run-time information) expressed in relationships between instances. This difference is reflected most clearly in the way that UML separates between class diagrams (dealing with types and their relations) and instance diagrams (dealing with instances and their relations).

Closely related to the strong separation between types and instances is the unfortunate instance notation in UML, as shown in the left part of Figure 3. From a structural (mathematical) perspective, it weakens the representational power of a language to represent a relation between two concepts[14] on one of the concepts involved instead of on the connection between them. This design weakness makes it practically impossible to express several levels of the instance-type relationships in UML. Of course, when you are modeling with the aim to create software, this is not a severe restriction, since you normally think of the types as classes and represent them in a class diagram. They represent the compile-time view of the system. The instances, on the other hand, represent the run-time view of the system. Instances are born in multitudes, and they live a hectic and often brief life, which is illustrated with partial snapshots in the form of UML instance diagrams. Here, UML reveals its close historical ties with the object-oriented community, which has been dominated by static, single-level typed languages such as C++ and Java.

What is needed in order to remedy this weakness is to notationally express the instance-type relationship in a way that reflects its true nature; namely, as a conceptual relationship. We will introduce a notation for the instance-type relationship in the next section.

Moreover, in ordinary language, types are generally referred to without a prefixing article (determined or undetermined) (e.g., this Volvo is a type of car), while instances generally are referred to with a determined or undetermined article (e.g., the car, this car, a car). In contrast, within the object-oriented modeling community, there is a tradition of denoting the inheritance relationship with is a (e.g., car is a vehicle), as expressed in the left part of Figure 5. This breaks the linguistic coherence of the model, since it compares car to a vehicle at the same type level.

The Unified Language Modeling Technique

Unified language modeling (ULM) (Naeve, 1997, 1999, 2001a) is a context-mapping technique that has been developed during the past decade. It is designed to visually represent a verbal description of a subject domain in a coherent way. Today, the ULM technique is based on the UML, which, as noted above, is a de facto industry standard for systems modeling.

In ULM, the resulting context maps have clearly defined and verbally coherent visual semantics, which makes it easy to cognitively integrate the conceptual relations and achieve a clear overview of the context. Moreover, making the context visually explicit provides important support for the conceptual calibration activities[15] that are necessary in order to achieve semantic collaboration. The ULM verbal-to-visual contextual representation technique has a crucial advantage compared to similar techniques, such as concept maps (Concept Maps, n.d.; Novak, n.d.) or topic maps (Topicmaps, n.d.), which have to rely on purely verbal semantics in order to convey their conceptual relationships.

In order to be able to correctly interpret the context maps of this chapter, we will give a brief description of some of the extra notation introduced in ULM compared to UML.[16]

As discussed earlier, UML represents the example-type (instance-type) relation on the instance itself, as shown in the left part of Figure 3, which shows that the depicted concept is an (unnamed) instance of type car. The right part of the figure shows the same relation represented in ULM. The dashed arrow (with a small filled head) represents the classification/instantiation and is pronounced is a when read

Figure 3. UML: A car is a(n instance of type) car

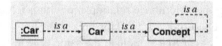

Figure 4. A car is a car is a concept is a concept is a ...

Figure 5. Traditional OO: Car is a vehicle. ULM: Car kind of vehicle

Vehicle		Vehicle
⬆ *is a*		⬆ *kind of*
Car		Car

along the direction of the arrow, and a when read in the opposite direction. Hence, the language interpretation of the right part of Figure 3 is "a car is a car", which is a purely tautological statement. Here, the indefinite article a serves as an instantiation operator (providing the example), and is a serves as a classification operator (providing the type of the example).

In this way, ULM decouples the description of the concept (the specific car instance) from the relationship to its type (car). This addition to classical UML achieves two important benefits:

- It makes it possible to describe several levels of the example-type relationship. Figure 4 shows an example of this, which cannot be expressed in classical UML.

- It corrects the unfortunate traditional notation from the object-oriented community, where is a denotes the generalization/specialization relationship, as shown in the left part of Figure 5. This relation instead should be called kind of, as shown in the right part of Figure 5.[17]

These notational changes open the way for descriptions that can combine relations in a diagrammatically correct way and that translate from the visual to the verbal in a coherent manner. Figure 6 shows an example of how this works. Here, we see how the statements "a car is a car" and "car kind of vehicle" are combined (both diagrammatically and verbally) into the statement, "a car is a kind of vehicle".

The basic visual to verbal coherence of the ULM technique is shown in Figure 7.

The statements "a fuel tank is a fuel-tank" and "fuel-tank part of car" are combined into the statement "a fuel tank is a part of a car", showing the difference between the gen/spec and the aggregation relationships. The former expresses the structure of a single instance ("a car is a kind of vehicle"), while the latter expresses a link between two instances of the corresponding types ("a fuel tank is a part of a car").

Figure 6. An example of the verbal-visual coherence of ULM

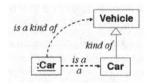

Figure 7. The basic verbal/visual correspondence of ULM

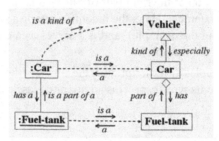

Notice also how the latter relationship is expressed in the opposite direction: The statement "car has fuel tank" is transported by the instantiation operator (the indefinite article a) into the statement "a car has a fuel tank".

Conzilla:
A Human Semantic Web Browser

During the past seven years, we have developed a prototype of a concept browser (Naeve, 2001a), called Conzilla (Palmér & Naeve, 2005; Conzilla, n.d.). Since Conzilla is designed with a clear object-oriented structure that separates the underlying logic from the presentation and style graphics, it can easily be adapted to different presentational styles and cognitive profiles.[18] Several Conzilla-based knowledge manifolds have been constructed (i.e., within the fields of mathematics, IT standardization, and interoperability among different systems for e-commerce) (ECIMF, n.d.).

A concept browser is a powerful tool with a multitude of potential applications, and Conzilla is attracting increased attention both on the national and international levels. Within the framework of the human Semantic Web, we are aiming to develop Conzilla into a generic information management tool by participating in collaborative projects that will expand the capabilities of the program within the rapidly converging areas of learning and knowledge management, focusing on the domains of e-learning, e-commerce, and e-administration.[19]

In February 2005, we released Conzilla2, a human Semantic Web browser, or a conceptual interface to the (machine) Semantic Web. Its main requirements are as follows:

Figure 7. The representation of Conzilla2 of the fact that "Eric knows Stephen"[20]

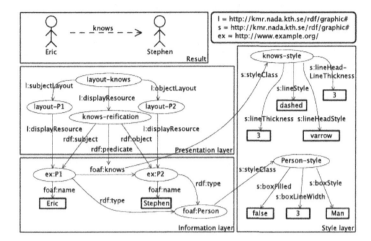

- It should serve as a collaboration tool for more or less formalized modeling techniques, most notably UML dialects.

- It should simplify the task of creating information according to various metadata standards.

- It should support customized presentations of information without requiring duplication or modification of information sources.

These requirements are fulfilled by choosing a three-layered approach for working with Semantic Web information in Conzilla; namely, the information, presentation, and style layers. Figure 8 shows these three representation layers resulting in the top-left context map, which displays the fact that Eric knows Stephen.

Human Semantic Queries on the Machine Semantic Web

As mentioned in a previous section, the Semantic Web offers unprecedented opportunities for precise querying and searching for information about various resources. Edutella (Nejdl et al., 2002; Nilsson, Naeve, & Palmér, 2004; Wilson, 2001) is a peer-to-peer network infrastructure for search and retrieval of information about resources on the Semantic Web, which takes advantage of these opportunities.

Figure 9. An Edutella query expressed in simplified RDF. It is directed toward the (machine) Semantic Web and not very understandable for humans.

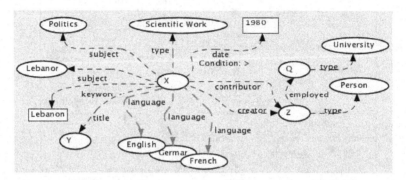

Edutella builds upon metadata standards defined for the World Wide Web (WWW) and provides an RDF-based metadata infrastructure for P2P applications, building on the JXTA framework (JXTA, n.d.).

To show the kind of queries that Edutella can manage, consider the query depicted in Figure 9 (as a simplified RDF graph). X represents the resource we are looking for, and the arcs are properties of that resource. In plain English, the query asks for the following (in counter-clockwise order):

All scientific works on the subject of politics, having Lebanon as subject or keyword, with a title (Y) written in English, German, or French, created or contributed to by a person (Z), employed at a university, and created after 1980.[21]

Edutella takes queries of the previous complexity, distributes them to peers that have declared themselves capable of answering this type of query, collects the answers, and returns them to the originator. It is possible that parts of the answers are located on different peers. In the example, the university employee information is perhaps not located on the same server as the resource metadata, but Edutella is able to handle these kinds of situations in a transparent manner (Nilsson, Naeve, & Palmér, 2004).

Although the Edutella query depicted in Figure 9 is logically precise and easy for machines to process, it is not very understandable for humans. When the queries are formulated by humans, as opposed to agents, for example, there is a need to represent them in a more humanly understandable form. Figure 10 shows the same Edutella query presented on the human Semantic Web through a query interface in

Figure 10. The same Edutella query presented on the human Semantic Web through a query-interface on Conzilla (with most of the information hidden)

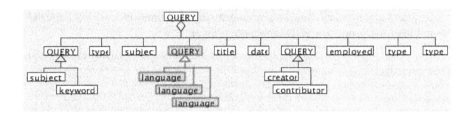

Conzilla. Here, the query is formulated as a Boolean tree, with "or" expressed as a UML generalization and "and" as a UML aggregation, which have the corresponding semantics.

Supporting the Concept-in-Context Methodology

The rapidly increasing internationalization and professionalism of higher education is dependent on the methodology and the quality of the supporting ICT tools. In this context, projects like Sakai (n.d.) and ELF (n.d.) are blazing a new trail. Instead of leaving the development of quality tools and services needed by the university to the commercial actors, these projects have taken the lead by having member institutions collaboratively develop an open source portals and learning systems/tools/services. Currently, more than 65 institutions from 10 countries are Sakai members and participate in the development of the Sakai system. In addition, many other schools, including K-12, community colleges, and universities, are interested in adopting the open source Sakai toolkit. Use of Sakai on a large scale at many universities provides a good opportunity to introduce new methodologies and new ways of teaching.

At the time of writing of this chapter, we are involved with Sakai in defining a project that aims to help students achieve better learning outcomes by the collaborative construction of kuman semantic learning Webs accessed through supportive, well-integrated, ICT-based frameworks and technologies. The project proposes integration of our concept-mapping methodology, called concept-in-context, into Sakai. This methodology encourages students and teachers to externalize what is being learned by expressing concepts and their relationships in various contexts. The methodology has been tested with various student groups at KTH (Blomqvist, Handberg, & Naeve, 2003) over the past few years with promising results.[22] The explicit aims of the concept-in-context methodology are the following:

- To capture the communication situation when several learners/teachers work collaboratively on a sheet of chapter or whiteboard to sketch their ideas/common understanding of an area.

- To assist teachers and students in expressing thoughts on learning material and learning processes at the conceptual level.

- To support the formation of new knowledge by relating it to already established knowledge.[23]

The concepts and concept relations in this methodology are collected into browsable maps providing an overview and a collaborative workspace. Individual concepts may be enriched with examples, such as connections to course material, rich explanations, and relations to other concepts. The maps will be accessible through tools that will be integrated into the Sakai framework.

A crucial feature of the concept-in-context methodology is that concepts have a life independent of their occurrence in context maps. Their properties can be highlighted in one or several maps, but, in most cases, their full nature lies beyond the digital domain. Hence, some knowledge always will remain tacit in the mind(s) of the individual or group responsible for expressing the concepts. Consequently, it is vitally important to keep track of who expressed what.

The contextual independence of concepts opens up the possibility of their reuse. For instance, concepts may be reused:

- By teachers in multiple courses, perhaps related to other concepts in the process.

- By learners for making connections and comments on what is learned. This could be for personal use as a way to communicate with fellow learners or to prove to someone else that you have reached a deeper level of understanding.

To support collaboration, maps and concepts cannot be owned exclusively. Consequently, when looking at a map or an individual concept, the user can choose to include or exclude various contributions made to it. Typically, a student investigates a map made by the teacher(s) and then chooses to include extensions from other fellow students in the same year or perhaps students that have taken the course in earlier years. The student may go on and make extensions and comments on the map, typically adding some concepts or relations among concepts. Before moving on, the student has to decide if his or her changes are for everyone to see, to be shared with a limited group of people, or not to be shared at all.

Conceptual Calibration

Semantic collaboration, as described in a previous section, can be approached in two fundamentally different ways: top-down or bottom-up. The top-down approach involves designing a common ontology from agreed-upon fundamental concepts, a process that basically requires the reaching of consensus among all participating stakeholders. The bottom-up approach, on the other hand, starts from the existing conceptual models of the participating calibration partners and tries to model both the similarities and the differences between these models. This is a more complex process than the top-down approach, but it has the great advantage that consensus does not have to be reached.

A bottom-up approach to achieving semantic collaboration can be carried out through the process of conceptual calibration described in (Naeve, 1997). This process consists of three different activities:

1.   Agreeing on what we agree on.
2.   Agreeing on what we don't agree on.
3.   Documenting 1 and 2 in a way that we agree on.

The Electronic Commerce Integration Meta-Framework

As an example of the conceptual calibration technique, we will consider the case of e-commerce systems, where the KMR group has been involved in a standardization project called ECIMF[24] (n.d.) within the CEN/ISSS Electronic Commerce workshop. The proliferation of mutually incompatible standards and models for conducting e-commerce (resulting from the isolated efforts of industry groups and standard bodies) has created quite the adverse effect from what was intended, when it comes to wide acceptance of electronic commerce, especially in the SME[25] market. The industry is looking for methods to meet the exploding demand for increased quality of service, reduction of manual labor and cost, and the requirements of nearly real-time reaction to changing market demands. However, the existing e-commerce frameworks require costly adjustments in order to fit a specific business model to that of a specific framework with the perspective that similar costs will follow if the business party wants to participate in other frameworks as well.

In response to these concerns from the industry, the CEN/ISSS Workshop for Electronic Commerce has carried out the E-Commerce Integration Meta-Framework (ECIMF) project,[26] which has aimed to deliver the following:

Figure 11. Overview of the ECMIF methodology

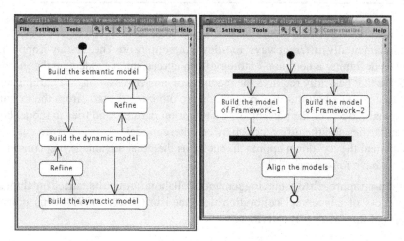

A meta-framework that offers a methodology, modeling language, and prototype tools for all e-commerce users to achieve secure interoperability of the service, regardless of system platforms and without major adjustments of existing systems.

An important premise of the project is the following definition of interoperability:

Interoperability, as seen from the business point of view, takes place when the business effects for the two involved enterprises are the same as if each of them were conducting a given business process with a partner using the same e-commerce framework.

The ECIMF project has built on the experiences from projects, such as ebXML (n.d.), UN/CEFACT Unified Modeling Methodology (n.d.), RosettaNet (n.d.), BizTalk (n.d.), and various Web services initiatives. An extended version of Conzilla has been used as an experimental platform for the project. The extensions were constructed specifically in order to support the conceptual calibration methodology that was described previously.

The ECIMF makes use of three different types of models: semantic, dynamic, and syntactic. For each e-commerce system involved, these models are constructed in a top-down manner, combined with an iterative process of refining the higher-level models, based on the additional information gathered in the process of modeling the lower levels, as shown in the left part of Figure 11. Here, we will illustrate briefly

Figure 12. The top windows show the semantic models of framework 1 (left) and framework 2 (right). The bottom window shows three Conzilla comparators. Highlighting the Agent/Party comparator shows the corresponding parts of the two models.

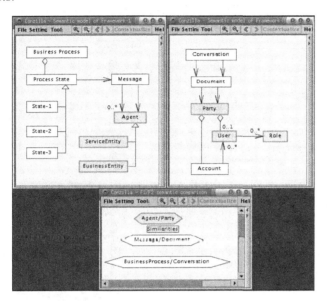

the alignment methodology of the semantic models, since it makes use of the bottom-up conceptual calibration technique described previously.

Figure 12 shows the Conzilla approach to the alignment of the two semantic models in a highly simplified artificial example. The left and right top windows of Figure 12 show UML diagrams of the two semantic models, and the bottom window shows three Conzilla comparators, called Agent/Party, Message/Document, and BusinessProcess/Conversation. Each comparator connects the corresponding concepts of the two models in such a way that, when the comparator is highlighted, so are the corresponding concepts. In Figure 12, the comparator Agent/Party has been highlighted, showing that Agent, ServiceEntity, and BusinessEntity in framework 1 correspond to Party, User, and Role in framework 2.

Moreover, each comparator is linked to a semantic comparison window, where the similarities and differences of the corresponding parts of the two models are described. For example, double-clicking the Agent/Party comparator (Figure 13) opens the corresponding semantic comparison window (bottom left), where the similarities and the differences between the Agent/Party sections of the two models are described. The dotted lines show that Agent corresponds to Party, while Ser-

Figure 13. Double clicking the Agent/Party comparator opens the semantic comparison window (bottom left), where the similarities and the differences between the Agent/Party sections of the two models are described.

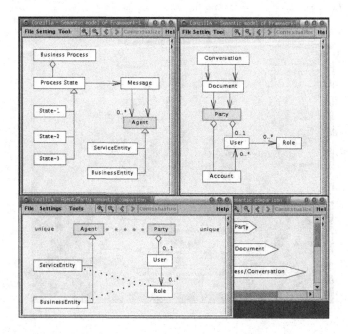

viceEntity and BusinessEntity correspond to Role. Highlighting a concept in any window (e.g., Agent, as in Figure 13) will highlight it and its corresponding concepts (in this case, Party) in all windows where these concepts appear.

As shown in Figure 14, in the semantic comparison window, the similarities are represented as metadata on the dotted line between the corresponding concepts, while the differences are represented as metadata on the "unique" labels.

Knowledge Creation on the
Human Semantic Web

The SECI Spiral of Knowledge Creation

In their award-winning 1995 book, *The Knowledge Creating Company*, Nonaka and Takeuchi introduce their theory of organizational knowledge creation. According

Figure 14. Similarities and differences between the concepts Agent and Party represented as metadata in the semantic comparative window

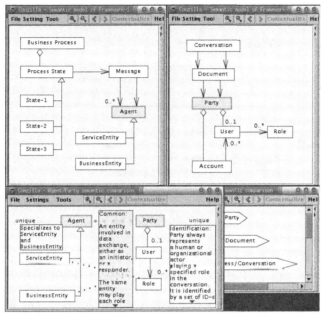

to them, the Cartesian split between subject and object, the knower and the known, has given birth to a Western view of an organization as a mechanism for information processing. While this view has proven to be effective in explaining how an organization functions, it does not really explain the concepts of innovation and knowledge creation. In the Nonaka-Takeuchi theory of knowledge creation, the cornerstone is the distinction between tacit and explicit knowledge. The dominant form of knowledge in the West is explicit knowledge, which can be transmitted easily across individuals, both formally and systematically. In contrast, the Japanese view knowledge as primarily tacit, something that is not easily visible and expressible but which is deeply rooted in an individual's actions and experiences.

According to Nonaka and Takeuchi (1995), the key to knowledge creation lies in the following four (SECI) modes of knowledge conversion, which occur when tacit and explicit knowledge interact with each other:

- **Socialization:** The process of sharing experiences (tacit knowledge), thereby creating new tacit knowledge.

Figure 15. The SECI sprial of knowledge creation

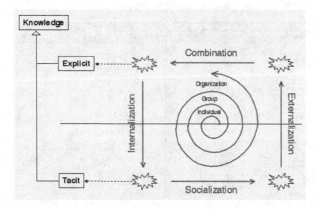

- **Externalization:** The process of articulation and conversion of tacit knowledge into explicit knowledge.

- **Combination:** The process of restructuring and aggregating explicit knowledge into new explicit knowledge.

- **Internalization:** The process of reflecting on and embodying explicit knowledge into tacit knowledge.

As illustrated in Figure 15, a knowledge-creating spiral occurs when these modes of interaction between tacit and explicit knowledge are elevated from the individual to the group and organizational levels. "Organizational knowledge creation, therefore, should be understood as a spiraling process that organizationally amplifies the knowledge created by individuals and crystallizes it as part of the knowledge network of the organization. This process takes place within an expanding community of interaction, which crosses intra- and inter-organizational levels and boundaries" (Takeuchi & Nonaka, 2004).

Nonaka and Takeuchi (1995) emphasize that, on the organizational level, the spiral of knowledge creation is driven by organizational intention (i.e., an organization's aspiration to achieve its goals). Moreover, they introduce the Japanese concept of ba, which roughly means place for interactions as a crucial enabler for effective knowledge creation. Within an organizational context, it is the role of managers to maintain the necessary manifestations of such ba in order to support the knowledge creation spiral and to make it efficient for the purposes of the organization.

Figure 16. The present structure of closed medical research

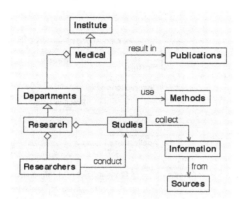

Globalizing the SECI Spiral

The human Semantic Web can be seen as a kind of ba for elevating the SECI spiral of knowledge creation to the global level, where groups of individuals or organizations that share similar intentions can interact and create new knowledge together. Sharing experiences with others through electronically mediated trusted interactions can support socialization[28] and generate new tacit knowledge, which then can be externalized and turned into explicit knowledge by creating context maps. Then, by making use of the concept-in-context methodology described in a previous section, these context maps can be elaborated on and extended by others, creating new explicit knowledge by combination. This explicit knowledge, in turn, can be reflected upon and internalized into new tacit knowledge, completing a full turn of the SECI spiral.

Open Research: A Scenario from the Medical Domain

The advent of informal Web publishing has created unparalleled possibilities of accessing the ongoing research work of others. In conjunction with the presently exploding Web logging activities (Mortensen & Walker, 2002), this is creating the foundations for a globally annotated open research culture (Seb's Open Research, n.d.), where the value of a specific research contribution will be judged by its off-spring (i.e., who will decide to reference or re-use it) and not by its offering (i.e., who will decide to publish it). The emergence of such an open research paradigm,

Figure 17. A possible structure for open medical research with validated feed-back

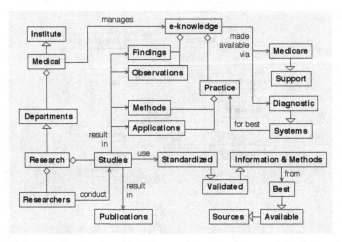

based on what Paquet (n.d.) calls personal knowledge publishing, is challenging the business models of many professional publishers (Smith, 1999), where authors are supposed to contribute for free, only for the pleasure of being allowed to publish the results of their work under the freely supplied peer review of their colleagues.

Here, I will discuss briefly a possible open research scenario from the medical domain,[29] which could bridge the present gap between medical research and practice. Figure 16 depicts the present state of closed research within the medical sector, as it would be described on the human Semantic Web.

As shown in Figure 16, a medical institute consists of research departments with researchers that conduct research studies, which result in publications. These research studies make use of methods and collect information that is available from different sources.

A future scenario for medical research, based on a variation of the open research paradigm is described in Figure 17. Here, in addition to the descriptions of Figure 16, it is shown that research studies result in findings, observations, methods, and applications that are part of the e-knowledge managed by the medical institute. This e-knowledge, in turn, is made available via medicare support and diagnostic systems for best practice, which enables the research studies to make use of standardized validated information and methods from the best available sources. Note that, in this case, the concept of open research should be interpreted as open research source, since it is the sources of research that are made open, while the research on this information is separated from its collection and maintenance. In this way, the human Semantic Web could provide a basis for a fundamental restructuring of the entire health care sector, which could be turned into a transparently documented and validated process supported by modern ICT tools, where medical practitioners would get easy access to the latest medical research findings. This is in sharp contrast to the closed research source situation of today, where medical research and practical health care are almost totally separated.

Enriching the Economy by Expanding the Value Ontology

Figure 18 shows a Conzilla map called taxonomy of value types, which was created about four years ago in connection with a project idea called ethical e-commerce (E2C) that we were discussing with one of our industry partners, but which, for various reasons, was not realized at the time. The aim was to make use of the human Semantic Web as a collaborative modeling environment and to try to set up a Conzilla-based ba for capturing as many of the different value-types as possible that are important to some of the stakeholders in our global future, including individuals, communities, and organizations on the national and international level. Then these stakeholders would create stakeholder-specific value profiles for different projects, with each value profile marked with information on the stakeholder(s) that created it.[30]

The E2C project could be subtitled "Enriching the Economy by Expanding the Value Ontology: Stakeholder-Specific Value Profiling as a Mediator of Market Exchange." The specific idea was to let the operator (= market-maker) of a so-called market hub (= electronic marketplace) announce that a certain percentage (e.g., 1%) of the turnover of the hub would be directed to a project that the customer would be free to choose. The system (based on Conzilla) would provide a menu of possible choices, and each project would be equipped with a set of value profiles issued by different

Figure 18. An embryo of an expanded-value ontology

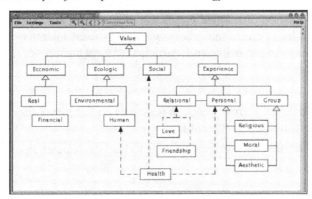

organizations, whose relevant metadata would be available from an inspection of the value-profile itself.

In this way, if you support Greenpeace, for example, then you would be free to choose a project that has an attractive Greenpeace value profile. The underlying idea is to supply the consumer with a whole set of group consensus-based, stake-holder-specific value profiles that have been developed by a conceptual calibration process, based on modeling of value types within the group. Such E2C groups, of course, would include (but not be limited to) various consumer groups. Then the consumer can make the choice according to the preferences (expressed in the form of a value profile) of the group in which s/he places the most trust.

The crucial challenge of this E2C scheme, as briefly outlined above, is to set things up so that it will be commercially profitable to act in an ethical way. Otherwise, this type of behavior will not spread among market stakeholders. Therefore, all sorts of information regarding the value-profiled activities on the market hub should be fed back automatically to the market-maker's advertising department, which can do things like display on its Web site today's contribution by their consumers toward "making the world a better place" by supporting the following value profiles with the following amount. In fact, I believe (as do the authors of the book, *Beyond Branding* [Ind, 2003]), that it will become very profitable for a market maker to show vigorous activity in the many "non-commercial" dimensions that are reflected in the expanded value ontology. Of course, consumer-centric value modeling will require a whole chain of supervisory activities, which, if designed appropriately, will have the potential to support the democratic process, as it evolves into new and uncharted electronic territory.

Negozilla: Negotiating a Sustainable Future for All

The human Semantic Web also provides the necessary ba for distributed global negotiations about creating a sustainable future for all inhabitants on this planet.[31] In order to initiate such negotiations in a playful and creative way, we plan to develop a Conzilla-based distributed global resource negotiation game that we call Negozilla. In order to create the necessary organizational intention for effective knowledge creation in Negozilla, each participant[32] must answer yes to the following two questions:

1.   Do you think that there are enough resources on this planet for every person that inhabits it to have a decent life?

2.   Are you prepared to contribute actively toward the realization of this goal?

If your answer to any one of these questions is no, you are not allowed to enter the game. Otherwise you are assigned your own knowledge patch (= group of layered context maps) and invited to a global negotiation table. Since all participants have agreed that "there is enough for everybody", and "we will work toward making it happen", it follows that there is no need for all the violence-based repressive barriers that we have erected in order to protect ourselves (and our assets) from ourselves. Therefore, all the destructive violence-supporting capital on this planet is freed up for redistribution and can be used to support more constructive activities. This is what the online negotiations of Negozilla will be dealing with. These activities will take place using the methods of "concept-in-context" and "conceptual calibration", described previously. The state of the negotiations and the agreed-upon actions and activities will be visualized and made available for public inspection on the Web. The Negozilla negotiations will consist of several activities/modeling, including the following:

1. **Modeling of ownership relations:** Ownership-maps will be constructed in order to achieve a global overview of the ownership structures on this planet and highlight uncharted areas of unknown ownership relations.

2. **Modeling of participator contributions and needs (describing what you have to offer and what you need):** This is similar to knowledge-gap learner modeling, which is based on modeling what you know and what you would like to know; it could be termed earth-inhabitant modeling, customizing your existence space, or capturing your specs for a decent life.

3. **Collaborative negotiations modeling using the conceptual calibration method:** This modeling will be aimed at expanding our global value ontology,[33] describing our various activities with certified value profiles, where certified means explicit and validated information about who (individual or group) has assigned this value profile to this activity/project as well as when this as-signment was made. Much effort will be spent on modeling and visualizing the correspondences between activities/projects, value profiles, and certifying bodies in various ways. The overall aim is to support the emergence of birds-of-a-feather types of interactions among groups of individuals and organiza-tions that have large overlaps in their respective assessments (value profiles) of a specific project. This presents a value-pulling way of establishing value chains that can contribute toward the overall goal of a decent life for all. By striving toward this goal (which, of course, can never be fully achieved), we contribute toward the construction of a transnational corporation that could be called Humanity Inc., where the Inc. stands for incorporated as individuals.

The most important predicted effect of Negozilla is that even though (or, in fact, just because) it is "just a game", it should be able to transparently provide descriptions of constructive scenarios for the future of all inhabitants on this planet in a way that is accessible for a substantial (and rapidly increasing) part of these inhabitants. In this way, Negozilla can be expected to externalize and make available some of the utopian visions of the future that are dangerously lacking in real politics and from which we can internalize and socialize the inspiring and innovative ideas that are so desperately needed in order to create a constructive and sustainable future for us all.

Summary and Conclusion

In this chapter, I have argued that, with the advance of new technologies like the Semantic Web, it becomes a necessity to change the knowledge and learning management paradigm from the current push approach to an individualized pull approach, focusing on the user rather than on the non-flexible standardized approaches of today. I have introduced the human Semantic Web, structured in the form of a knowledge manifold and conceptually described in terms of unified language modeling, and I have argued that it has the representational and presentational power to effectively support the knowledge-pulling paradigm.

Moreover, I have introduced semantic isolation, coexistence, and collaboration as three distinctive levels of semantic interoperability, and I have explained how our conceptual Web browser, Conzilla, can help to achieve semantic collaboration in a bottom-up way by building ontological bridges between different conceptual models, using the conceptual calibration technique. Finally, I have introduced the Nonaka-Takeuchi theory of knowledge creation and shown how the human Semantic Web could provide an interaction space for elevating the SECI spiral of knowledge creation to the global level. In three different futuristic scenarios, I have tried to outline what kind of impact there would be if knowledge were created and shared collaboratively on the global level instead of being kept secret for various reasons.

Two thousand five hundred years ago, Pythagoras taught us that unselfish knowledge is the best way to purify our souls. Today, economists and politicians tell us that selfish knowledge is the best way to fill our wallets. Hence, the catharsis-oriented knowledge philosophy of the Pythagoreans has been complemented with the utility-oriented knowledge economy of the modern information society. The vision of this emerging knowledge economy has been formulated convincingly in the book, *Transforming E-Knowledge* (Norris, Mason, & Lefrere, 2003), where it is stated that:

In the Knowledge Economy, those individuals and enterprises that share and process their knowledge effectively have a great advantage. To keep up, most of us will need a quantum leap in our ability to manage knowledge. This won't happen without a genuine transformation in the ways in which we appraise what we know, what we can do with it, and what we need to know. [...] Through this transformation, learning and knowledge management will be fused in both theory and practice. This synthesis will form the core of a new social and economic system based on knowledge sharing. This transformation is underway. Participation in shaping the transformation is mandatory for all hoping to achieve success in the Knowledge Economy.

Although the utility-oriented knowledge economy is strategically important for our future, we cannot afford to neglect the catharsis-oriented knowledge philosophy, if the quality of the learning process is to be maintained.[34] The great strategic challenge upon which our future on this planet hinges is to transcend these opposing knowledge perspectives and achieve a dialectical synthesis of the selfish and unselfish views of knowledge. In this chapter, I have tried to indicate how the human Semantic Web could contribute to this synthesis — an aspiration that inspires the work of my entire research group.

Acknowledgments

I acknowledge my gratitude to the members of the KMR group and especially to Mikael Nilsson and Matthias Palmér for their contributions to many of the subjects that have been discussed in this chapter. I am also grateful to Miltiadis Lytras without whose persuasive powers this article would not have been written. Finally, I acknowledge the contributions of several members of our international networks, notably WGLN (Wallenberg Global Learning Network; see http://www.wgln.org), Prolearn (see http://www.prolearn-project.org), SIGSEMIS (see http://www.sigsemis.org), and Sakai (see http://www.sakaiproject.org).

References

BizTalk. (n.d.). Retrieved from http://www.microsoft.com/biztalk/techinfo/BizTalkFramework20.doc

Blomqvist, U., Handberg, L., & Naeve, A. (2003, May). New methods for focusing on students' learning process and reflection in higher education. In *Proceedings of the 28th IUT (Improving University Teaching) Conference*, Växjö.

Concept maps. (n.d.). Retrieved from http://www.graphic.org/concept.html

Confolio. (n.d.). Retrieved from http://www.confolio.org

Conzilla. (n.d.). Retrieved from http://www.conzilla.org

Demo-editor. (n.d.). Retrieved from http://knowgate.nada.kth.se:8180/SHAME/DemoEditor.jsp

Dublin Core Metadata Initiative. (n.d.). Retrieved from http://dublincore.org

ebXML. (n.d.). Retrieved from http://www.ebxml.org

ECIMF (Electronic Commerce Integration Meta-Framework). (n.d.). Retrieved from http://www.ecimf.org

Edutella. (n.d.). Retrieved from http://edutella.jxta.org

ELF (E-Learning Framework). (n.d.). Retrieved from http://www.elframe work.org

e-Europe. (n.d.). Retrieved from http://europa.eu.int/information_society/eeurope/index_en.htm

Grace, A., & Butler, T. (2005). Learning management systems: A new beginning in the management of learning and knowledge. *IJKL, 1*(1-2).

Gruber, T. (2004). Every ontology is a treaty — a social agreement — among people with some common motive in sharing. *AIS SIGSEMIS Bulletin, 1*(3).

Ind, N. (Ed.). (2003). *Beyond branding: How the new values of transparency and integrity are changing the world of brands*. Kogan Page Limited.

JXTA. (n.d.). Retrieved from http://www.jxta.org

KMR (Knowledge Management Research) Group. (n.d.). Retrieved from http://kmr.nada.kth.se

LOM-RDF-binding. (n.d.). Retrieved from http://kmr.nada.kth.se/el/ims/metadata.html

Mortensen, T. & Walker, J. (2002). *Blogging thoughts: Personal publication as a research tool*. Retreived from http://www.intermedia.uio.no/konferanser/skikt-02/docs/Researching_ICTs_in_context-Ch11-Mortensen-Walker.pdf

Naeve, A. (1997). *The garden of knowledge as a knowledge manifold: A conceptual framework for computer supported subjective education*. Department of Numerical Analysis and Computer Science, KTH, Stockholm. Retrieved from http://cid.nada.kth.se/sv/pdf/cid_17.pdf

Naeve, A. (1999). *Conceptual navigation and multiple scale narration in a knowledge manifold*. Department of Numerical Analysis and Computer Science. Retrieved from http://cid.nada.kth.se/sv/pdf/cid_52.pdf

Naeve, A. (2001a, October 24-26). The concept browser: A new form of knowledge management tool. In *Proceedings of the Second European Web-Based Learn-*

ing Environment Conference (WBLE 2001), Lund, Sweden (pp. 151-161). Retrieved from http://kmr.nada.kth.se/papers/ConceptualBrowsing/Concept-Browser.pdf

Naeve, A. (2001b, October 24-26). The knowledge manifold: An educational architecture that supports inquiry-based customizable forms of e-learning. In *Proceedings of the Second European Web-Based Learning Environment Conference (WBLE 2001)*, Lund, Sweden (pp. 200-212). Retrieved from http://kmr.nada.kth.se/papers/ConceptualBrowsing/ConceptBrowser.pdf

Naeve, A., Nilsson, M., & Palmér, M. (2001, July). The conceptual Web: Our research vision. In *Proceedings of the First Semantic Web Working Symposium*, Stanford, CA. Retrieved from http://www.semanticweb.org/SWWS/program/position/soi-nilsson.pdf

Naeve, A. et al. (2002, November). *En publik e-lärandeplattform byggd på kunskapsmångfalder, öppen källkod och öppna IT-standarder (A public e-learning platform based on knowledge manifolds, open source and open, international ICT standards)*. Report to the Swedish Netuniversity. Retrieved from http://kmr.nada.kth.se/papers/SemanticWeb/Natuniv-KMR.pdf

Naeve, A., Nilsson, M., Palmér, M., & Paulsson, F. (2005). Contributions to a public e-learning platform: Infrastructure, architecture, frameworks and tools. *International Journal of Learning Technology, 1*(3), 352-381.

Nejdl, W. et al. (2001). *PADLR (Personalized Access to Distributed Learning Repositories)*. Proposal to WGLN. Retrieved from www.learninglab.de/pdf/L3S_padlr_17.pdf

Nejdl, W. et al. (2002, May 7-11). Edutella: A P2P networking infrastructure based on RDF. In *Proceedings of the 11th World Wide Web Conference (WWW 2002)*, HI. Retrieved from http://kmr.nada.kth.se/papers/SemanticWeb/p597-nejdl.pdf

Nilsson, M., Naeve, A., & Palmér, M. (2004). The Edutella P2P network: Supporting democratic e-learning and communities of practice. In R. McGreal (Ed.), *Online education using learning objects*. New York: Routledge-Falmer.

Nilsson, M., Palmér, M., & Naeve, A. (2002, May 7-11). Semantic Web metadata for e-learning: Some architectural guidelines. In *Proceedings of the 11th World Wide Web Conference*, HI. Retrieved from http://kmr.nada.kth.se/papers/SemanticWeb/p744-nilsson.pdf

Nonaka, I. & Takeuchi, H. (1995). *The knowledge-creating company: How Japanese companies create the dynamics of innovation*. New York: Oxford University Press.

Norris, D., Mason, J., & Lefrere, P. (2003). *Transforming e-knowledge*. Ann Arbor, MI: Society for College and University Planning.

Novak, J. D. (n.d.). *The theory underlying concept maps and how to construct them*. Retrieved from http://cmap.coginst.uwf.edu/info/

Odell & Martin. (1998). *Object-oriented methods: A foundation.* Prentice Hall.

OWL (Web Ontology Language). (n.d.). Retrieved from http://www.w3.org/TR/owl-features

Palmér, M., & Naeve, A. (2005, July 18-22). Conzilla: A conceptual interface to the semantic Web. In *Proceedings of the 13th International Conference on Conceptual Structures (ICCS 2005)*, Kassel. Springer.

Palmér, M., Naeve, A., & Paulsson, F. (2004, May). The SCAM-framework: Helping applications to store and access metadata on the semantic Web. In *Proceedings of the First European Semantic Web Symposium*, Heraklion, Greece. Retrieved from http://kmr.nada.kth.se/papers/SemanticWeb/SCAM-ESWS.pdf

Paquet, S. (n.d.). *Personal knowledge publishing and its uses in research.* Retrieved from http://radio.weblogs.com/0110772/stories/2002/10/03/personalKnowledgePublishingAndIts UsesInResearch.html

Pettersson, D. (2000). *Aspect filtering as a tool to support conceptual exploration and presentation.* CID/NADA/KTH. Retrieved from http://kmr.nada.kth.se/papers/ConceptualBrowsing/AspectFiltering-exjobb.pdf

Poincaré, H. (1905, 1952). *Science and hypothesi*s. New York: Dover Publishing.

Powell, A., Nilsson, M., Naeve, A., & Johnston, P. (2004). *DCMI: Abstract model* (working draft). Retrieved from http://dublincore.org/documents/abstract-model

Prolearn. (n.d.). Retrieved from http://www.prolearn-project.org

RDF (Resource Description Framework). (n.d.). Retrieved from http://www.w3.org/RDF

RDFS (RDF-Schema). (n.d.). Retrieved from http://www.w3.org/TR/rdf-schema

RosettaNet. (n.d.). Retrieved from http://www.rosettanet.org

Rumbaugh, J., Jacobsson, I., & Booch, G. (1999). *The unified modeling language reference mannual.* Addison Wesley Longman.

Sakai. (n.d.). Retrieved from http://www.sakaiproject.org

SCAM. (n.d.). Retrieved from http://scam.sourceforge.net

Seb's Open Research. (n.d.). Retrieved from http://radio.weblogs.com/0110772

Semantic Web Initiative. (n.d.) Retrieved from http://www.SemanticWeb.org

SHAME. (n.d.). Retrieved from http://kmr.nada.kth.se/shame

SIGSEMIS. (n.d.). Retrieved from http://www.sigsemis.org

Smith, J. W. T. (1999, April). The deconstructed journal: A new model for academic publishing. *Learned Publishing, 12*(2). Retrieved from http://library.kent.ac.uk/library/papers/jwts/d-journal.htm

Takeuchi, H., & Nonaka, I. (2004). *Hitotsubashi on knowledge management*. Wiley & Sons.

Topicmaps. (n.d.). Retrieved from http://www.topicmaps.net and http://www.top-icmaps.org

UDBL (Uppsala Data Base Laboratory). (n.d.). Retrieved from http://www.dis.uu.se/~udbl

ULL (Uppsala Learning Lab). (n.d.). Retrieved from http://www.ull.uu.se

UML (Unified Modeling Language). (n.d.). Retrieved from http://www.uml.org

UN/CEFACT. (n.d.). Retrieved from http://www.unece.org/cefact

VWE (Virtual Workspace Environment). (n.d.). Retrieved from http://www.vwe.nu

WGLN (Wallenberg Global Learning Network). (n.d.). Retrieved from http://www.wgln.org

Wilson, S. (2001, September). *The next wave: CETIS interviews Mikael Nilsson about the Edutella project*. Centre for Educational Technology Interoperability Standards (CETIS). Retrieved from http://kmr.nada.kth.se/papers/Semantic-Web/TheNextWave.pdf

Wittgenstein, L. (1953). *Philosophical investigations*. Oxford: Basil Blackwell.

Endnotes

[1]   Throughout this chapter, the term we (when not used to involve the reader in the discussion) will refer to the Knowledge Management Research (KMR) Group at KTH, which I am leading.

[2]   As opposed to muscular knowledge, which could be defined as efficient reflexes. The word fantasy is used instead of the more or less synonymous word conceptualization in order to emphasize that the conceptual structures are constructed from within.

[3]   The technical basis for this is the description languages RDF(S) (n.d.) and OWL (n.d.).

[4]   For example, through the Edutella infrastructure (Nejdl et al., 2002; Edutella, n.d.).

[5]   Such as AMOS/PSELO developed by Uppsala Data Base Laboratory (UDBL, n.d.).

[6]   An important step toward semantic collaboration is abstract modeling, which allows both sides of an ontological bridge to be treated as instantiations of the

same abstract model. See Powell, Nilsson, Naeve, and Johnston (2004) for an application to the Dublin Core Metadata Initiative (n.d.).

[7] For a more detailed description of these matters, the reader is referred to Naeve, Nilsson, Palmér, and Paulsson (2005).

[8] In KM terminology, we use the term knowledge object when we assume the perspective of the teacher(s), the term information object (or learning object) when we assume the perspective of the learner(s), and the term resource object when want to remain neutral in this respect.

[9] This supports the separation of content from context, which promotes the reuse of content across different contexts.

[10] Further discussed in Nilsson, Palmér, and Naeve (2002).

[11] Based on the UML (Unified Modeling Language, n.d.).

[12] The power of thinking lies in knowing what not to think about.

[13] That is, the conditions of its definition.

[14] In this case, the property that something is to be regarded as an instance of something else, which is to be regarded as its type.

[15] Described in the section "Conceptual Calibration."

[16] Technically speaking, ULM can be regarded as a profile of UML, which defines some special notation that is useful in order to draw how we talk about things.

[17] In UML, this relation is called gen/spec (generalization/specialization), which gives no clue as to how to read out the relations in a coherent way. Both is a and kind of are used for reading the gen/spec arrow along its direction.

[18] Conzilla is being developed as an open source project at Sourceforge and can be downloaded from http://www.conzilla.org.

[19] In accordance with the e-Europe initiative (e-Europe, n.d.), we also are aiming for Conzilla to support increased e-accessibility by enabling it to configure itself to different cognitive profiles.

[20] This picture is taken from Palmér and Naeve (2005) where Conzilla2 is described in detail.

[21] Note that there are several occurrences of or in this transcription. However, this information is not explicit in the figure; it is represented separately.

[22] Mainly students in the media technology program.

[23] This is achieved by encouraging reuse, annotation, and refinement of concepts.

[24] Electronic Commerce Integration Meta-Framework.

[25] Small- and medium-sized enterprises.

[26]   Between February 2001 and February 2003.

[28]   Of course, the critical part of this process is the trust part, which is far from present on the Web of today. However, the SW initiative has created the prerequisites for building the necessary Web of trust, since on the SW, every resource is uniquely identifiable.

[29]   This scenario has been worked out in collaboration with Göran Agerberg.

[30]   Who is probably the most important single piece of metadata on the Web.

[31]   Of course, this is closely related to the E2C project described in the last section.

[32]   Note that participator stands for both individuals and organizations. Any organization can enter the Negozilla game, provided that its executives answer yes to the two entrance questions.

[33]   As described in the section titled "Enriching the Economy by Expanding the Value Ontology."

[34]   This is known by everyone that is deeply involved in education.

The chapter was previously published in the International Journal on Semantic Web & Information Systems, 1(3), 1-30, July-September 2005.

Section II

Frameworks and Methodologies

Chapter III

General Adaptation Framework:
Enabling Interoperability for Industrial Web Resources

Olena Kaykova, University of Jyväskylä, Finland

Oleksiy Khriyenko, University of Jyväskylä, Finland

Dmytro Kovtun, University of Jyväskylä, Finland

Anton Naumenko, University of Jyväskylä, Finland

Vagan Terziyan, University of Jyväskylä, Finland

Andriy Zharko, University of Jyväskylä, Finland

Abstract

Integration of heterogeneous applications and data sources into an interoperable system is one of the most relevant challenges for many knowledge-based corporations nowadays. Development of a global environment that would support knowledge transfer from human experts to automated Web services, which are able to learn, is a very profit-promising and challenging task. The domain of industrial maintenance is not an exception. This chapter outlines in detail an approach for adaptation of heterogeneous Web resources into a unified environment as a first step toward interoperability of smart industrial resources, where distributed human experts and learning Web services are utilized by various devices for self monitoring and self diagnostics. The proposed General Adaptation Framework utilizes a potential of the Semantic Web technology and primarily focuses on the aspect of a semantic adaptation (or mediation) of existing widely used models of data representation to RDF-based semantically rich format. To perform the semantic adaptation of industrial resources, the approach of two-stage transformation (syntactical and semantic) is elaborated and implemented for monitoring of a concrete industrial device with underlying XML-based data representation model as a use case.

Introduction

At the current stage of ICT development, there is a diversity of heterogeneous systems, applications, standards of data representation, and ways of interaction. All those systems were tailored for particular tasks and goals. The world is heterogeneous, and modern industry is looking for fast, global solutions related to knowledge management, enterprise application integration, electronic commerce, asset management, and so forth. However, in spite of advancements in data processing and acquisition, it is still difficult to automatically process and exchange data among the heterogeneous systems. Various industrial standards, which have been created and implemented by different consortia, appear not to be sufficient for growing interoperability demands.

Taking into account a great variety of possible types of information resources, data formats, and ways of data accessing and acquisition, an integration of such resources into a unified environment is an important development challenge (BMC Press, 2003; Khanna, 2004).

Basically, the integration tasks can be solved by adaptation of data from heterogeneous formats to some commonly accepted and semantically reached format (i.e., adaptation of heterogeneous applications and data originally represented according to a standard different from the common standard.

The integration process may include the following key functions (Apte, 2002; Sun Press, 2003):

* **Extracting, transformation, and loading:** For building data warehouse or operation data stores and giving to an end user/application a possibility to work with integrated data.

* **Data replication:** To allow heterogeneous servers and databases to share data in real time.

- **Data synchronization:** To allow sharing of data among servers and remote devices when connectivity is temporary.

Application adaptation is a special part of the general integration task. The data are generated by different applications with the following specific features:

- Application functions
- Application APIs
- Application interfaces

All variations of these features have an effect on the process of adaptation and the architecture of adaptation framework.

During the last several years, major efforts in solving the challenge of enterprise application integration have focused on the domain of Web services; that is, loosely coupled Internet and intranet applications developed according to the requirements of W3C's Web Services Architecture Working Group. So far, standardization efforts of W3C in this direction have resulted in SOAP (2000), WSDL (2001), and UDDI (2004) specifications. Industry currently supports these standards as a solid solution for a wide variety of tasks from the EAI domain. A service-oriented approach is actively used in modeling business-to-business tasks; Business Process Execution Language for Web services (BPEL4WS, 2003) is used the most widely nowadays.

Semantic Web is a relatively new initiative within the W3C standardization effort to enable machine interpretable metadata on the Web. It provides standards and tools to enable explicit semantics of various Web resources, based on semantic annotations and ontologies. Integration in general is considered a killer application of Semantic Web technology, which particularly can be interpreted as heterogeneous data integration, Enterprise Application Integration, and Web service integration, among other interpretations. In contrast to ICT, the semantic technologies represent meanings separate from data, content, or program code, using the open standards for the Semantic Web. They are language-neutral, machine-interpretable, sharable, and adaptive, and allow ontology-based integration of heterogeneous resources. Automated knowledge accumulation and sharing is becoming the most profitable kind of business for modern knowledge-driven enterprises.

Academic community has actively utilized concepts of the Semantic Web for further development of the potential of service-oriented analysis and underlying standards. Extending current XML-based standards for Web services by explicit semantics would make automated discovery or composition of Web services possible. The recent efforts in the domain of Semantic Web services are represented by three major projects: OWL-S (2003), METEOR-S (2005; Sivashanmugam, Miller, Sheth, &

Verma, 2004), and WSMO (2005), and associated initiatives such as SWWS (2005), SWSI/SWSA (2005), and interoperability initiatives between some of these (Lara, Roman, Polleres, & Fensel, 2004; Paolucci, Srinivasan, & Sycara, 2004). WSMO and several related activities are being performed within the European Adaptive Services Grid (ASG, 2005) project. CASCOM European project (2005) also can be mentioned as one of the significant projects of the concerned domain, which is based on an interdisciplinary combination of intelligent agent, Semantic Web, peer-to-peer, and mobile computing technologies.

One of the domains, where knowledge accumulation and its timely delivery are crucial, is industrial maintenance (Automation, 2003). Development of a global environment, which would support automation of knowledge management for industrial maintenance, is a very profit-promising and challenging task. The latter is what the SmartResource[1] project aims at in the research and development efforts of Industrial Ontologies Group.[2]

The intention of the SmartResource team is to provide tools and solutions to make heterogeneous industrial resources (files, documents, services, devices, processes, systems, human experts, etc.) Web-accessible, proactive, and cooperative in a sense that they will be able to analyze their state independently from other systems or to order such analysis from remote experts or Web services in order to be aware of their own condition and to plan behavior toward effective and predictive maintenance.

This chapter presents an approach and a case study performed by the SmartResource team within an industrial maintenance domain aimed to design a possible architecture for interoperability of heterogeneous industrial resources, based on Semantic Web standards. Emphasis is made on a General Adaptation Framework, which is envisioned to enable reusable solutions and components for automatic adaptation of different types of resources and their data formats to the Semantic Web environment.

The structure of the further content is the following. The next section introduces a global understanding environment as a background concept for future implementation and also briefly describes stages of architectural design for it. The third section provides more design and implementation details about the Adaptation Stage for the target environment design. Then the general approach to building semantic adapters for industrial resources is given. The section describes the challenge itself, goes deeper into the details of the two-stage transformations between data models, and presents its pilot implementation results for a use-case scenario. The fifth section contains conclusions that follow from the performed research and development, and finally, the last section comprises additional discussion around the work done: practical usability of the results, their possible application areas, and plans for further development.

Proactive Self-Maintained Resources in the Semantic Web

The contribution of the ongoing SmartResource project (2004 to 2006), together with appropriate research effort, includes prototype implementation of distributed Semantic Web enabled maintenance management environment with complex interactions of components, which are devices, humans (experts, operators), and remote diagnostic Web services. The environment will provide automatic discovery, integration, condition monitoring, remote diagnostics, and cooperative and learning capabilities of the heterogeneous resources to deal with maintenance problems. Maintenance (software) agents will be added to industrial devices, which are assumed to be interconnected in a decentralized peer-to-peer network and which can integrate diagnostic services in order to increase the maintenance performance for each individual device. The maintenance case is expected to demonstrate the benefits and possibilities of a new resource management framework and Semantic Web technology in general. An approach to that case harnesses the potential of emerging progressive technologies, such as Semantic Web, agent technology, machine learning, Web services, and peer-to-peer.

The Background Concept: A Global Understanding Environment

Global understanding environment (GUN) (Terziyan, 2003) is a concept used to name a Web-based resource welfare environment, which provides a global system for automated care over (industrial) Web-resources with the help of heterogeneous, proactive, intelligent, and interoperable Web services. The main players in GUN are the following resources: service consumers (components of service consumers), service providers (components of service providers), and decision makers (components of decision makers). All these resources can be artificial (tangible or intangible) or natural (human or other). It is supposed that the service consumers will be able to: (1) proactively monitor their own state over time and changing context; (2) discover appropriate decision makers and order from them remote diagnostics of their own condition, and then the decision makers automatically will decide which maintenance (treatment) services are applied to that condition; and (3) discover appropriate service providers and order from them the required maintenance. Main layers of the GUN architecture are shown in Figure 1.

Industrial resources (e.g., devices, experts, software components, etc.) can be linked to the Semantic Web-based environment via adapters (or interfaces), which include (if necessary) sensors with digital output, data structuring (e.g., XML), and semantic adapter components (XML to Semantic Web). Agents are assumed to be assigned to

Figure 1. Layers of the GUN architecture

each resource and are able to monitor semantically reached data coming from the adapter about states of the resource, decide if more deep diagnostics of the state is needed, discover other agents in the environment that represent decision makers, and exchange information (agent-to-agent communication with semantically enriched content language) in order to get diagnoses and decide if a maintenance is needed. It is assumed that decision-making Web services will be implemented, based on various machine-learning algorithms, and will be able to learn, based on samples of data taken from various service consumers and labeled by experts. Use of agent technologies within the GUN framework allows mobility of service components between various platforms, decentralized service discovery, FIPA communication protocols utilization, and MAS-like integration/composition of services (Ermolayev, Keberle, Plaksin, Kononenko, & Terziyan, 2004).

Main Stages Toward Smart Resources

We have divided the implementation of the GUN concept for the maintenance domain into the following three stages: adaptation, proactivity, and networking. Each stage assumes design of a more enhanced version of the maintenance environment.

The adaptation stage defines Semantic Web-based framework for unification of maintenance data and interoperability in the maintenance system by adding explicit semantics into existing data representation formats. The semantics (metadata), which are intended to be added to the data that describe corresponding industrial resources, include knowledge about their state, condition, and diagnosis in temporal and contextual space. Further, the semantically reached resource descriptions will be used as input to decision-making components (e.g., Jess-based [Jess, 2005]) of software agents. The research and development tasks of this stage include development of a generic semantic adapter mechanism (General Adaptation Framework) and supporting ontology (Resource State/Condition Description Framework) for different types of industrial resources: devices, software components (services), and humans (operators or experts). The key technology, which is utilized during the adaptation stage, is the Semantic Web.

The proactivity stage focuses on an architectural design of agent-based resource management framework and on enabling a meaningful resource interaction. Its research and development tasks include adding software agents (maintenance agents) to the industrial resources, which enables their proactive behavior. For this purpose, Resource Goal/Behavior Description Framework has to be designed, which will be the basis for making the resource's individual behavioral model. The model is assumed to be processed and executed by the RGBDF engine used by the Maintenance Agents. An agent-based approach for management of various complex processes in the decentralized environments is being adopted and popularized currently in many industrial applications. Presentation of the resources as agents in the multi-agent system and use of technologies and standards developed by the agent research community seems to be a prospective way of industrial systems development. Creation of a framework for enabling resources' proactive behavior and such agent features as self-interestedness, goal-oriented behavior, ability to reason about itself and its environment, and communicating with other agents can bring a value to the next-generation industrial systems.

The objective of the Networking Stage comprises complex behavior/interaction scenarios of Smart Resources (agent-augmented device, expert, and service) in a global decentralized networked environment. The scenarios assume agent-based interoperation of multiple devices, multiple services, and multiple experts, which allows discovery of necessary experts in peer-to-peer network, using their experiences to learn remote diagnostics Web services, making online diagnostics of devices by integrating diagnoses from several services, learning models for a device diagnostics based on online data from several distributed samples of similar device, and so forth. Emerging peer-to-peer technology and similar network architectures suit well the increasingly decentralized nature of modern companies and their industrial and business processes, whether it is a single enterprise or a group of companies (Terziyan & Zharko, 2003). The set of attractive features of the peer-to-peer model includes decentralization, scalability, and fault-tolerance, along with low administration expenses. Client/server architectures with centralized management policies increasingly fail with big amounts of nodes because of their complexity and extremely high demands on computing resources. Distributed content management systems address the need to access content wherever it resides, produce content while maintaining control over it, and collaborate efficiently by sharing real-time data within a distributed network of stakeholders.

This paper describes in detail the results of the first mentioned stage and represents the second stage as plans for future (in the last section). The third stage of detailed research and implementation of the GUN vision (networking) remains as a planned perspective.

Essentials of a Resource Adaptation

Semantic Data Model

We cannot say yet that Semantic Web technology as such is mature enough to be accepted by industry on a large scale. The reasons for that are analyzed in (Kaikova, Khriyenko, Kovalainen, & Zharko, 2004; Khriyenko & Terziyan, 2004; Terziyan, 2005; Terziyan & Kononenko, 2003; Terziyan & Zharko, 2003), and recent prognoses state the same (Cardoso, Miller, Su, & Pollock, 2005). Some standards still need modifications as well as appropriate tool support. For example, Semantic Web technology offers a Resource Description Framework (RDF) as a standard for semantic annotation of Web resources. It is expected that Web content with an RDF-based metadata layer and ontological basis for it will be enough to enable interoperable and automated processing of Web data by various applications. However, emerging industrial applications consider machines, processes, personnel, services for condition monitoring, remote diagnostics, and maintenance, for example, to be specific classes of Web resources and, thus, a subject for semantic annotation. Such resources are naturally dynamic, not only from the point of view of changing values for some attributes (state of resource) but also from the point of view of changing status labels (condition of the resource). Current RDF still needs temporal and contextual extensions (Nikitin, Terziyan, Tsaruk, & Zharko, 2005).

This motivates one of the objectives of SmartResource activities during the Adaptation Stage, which is Resource State/Condition Description Framework (RSCDF), as an extension to RDF, which introduces upper ontology (semantic standardized data model) for describing such characteristics of resources as states and corresponding conditions, dynamics of state changes, target conditions, and historical data about previous states. These descriptions are supposed to be used by external Web services (e.g., condition monitoring, remote diagnostics, and predictive maintenance of the resources). Pilot version of RSCDF and appropriate schema developed using the

Figure 2. Conceptual meaning of the resource state/condition description framework

freeware open source Protégé[3] tool are presented in Kaykova, Khriyenko, Naumenko, Terziyan, and Zharko (2005). Querying specifics of RSCDF was analyzed in (Nikitin, Terziyan, Tsaruk, & Zharko, 2005). Figure 2 depicts the conceptual meaning of RSCDF: it is an RDF-compliant semantic representation format for a resource's historical (life-cycle) data.

RSCDF inherits from RDF an approach of modeling a problem domain utilizing interrelated hierarchies of classes and properties. Special emphasis in RSCDF is made on context-sensitive semantic descriptions of Web resources. This approach endows the resulting data models with high extensibility and originally aims at providing a semantically rich descriptive data (metadata) about a corresponding resource to a new-generation (intelligent) software processing tools.

To utilize the RSCDF advantages in domains other than industrial maintenance, a simplified version of RCSDF called context description framework (CDF) (Khriyenko & Terziyan, 2005) has been designed, which includes only the following basic new components comparable to RDF: (1) contextual representation of RDF triplet statement (subject-predicate-object-context), where the context is represented with a container of RDF statements; (2) the definition of a property in RSCDF schema in addition to definition of a domain and a range will also include the definition of a context of the property as the set of possible properties from the context container for this property (see Figure 3).

Figure 3. Basics of the RSCDF extension in comparison to RDF

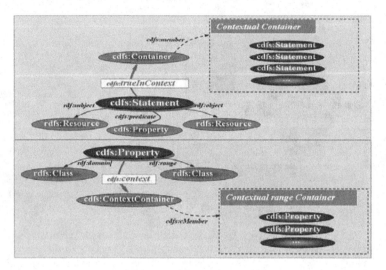

General Adaptation Framework

Another obstacle for the Semantic Web standardization effort relates to the fact that, despite many industrial companies and consortiums having realized that a explicit description of semantics of data and domain modeling is necessary for application integration, they still have used for that purpose their company/consortia-specific standards or XML language that are inappropriate for global integration. Even realizing that the Semantic Web is providing really global standards, it is already too late and too labor- and resource-consuming to transform manually huge amounts of already modeled metadata from a local to a global standard. One possible solution would be to design semantic adapters that enable semi-automatic transformation from company-specific standards to Semantic-Web standards. This motivates the second objective of the SmartResource Adaptation Stage, which is a design of the General Adaptation Framework aimed to provide a methodology for designing adapters from various data formats to RSCDF and back. The pilot version of the task and its solution are presented as deliverables of the SmartResource project,[4] along with concrete test implementations of the approach of General Adaptation —adapters for three different samples of heterogeneous resources (device data, expert interface, Web service). The conceptual picture of General Adaptation Framework is shown in Figure 4.

Figure 4. General Adaptation Framework illustrated

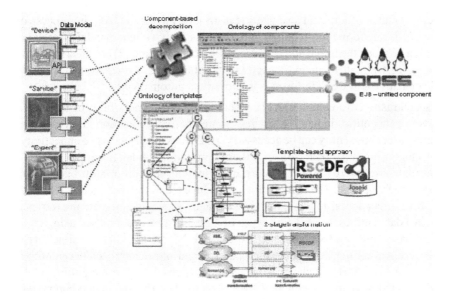

In the approach of General Adaptation, we distinguish two aspects of adaptation: data model transformation and application programming interface (API) adaptation, as it was mentioned in the introduction. The first aspect focuses on a transformation of resource data stored in a specific data model (relational database, family of XML-based standards, UML, etc.) to a unified semantically rich format (in our case, to RSCDF), and vice versa. For this purpose, we utilize a method of two-stage transformation, which assumes mapping of a specific data model to a corresponding canonical form from the same family of data representation standards. If, for instance, we need to transform an XML schema to RSCDF, first we have to define the XML canonical schema and make a mapping to it.

The strength of the two-stage transformation is in reuse of a variety of existing powerful tools for data model mapping[5] and also in simplification of the data model mapping process for potential customers (owners of resources that are intended to be integrated into the target maintenance environment). The owners do not have to think about complicated ways to transform their data models to RDF-based standards; they just have to map their data model to the canonical one within the same standard (e.g., XML). After native-to-canonical data model mapping, the template-based approach of semantic transformation from a canonical form to RSCDF is applied according to GAF. This approach is based on automated generation of XML serialized RSCDF instances, which are determined from the ontology of templates. The ontology stores classified pairs of correspondence between canonical and RSCDF patterns, chunks of terminal strings of text. In fact, thanks to GAF, the process of data model transformation requires only two relatively simple manual efforts: (1) mapping between the initial and canonical data schemata and (2) engineering of the ontology of templates. Having these two activities done, the data transformation between native and RSCDF formats is carried out automatically.

The second aspect of adaptation (API adaptation) relates to a possibility of automated access to data entities in native storages through native application interfaces. For instance, a database entity can be accessed via ODBC (Open Database Connectivity) connectors using functional calls in different programming languages. To access a certain database record for further data transformation, an appropriate programming component must exist. The component either can execute native functional calls or perform a direct access to the native data storage. Hence, to automate the retrieval of native data entities, the existing types of APIs must be decomposed using component-based analysis (Nierstrasz & Dami, 1995; Nierstrasz, Gibbs, & Tsichritzis, 1992; Teschke & Ritter, 2001), classified and arranged into a centralized/decentralized library (Lucena, 2001). Such components, in a vision of GAF, are building blocks for automated assembly of concrete adapter on the fly. The automated component integration is performed using ontology of components, and the resulting adapter is run as an EJB[6] (Enterprise Java Bean) component on a JBoss Application server[7] in our implementation.

To a have a comprehensive framework for adaptation of resources, ontology of templates and ontology of components must be closely interrelated due to high dependency between data models and methods of accessing the corresponding data.

SmartResource Prototype Environment

For a practical testing of the developed General Adaptation approach, the first version of the target prototype environment has been implemented. The environment can be launched on one or several workstations, which meets the specified installation requirements. Figure 5 illustrates the architecture of the implemented prototype environment.

For the process of software engineering, the latest and most powerful freeware and open source tools and technologies have been used. The whole environment is based on Java 2 Platform, Enterprise Edition[8] (J2EE) and was developed using Eclipse[9] Integrated Development Environment, together with the Poseidon[10] UML-based modeling tool. Versioning control was carried out with the help of the CVS[11] tool. As mentioned, for testing the approach of General Adaptation Framework and the

Figure 5. Architecture of the SmartResource prototype environment, v. 1.0

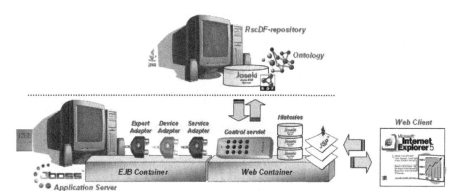

RSCDF format, three sample adapters were implemented (for a device, an expert, and a Web service). Their logic was encapsulated in three Enterprise Java Beans (EJB) and executed on the JBoss application server. Specification of the KF-330 Blow Molding Machine was used for simulation of the device data (seven device parameters). Device states were generated in a form of XML entities according to the corresponding XML schemata (three different schema variations plus a canonical one). State and condition resource data have been encoded in RSCDF after the transformation and stored in a remote Joseki[12] RDF server. For creation of a local history cache, Jena[13] classes were used. Code that coordinated coherent work of the adapters and provided a control/monitoring over them was executed in the control Java Servlet.[14] Visualization of the internal processes of the prototype environment was organized using a set of Java Server Pages[15] (JSP). Demonstrations were carried out using Internet Explorer Web browser.

Web service adapter incorporated a simple sample of learning algorithm (KNN method) wrapped by a Web service container using Axis[16] and Lomboz[17] (see Figure 6). The adapter using generated SOAP-client simulated software agents' requests for learning and diagnostics. For RSCDF-XML transformations, the adapter used the approach of two-stage transformation with RDQL-templates.

In the implementation of the human expert adapter, a two-stage transformation and User Interface Templates were used for flexible building of a specific human interface (Figure 7). Involvement of the JFreeChart[18] open Java library allowed generating images for representation of the device states. Human Expert is requested for diagnostics via e-mail.

Figure 6. Implementation architecture of the Web service adapter

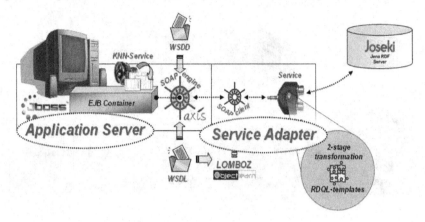

Figure 7. Implementation architecture of the human expert adapter

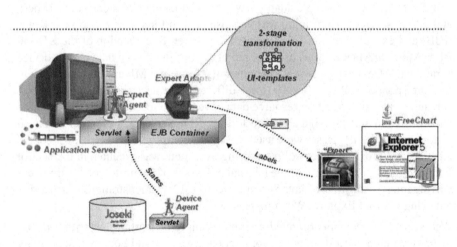

Implementing General
Adaptation Framework

Challenges

There is a variety of resources intended for integration into a common SmartRe-source environment. For more efficient analysis, all resources were divided into three basic classes: devices, services, and humans. These resources represent real-world objects that should interact in a certain way according to appropriate business models. The adaptation of such heterogeneous resources in common sense lies in providing an environment that would allow them to communicate in a unified way via standard protocol.

The primary intention behind the General Adaptation Framework (GAF) is a design of common framework for adaptation of heterogeneous resources. The design of the framework will be divided into two layers:

1.   Structured software design for modules, classes, behavior, and protocols

2.   Semantic adaptation of different formalizations of the problem domain edges

A semantic transformation is one of the key problems in the development of the General Adaptation Framework. We assume that semantic annotation of data that are used in communication between heterogeneous software components based on common ontology (Farrai, Lewis, & Langendoen, 2002) will enable interoperability (Malucelli & Oliveira, 2003).

At the moment, an arbitrary number of standards exists; these standards define each other on different levels of abstraction and, thus, form a hierarchy. There are many data models, and one of them that recently has gained wide adoption is Extensible Markup Language (XML). The older and more tested data representation standard is Relational Model. The novel data representation standards that focus primarily

Figure 8. Two-stage transformation

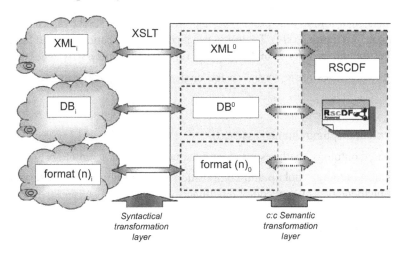

on semantics are RDF and OWL. All these data representation standards first have to be analyzed in order to understand the essence of semantic transformation. As we can see, the standards provide specifications as guidelines to formalization of various problem domains. For a concrete problem domain, the necessary schemata are constructed as a formalized domain model based on the corresponding specifications. Content (documents, database records, any structured data) that includes a set of facts within the chosen problem domain are structured according to the developed schemata and specifications. More abstract models define the more specific ones. In different cases, an arbitrary number of models can be found in chains and layers. In this perspective, the semantic transformation results in extraction of data semantics independently from a particular data representation standard. This approach must be used to allow encoding of these data to another representation standard without losing the meaning.

During the semantic transformation process, transforming object/module involves a format's metadata (schemas) and transformation rules. Schemas, rules, and underlying ontologies constitute a framework for semantic transformation. Semantic transformation defines a functionality to work with semantics of:

- Adapter functionality (services provided by an adapter)
- Data representation standards and models of adapter systems
- Software interface standards of adapted systems
- Configuration properties of an adapter runtime environment

Given that unambiguous semantic description of resources that are supposed to be machine-processable, an automated adapter composition will be possible. However, an unambiguous semantic description requires a human to map the meaning of concepts and relations, unless this mapping already exists in some ontology. Tools will be needed to simplify the process of mapping for human (Kaykova, Khriyenko, Kovalainen, & Zharko, 2004). Tools will use faceted classification adapted for each particular domain in order to make the most relevant concepts easily accessible.

The following cases are essential in the context of automated semantic adaptation:

1. Explicit mapping (human assisted)
2. Shared ontology (both resources are mapped to the same ontology)
3. Shared ontology lookup and composition (may be wrapped as a service or implemented as an embedded functionality)

Pilot Implementation of Semantic Adapters

Two-Stage Transformation

The SmartResource domain needs RDF and its RSCDF extension as a basis for the formalization. Concept definitions that are also necessary are included in RSCDF schema (Resource State/Condition Description Framework, see detailed description in Kaykova, Khriyenko, Naumenko, Terziyan, & Zharko [2005]). To meet the challenge of semantic adaptation, an ontology-based approach is used to define the semantics. This involves associating a commonly used meaning to the definition of adapter properties, functionality, configuration, and corresponding metadata standards.

The SmartResource addresses the adaptation challenge using the two-stage transformation:

- Syntactical transformation
- Canonical-to-canonical semantic transformation

Such a technique seems reasonable, because the division into two independent phases facilitates the whole transformation process. This is possible in cases where tools for (semi)automatic syntactical transformation exist. A specific canonical form for a given domain description should be available for every data representation standard so that a transformation is performed between different schemas of the same data model.

XSLT-based transformation is a good example of syntactical transformation of XML files. In our case, XSLT is used for syntactical transformation among different XML-schemas (XPATH expressions are also a possible solution). Each document of a certain standard (for XML it is XMLi) is transformed into a corresponding canonical form (for XML, it is XML0) during the syntactical transformation stage, as shown in Figure 8. During the second stage (canonical-to-canonical semantic transformation), the canonical form (e.g., XML0) is transformed into the unified semantic canonical form, which is RSCDF in our case.

The two-stage transformation assumes functioning in both directions; that is, the RSCDF-XML0-XMLi path of the transformation is equally in the scope of the analysis. There are few projects that have elaborated pilot methods of transforming RDF to XML (Miller & Sperberg-McQueen, 2004; XR homepage, 2004). Since RSCDF is an enhanced subset of RDF, it also is possible to adopt these methods.

Once the mechanism of transformation from RSCDF to XML and XML to RSCDF has been designed, it is possible to use standard approaches for future transformations

Figure 9. XML transformation in MapForce, adopted

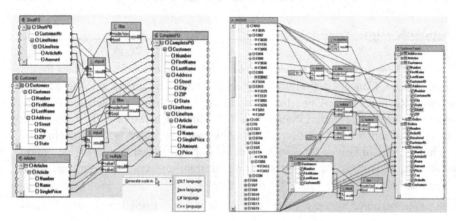

(to other existing standards). We assume such approach to decrease the complexity of a whole transformation task, because existing tools and standards of syntactical transformation can be reused and utilized. Canonical form limits variety of syntactical representation of the same domain to a strict syntactical form and allows a template-based approach for semantic transformation.

From the existing commercial tools that provide transformation of XML to other formats, Altova MapForce can be mentioned.[19] This commercial tool allows XML to XML transformation based upon two XML schemas (Figure 9, left picture). It also might be necessary to perform some processing functions to pipe data from source to target.

MapForce allows mapping between XML and Relational database, too (Figure 9, right picture). The process of mapping starts from the loading of database schema and XML schema. Then, an engineer manually fulfills matching between XML elements and database entities. While mapping, it might be necessary to use processing functions.

Canonical Forms

The development of the canonical forms for a particular problem domain involves domain experts and takes into account existing formalizations of the same problem domain. As an example of the latter, Paper IXI,[20] a consortia-wide XML-based standard for Paper Mill model, can be mentioned.

The domain, which is in focus of the SmartResource activities, is related to the paper industry, paper machines, and a process of paper manufacturing. The first stage of the development of a canonical form for this domain will be elaboration of a conceptual model for it. First, the domain description in a natural language must exist. It can be made separately, or existing specifications can be used. The main point is that this description must contain all important aspects of the problem domain. For our domain, the description can include such phrases as "a paper machine produces paper, uses cellulose," and so forth.

The domain decomposition follows the domain description and is based on it. In that stage, entities, classes, properties, relations, and behaviors of the problem domain are distinguished. After the necessary decompositions, the domain formalization is performed using any appropriate data models. It can be ER (entity relationship) diagrams, UML, Ontology, and so forth.

Then, analysis of data representation format, which will be used for the canonical form, should be performed. It includes analysis of the data format type (XML, text file, Excel table, Oracle database, etc.), types of APIs that can be used in the domain (SQL-queries, Java DOM API, XQuery, etc.), access methods to data (JDBC, OLE, etc.), and types of standards that are used to represent a format (ASCII, W3C-family standards).

The first stage of the canonical-to-canonical semantic transformation is a metadata analysis. This stage includes analysis of data schema used in the canonical form (elements, relationships, types, etc.), possible variations (XML tags or values, etc.), and hierarchy of elements and restrictions (nesting of classes, range, etc.).

A further stage of the canonical-to-canonical semantic transformation is an analysis of standard that has been chosen for the canonical representation form. This stage includes analysis of standard specification (syntax, vendors, schema, etc.), analysis of existing formal theory (relational algebra, frame model, etc.), analysis of existing

Figure 10. Example of syntactical transformation

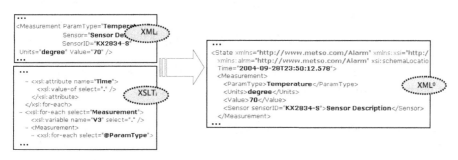

methods of transformation (XSLT, production rules, etc.), and analysis of capabilities and restrictions (possibilities of formalization, querying, etc.).

The final step of the canonical-to-canonical semantic transformation is concerned with data-mapping rules. This paper considers a use case of XML-RDF transformation. This stage requires efforts for determining a protocol of transformation (elements and types matching); representation format for the rules (Ontology, XSLT, etc.); and percentage of manual, semiautomatic, and automatic matching actions.

In the SmartResource pilot implementation, according to the approach of the two-stage transformation, canonical XML schema was designed and another three different XML schemata were used for testing the phase of syntactical transformation. Those three schemata were dedicated to describe the same semantics (physical measurements), using different structural organization and syntactic elements (XML attributes and tags). The canonical schema is designed to incorporate a unification of all semantically significant XML tags and to represent a single syntactical option for them. To perform syntactical transformation to the common XML canonical form, for each of the three XML schemata, corresponding XSLT files were generated using MapForce trial version. Figure 10 contains fragments of one XMLi file, corresponding XSLTi used for transforming, and the fragment of the resulting XML file in the canonical form.

The mechanism of transformation requires the following analyses to be done: analysis of possible approaches (tools, APIs, services, etc.), estimation of cost for particular approach (time for development, price of the product, etc.), and study of interoperability and extensibility of the chosen approach (supported platforms, extensible API, etc.). For transformation, existing tools can be used, or, if reasonable, these tools can be developed from scratch. The most popular APIs used in transformation of XML are XSLT, SAX, and DOM. In the case of RSCDF, the functionality for implementation must be defined; either it will be XML-to-RDF transformation or more.

Use Case Scenario

Since many details about the SmartResource pilot implementation have been covered in Section 3, here we give just an example of the whole cycle of adaptation that takes place in the pilot environment. Some implementation details that have not been mentioned previously are given also.

The use case scenario that is used for testing the pilot implementation is based on the interaction procedures among heterogeneous Device, Service, and Expert (see Figure 11).

The scenario includes device diagnostics by a human expert that watches the device history through the expert adapter and puts diagnostic labels on the device states

Figure 11. Use case scenario of the SmartResource I

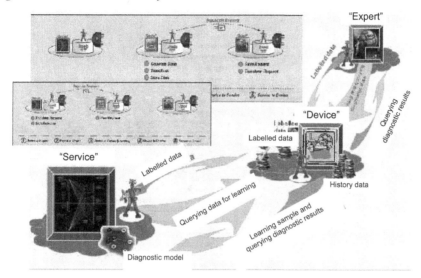

after analysis. The labeled data in the RSCDF format is stored in the history of the device and further is used for a learning procedure with the service. In order to meaningfully read the device history, service utilizes the corresponding adapter.

Thus, the tasks of the three adapters generated using General Adaptation Framework, are as follows:

1. Transform XML-based descriptions of the device history into the appropriate RSCDF form (instances).

2. After that, on the request of the expert (diagnostics) or service (learning/diagnostics), the adapter has to transform device data from the RSCDF form to the representation that is more convenient for the expert/service. Feedback of the expert or service has to be converted again into RSCDF for further reading by the device logics.

Let us describe the sequence of operational steps that occur according to the use case scenario. The corresponding sequence diagram created with the Poseidon UML modeling tool is presented in Figure 12. In the figure, four acting objects of the scenario are shown: Service Prototype, Device Prototype, Expert Prototype, and a Human User actor. The prototypes comprise corresponding adapters, and a simple logic of interaction among each other is used for testing the adapters. The Human User actor represents a Web-browser-based user interface designed for monitoring

Figure 12. Sequence diagram of the SmartResource I use case scenario

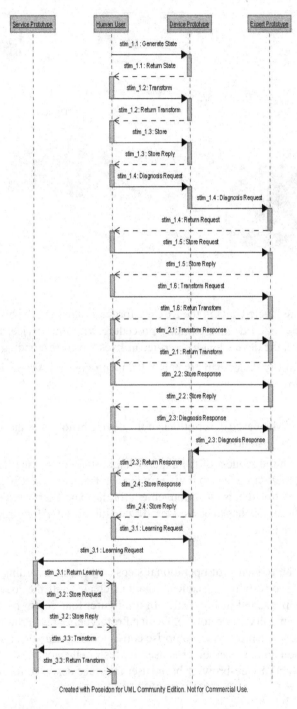

Created with Poseidon for UML Community Edition. Not for Commercial Use.

and controlling the functionality of the adapters. The user interface is implemented as HTML image maps (a couple of them can be seen in Figure 11).

The use case scenario comprises five interaction phases: (1) device-to-expert, (2) expert-to-device, (3) device-to-service (learning), (4) device-to-service (diagnostics), and (5) service-to-device. Each of them tests a concrete functionality of the adapters and interoperability among the underlying heterogeneous components. In the sequence diagram, just one to three interaction phases are included, because five and six duplicate the dialog of the device with expert (one and two). Each interaction phase is divided into a sequence of stimuli that denote atomic interactions among the actors of the diagram. Each stimulus has a name pattern — stim_X.Y — followed by the name of atomic interaction, where X denotes a number of the interaction phase and Y the number of the atomic interaction. For example, stim_1.2: Transform denotes a stimulating request sent by a user for invocation of the logic of the Device Adapter. In this chapter, we show stimuli from the sequence diagram that relate to the Device Adapter. The first one is stim_1.1:ReturnState, which denotes a process when Device Prototype returns a generated device state to the user in a form of chart that has underlying XML (canonical form mentioned in a previous subsection) representation (see Figure 13).

Stimulus stim_1.2:ReturnTransform is also worth mentioning, because it reflects sending results of the transformation process performed by the Device Adapter to the user in a form of RSCDF instances. All classes, which constitute the device adapter, are packaged into one template package (see Figure 14). Logically, the classes could

Figure 13. Device state represented in XML and in a chart

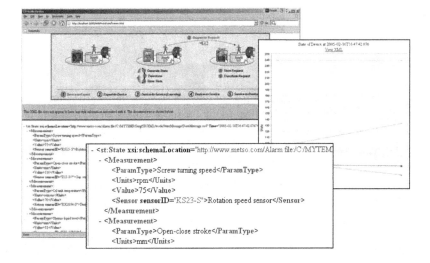

Figure 14. UML diagram of classes for a semantic adapter of a device

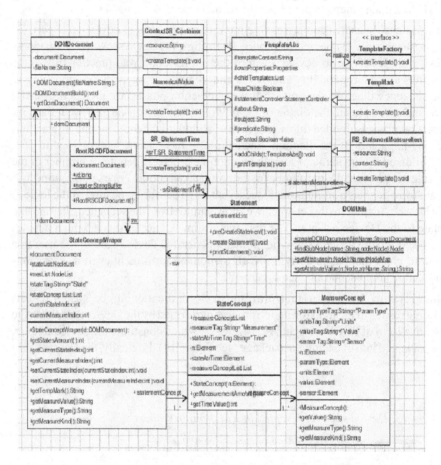

be divided into four parts. The first part of classes corresponds to the logic, which reflects the structure of the RSCDF document; the second one reflects the structure of the original XML document and encapsulates the logic of processing this structure; the third one represents the engine that plays the role of RSCDF document builder; and the fourth one is the set of reusable utilities for DOM processing.

For implementation of the second phase (XML0-RSCDF canonical-to-canonical semantic transformation), the method based on templates was applied. During the analysis of the RSCDF document, reusable templates can be extracted. For instance, from a RSCDF document, two types of templates were distinguished: structural (patterns) and tag. Structural templates reflect the structure of the RSCDF graph ac-

Figure 15. Template-based transformation

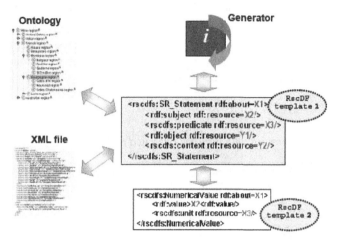

cording to its schema. Depending on a canonical XML document, some branches of the RSCDF graph have the same structure and could be cloned while processing.

On the other hand, the tag templates correspond to the RSCDF classes. In fact, tag template represents some classes from RSCDF schema; for example, SR_Statement, Context_SR_Container, SR_Container, NumericalValue, TempTempMark. Tag templates are "bricks," which are used by the adapter to produce the RSCDF document. Tag template has a body and a changing part, which can have different types:

- Link to other tag template
- Link to XML data
- Link to ontology data
- Generated value

Figure 15 represents an example of the tag template. The variable Xn is obtained during a run-time either from ontology or the XML file, or generated by the generator. The variable Yn is obtained from the identifier of from some other template. This means that if an RSCDF tag depends on some other RSCDF tag, then it will be generated after the latter one. In this way, the adapter recursively calls methods of template creation until it will reach the leaf nodes.

Using tag and structural templates, the device adapter performs semantic transformation. This approach provides a possible way to implement the logic of semantic transformation from canonical XML to RSCDF format.

For modularity of the approach and for a possibility of easy modeling over templates, all necessary lexical concepts that will be used further in manual or semi-automated (in perspective) manipulation, are defined in ontology (see Figure 16).

Figure 17 presents an example of a template for NumericalValue concept from the ontology with defined XML serialization form, which can be reused in semantic (canonical-to-canonical) XML-RSCDF transformation.

Figure 16. Sample ontology of templates designed in Protégé

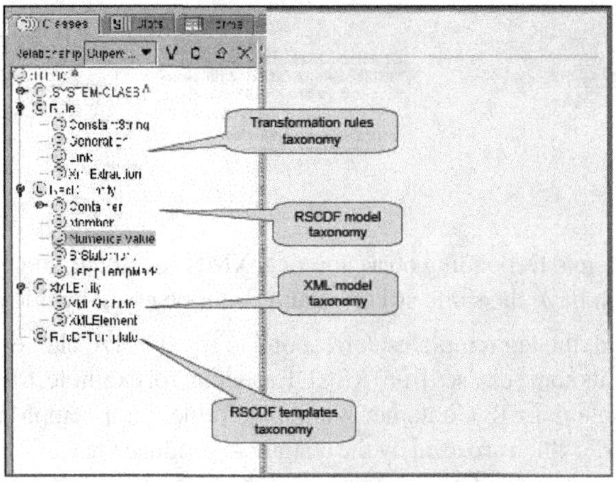

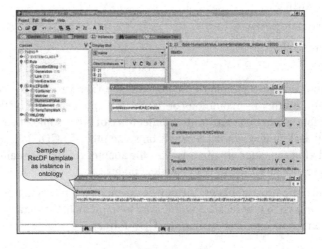

Figure 17. Example of a template definition in Protégé

Conclusion

Research efforts have been made to explore the potential of the emerging and promising Semantic Web technology in a challenge of adaptation of existing widely adopted models of data representation to emerging RDF-based ones. In contrast to ICT, the semantic technologies represent meanings separate from data, content, or program code, using the open standards for the Semantic Web. They are language-neutral, machine -interpretable, sharable, and adaptive, allowing ontology-based integration of heterogeneous resources.

During the adaptation stage that has been described in detail in this paper, we succeeded in implementation and prototype testing of the semantic modeling approach for the challenge of semantic adaptation of conventional data representation models (taking XML as an example) to the upcoming RDF-based models. The ultimate goal is to develop efficient semantic modeling methodology in order to simplify the relevant problem of integration of legacy systems that currently are used to manage digital aspects of enterprise resources to an automated, agent-based environment. Currently, this problem has been attacked in its two major points: data model transformation and integration of application programming interfaces. The latter remains unexplored, but application of semantic modeling with design of necessary ontology of components (the main granules for the composition processes) has become an indubitable direction for the efficient solution. The novel combination of the semantic modeling (ontology of components) with the component-based decomposition (the latter has developed for more than 10 years) is assumed to increase significantly the efficiency of the component-oriented analysis toward automation of the enterprise application integration.

The introduction of the semantic modeling element (ontology of data model templates — structural patterns and interrelations among them) into the process of data model transformation is anticipated to be a basis for tools that will allow an automation of the transformation. Also, the competent decomposition of the data model transformation process into two stages (mapping of a native format to a canonical one and mapping of the canonical model to a semantic one) will relieve resource providers of the complexities of semantics (facilitating the adoption of the Semantic Web technology) and will harness existing model mapping tools.

As for the semantic format based on the developed Resource State/Condition Description Framework, its presentation is intended to initiate a useful enhancement of the RDF standard in regard to its applicability to highly dynamic resource maintenance environments. A current version of the RSCDF schema, which contains contextual and temporal extensions, and adapters from and to RSCDF format are assumed to be a good case to facilitate the Semantic Web technology industrial adoption.

Discussion and Future Work

One of the goals of the SmartResource activity is a demonstration of the benefits and possibilities that the Semantic Web technology potentially can bring to the industry. The trend within worldwide activities related to Semantic Web definitely shows that the technology has emerging growth of interest in both academia and business during a quite small time interval. The stage of the technology (according to highly qualified expert evaluations [Davis, 2004]) is called now "from skepticism and curiosity to enthusiasm: People are now asking 'How questions as opposed to 'Why' and 'What.'" Moreover, prognoses show that "semantic solutions, services and software markets will grow rapidly topping $60B by 2010" (Davis, 2004). Semantic technologies are building blocks of the next megawave of economic development — distributed intelligence — and now is the time for semantic technology investments to strengthen portfolios.

Usability of the SmartResource Results

The developed methodology of resource adaptation and its prototype implementation can be used by ICT industries in tasks related to the problem of Enterprise Application Integration and to less global problems of legacy application adaptation, for example. In addition, the proposed solution is compatible with the existing open W3C standard RDF, which provides rich semantic descriptions to resource data and, hence, enables resource maintenance by future specialized intelligent Web services or applications.

To apply the developed approach for the previously mentioned tasks, the following steps must be performed:

- Development of the library (centralized or decentralized storage) of reusable programming components according to the decomposition model recommended in GAF. In the development process, both large and small software development companies can participate, applying their unique expertise in specific component implementations and providing it to the world for a certain price. The great advantage of the component owners is that, according to GAF, their components are meant to be discovered and linked to the specific adapter automatically, thanks to the ontology of the components.

- Ontology of the software components must be engineered to automate the process of their search and acquisition. For this purpose, the existing types of components must be systematized, which requires involvement of a comprehensive player from the software market.

- Development of the ontology of templates, which contains a hierarchy of primitives from the canonical forms of different data models (XML, relational database, UML, etc.) and mappings among them. Decomposition of the existing data models into hierarchies of corresponding primitives requires extensive expertise in the field of domain modeling. A large software development company, using the described technology, could provide tools of automated transformation among different data models.

Communication providers can benefit from the available project results in the following way. GAF assumes adaptation and integration of the remote applications, too. This means that to assemble the necessary adapters, the software components, which provide networked connectivity, must be available in the library/ontology of the components. Therefore, software development companies would implement a specific components connector bound (configured) to a concrete communication provider that will be placed in the library and further used by adapter purchasers. In the prototype implementation, conventional information networked channels are used for connectivity among adapters; e-mail services are used to deliver diagnostic requests to a human expert. The diagnostic request also was tested on a reach/availability from the mobile communicator and the diagnostic interface. In the implementation plans, there is an SMS-driven human expert notification that is also very functionally beneficial for communication providers.

Another opportunity of the results application is appropriate in the environment of heterogeneous communication operators, where interoperability is required for proper transaction transfer among operators and for integral representation of a state-of-communication system or a mobile user's state/condition. However, this needs additional analysis of the results in the mentioned context.

Application Areas

The designed General Adaptation Framework and its implementation due to its original universality are supposed to find applications in various domains in which distributed heterogeneous resources exist, and problems of interoperability and integration into dynamic open environments are emerging.

Besides its main application area (integration of industrial assets), more than once the SmartResource activity results were analyzed in the context of such application areas as wellness (integration of human patients with embedded medical sensors, doctors/experts, and medical Web services), ecology (natural environment with sensors, human experts in an environmental monitoring, and Web services for environmental diagnostics and prediction), organizational management (staff/students with corresponding monitored organizational data, managers, and automated systems for organizational diagnostics and management), video security systems (objects under observation, monitoring experts, and video/image automated processing tools), and so forth.

Expert analysis of recent results and further brainstorming session have revealed their applicability in the sports domain. Currently, many kinds of human wearable and implanted sensors exist, and their integration could provide a comprehensive data set about the dynamics of a sportsman's state. The SmartResource General Adaptation Framework, in this case, could be applied to the adaptation of the heterogeneous sensors to a unified environment and their data integrated to a comprehensive semantic data model. Data stored with these assumptions can be available to sophisticated analytical software (even remote) or human experts, which also are supposed to be integrated to the same medium. As a concrete use case, we can consider, for example, some neuro-fuzzy online predictor that analyzes a track of ski-jumpers' state changes, and gives real-time instruction (e.g., about correct posture). The real-time instruction is very helpful for different sportsmen (e.g., swimmers, runners, water-jumpers, bodybuilders, etc.) during their training; the corrections of the loading are made, depending on the context (human condition, endured traumas, weather conditions, etc.). The output diagnosis of the decision-making service can be not so demanding to a response time, like a generation of a monthly or yearly individual training schedule. The latter has been formalized, classified, and specified rather well by now, which makes it easy to represent in a form of ontology. Sportsmen training and instructing is a very relevant domain for automated learning services, which, after the adaptation, can learn on the unified sportsmen training data and act as an expert service in the future.

The next application area covers various enterprise-wide knowledge management systems and research and development activities management systems, which integrate numerous heterogeneous companies' branches and coordinate their processes, providing an integral and unified representation interface. Enterprise resources planning (ERP) is a more concrete example of an application area; a representation of the state of resources through the whole enterprise in the integral view is a current challenge for many large companies today (e.g., integration of reports in Excel, XML, and different standards into one). Very often, within one big company, product or project data that are distributed among many filial parts in heterogeneous formats/systems must be transformed to a common format to enable determining the similarities and intersections among the products and projects.

Another application area is "Tender Management" (i.e., the evaluation of subcontractors). Companies such as Microsoft could utilize the project results for building a management system of the tender activities carried out among numerous heterogeneous third-party vendors. For this, the restrictions on the specification of the required component/subsystem are formalized in a unified form (according to our solution, it will be RDF/RSCDF) to enable automated semantic match with a corresponding description of the third-party vendor solutions.

Statistical information gathering (e.g., in the automobile industry) also is a possible implementation area. Manufacturers could accumulate statistical data, integrating sensor/alarm data from embedded blocks inside car systems. Integration of heterogeneous data takes place here, and its further analysis would help in planning production strategies.

Further Development

Semantic Web standards are not yet supporting semantic descriptions of resources with proactive behavior. However, as our research shows (Kaikova, Khriyenko, Kononenko, Terziyan, & Zharko, 2004), to enable effective and predictive maintenance of an industrial device in a distributed and open environment, it will be necessary to have autonomous agent-based monitoring over a device state and condition as well as support from remote diagnostics Web services. This means that the description of a device as a resource also will require a description of proactive behavior of autonomous condition monitoring applications (agents, services) toward effective and predictive maintenance of the device. For that, we recently have developed another extension of RDF, Resource Goal/Behavior Description Framework (RGBDF), to enable explicit specification of maintenance goals and possible actions toward faults monitoring, diagnostics, and maintenance. Based on RSCDF and RGBDF and appropriate ontological support, we also plan to design RSCDF/RGBDF platforms for Smart Resources (devices, Web services, and human experts) equipped by adapters and agents for proactivity, and then to apply several scenarios of communication among the platforms toward learning Web services based on device data and expert diagnostics to enable automated remote diagnostics of devices by Web services (see Figure 18).

Another challenge for the Semantic Web is the contradiction between the concept of centralized and shared ontology to enable global interoperability and the decentralized nature of today's global businesses. Actually, the heterogeneity of ontologies is already the fact, which prevents inter-consortia interoperability. Discovering necessary resources or services in the network, which is heterogeneous on the ontology level, requires specific solutions, among which semantic peer-to-peer resource discovery and context-sensitive ontologies could be an option. One of the targets for our project is a planned implementation of such condition monitoring, remote diagnostics, and predictive maintenance scenarios, which can be managed in a decentralized P2P heterogeneous environment. The scenarios assume agent-based interoperation of multiple devices, multiple services, and multiple experts, which allows the discovery of necessary experts in P2P networks, using their experiences to learn remote diagnostics Web services, making online diagnostics of devices by integrating diagnoses from several services, learning models for a device diagnostics based on online data from several distributed samples of similar device, and so forth.

Figure 18. Preliminary architecture of the SmartResource prototype environment v.2.0

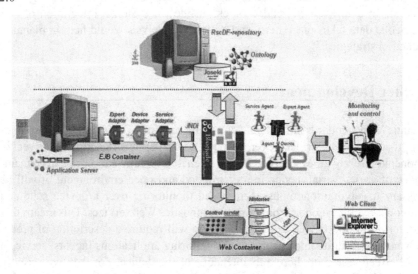

Figure 19. Evolution of RDF towards GUN platforms through dynamics and proactivity

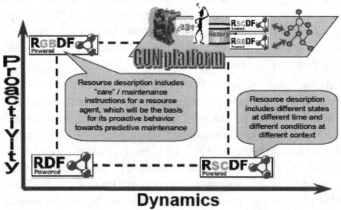

In general, the project's efforts strive to catalyze the evolution of RDF toward two directions: RSCDF (dynamics and context awareness) and RGBDF (proactivity and self-maintenance); the ultimate result has to be a set of open standards that enable the GUN architecture (Figure 19).

As mentioned previously, the GUN environment is meant for online condition monitoring and predictive maintenance of various industrial resources. Utilization of RSCDF and RGBDF allows the creation of agent-driven GUN platforms for each industrial resource, where all data related to monitoring, diagnostics, and maintenance of the resource will be collected in the resource history (lifeblog) and managed by the resource agent (Terziyan, 2005b).

Acknowledgment

This research has been performed as part of the SmartResource (Proactive Self-Maintained Resources in Semantic Web) project in Agora Center (University of Jyväskylä, Finland) and funded by TEKES, an industrial consortium of the following companies: Metso Automation, TeliaSonera, TietoEnator, and Science Park.

References

Adaptive Services Grid (ASG) project. (2005). Retrieved from http://asg-platform. org

Apte, A. (2002). *Java connector architecture: Building enterprise adaptors*. Sams Publishing. ISBN 0-672-32310-9, p. 360.

Automation. (2003). *Metso Automation's Customer Magazine*, (1), 7-9.

BMC Press. (2003). *Enterprise application integration: The risks behind the rewards* (white paper). Retrieved from http://www.bmc.com

Business process execution language for Web Services (BPEL4WS) Version 1.1. (2003). Retrieved from http://www-128.ibm.com/developerworks/library/ws-bpel

Cardoso, J., Miller, J., Su, J., & Pollock, J. (2005). Academic and industrial research: Do their approaches differ in adding semantics to Web services? In J. Cardoso & A. Sheth (Eds.), *Proceedings of the First International Workshop on Semantic Web Services and Web Processes Composition (SWSWPC 2004)* (Vol. 3387, pp. 14-21). Heidelberg: Springer-Verlag.

Context-aware business application service co-ordination in mobile computing environments — CASCOM project. (2005). Retrieved from http://www.ist-cascom.org

Davis, M. (2004, September). The business value of semantic technology. In *Proceedings of the Second Annual Semantic Technologies for E-Government Conference,* McLean, VA.

Ermolayev, V., Keberle, N., Plaksin, S., Kononenko, O., & Terziyan, V. (2004). Towards a framework for agent-enabled semantic Web service composition. *International Journal of Web Services Research, 1*(3), 63-87.

Farrar, S., Lewis, W., & Langendoen, T.A. (2002, March 10-13). A common ontology for linguistic concepts. In *Proceedings of the Knowledge Technologies Conference*, Seattle, WA.

Jess, the rule engine for the Java platform. (2005). Retrieved April 10, 2005, from http://herzberg.ca.sandia.gov/jess

Kaikova, H., Khriyenko, O., Kononenko, O., Terziyan, V., & Zharko, A. (2004). Proactive self-maintained resources in Semantic Web. Eastern-European *Journal of Enterprise Technologies, 2*(1), 4-16.

Kaykova, O., Khriyenko, O., Kovalainen, M., & Zharko, A. (2004, February 17-19). Visual interface for adaptation of data sources to semantic Web. In *Proceedings of the IASTED International Conference on Software Engineering (SE 2004)*, Innsbruck, Austria (pp. 544-547). ACTA Press.

Kaykova, O., Khriyenko, O., Naumenko, A., Terziyan, V., & Zharko, A. (2005). RSCDF: A dynamic and context-sensitive metadata description framework for industrial resources. *Eastern-European Journal of Enterprise Technologies, 3*(3), 1729-3774.

Khanna, R. (2004). *Top challenges in integration projects* (white paper). ITtollbox EAI. Retrieved from www.ittool box.com

Khriyenko, O., & Terziyan, V. (2004, June 24-26). OntoSmartResource: An industrial resource generation in semantic Web. In R. Schoop, A. Colombo, R. Berhardt, & G. Schreck (Eds.), *Proceedings of the Second IEEE International Conference on Industrial Informatics (INDIN '04)*, Berlin, Germany (pp. 175-179).

Khriyenko, O., & Terziyan, V. (2005). *Context description framework for the Semantic Web* (working draft). Retrieved from http://www.cs.jyu.fi/ai/papers/JBCS-2005.pdf

Lara, R., Roman, D., Polleres, A., & Fensel, D.A. (2004, September 27-30). A conceptual comparison of WSMO and OWL-S. In *Proceedings of the European Conference on Web Services*, Erfurt, Germany (pp. 254-269).

Lucena, V. (2001). Facet-based classification scheme for industrial automation software components. In *Proceedings of the Sixth International Workshop on Component-Oriented Programming (WCOP 2001)*, Budapest, Hungary.

Malucelli, A., & Oliveira, E. (2003, November 7-8). Ontology-services to facilitate agents' interoperability. In *PRIMA '03: Proceedings of the Sixth Pacific Rim International Workshop On Multi-Agents (LNAI)*, Seoul, Korea. Springer-Verlag.

METEOR-S: Semantic Web Services and processes. (2005). LSDIS Lab, University of Georgia. Retrieved from http://lsdis.cs.uga.edu/ and http://swp.semantic-web.org

Miller, E., & Sperberg-McQueen, C.M. (2004, August 3). On mapping from collo-quial XML to RDF using XSLT. In *Proceedings of the W3C Extreme Markup Languages,* Montreal, Canada.

Nierstrasz, O., & Dami, L. (1995). Component-oriented software technology. In O. Nierstrasz & D. Tsichritzis (Eds.), *Object-oriented software composition* (pp. 3-28). Prentice Hall.

Nierstrasz, O., Gibbs, S., & Tsichritzis, D. (1992). Component-oriented software development. *Communications of the ACM, 35*(9).

Nikitin, S., Terziyan, V., Tsaruk, Y., & Zharko, A. (2005). Querying dynamic and context-sensitive metadata in Semantic Web. In V. Gorodetsky, J. Liu, & V.A. Skormin (Eds.), *Proceedings of the International Workshop on Autonomous Intelligent Systems: Agents and Data Mining (AIS-ADM-2005)* (pp. 200-214). Springer.

Ontology Web language for Web Services (OWL-S) 1.0. (2003). Retrieved from http://www.daml.org/services/owl-s/1.0

Paolucci, M., Srinivasan, N., & Sycara, K. (2004). Expressing WSMO mediators in OWL-S. In *Proceedings of the International Semantic Web Conference (Workshop Notes VI: Semantic Web Services)* (pp. 120-134).

Semantic Web Enabled Web Services (SWWS) project. (2005). Retrieved from http://swws.semanticweb.org

Semantic Web Services Initiative/Semantic Web Services Architecture. (2005). Retrieved from http://www.daml.org/services/swsa

Simple object access protocol (SOAP) 1.1. (2000). Retrieved from http://www.w3.org/TR/soap

Sivashanmugam, K., Miller, J., Sheth, A., & Verma, K. (2004). Framework for Semantic Web process composition. *International Journal of Electronic Commerce, 9*(2), 71-106.

Sun Press. (2003). *J2EE connector architecture specification, v. 1.5.* Sun Micro-systems Inc. Retrieved from http://www.sun.com

Terziyan, V. (2003). Semantic Web services for smart devices in a "global understand-ing environment." In R. Meersman & Z. Tari (Eds.), *On the move to meaningful Internet systems 2003* (Vol. 2889, pp. 279-291). Springer-Verlag.

Terziyan, V. (2005a). Semantic Web Services for smart devices based on mobile agents. *International Journal of Intelligent Information Technologies, 1*(2), 43-55.

Terziyan, V. (2005b, March 8-9). SmartResource: Utilizing semantic Web services to monitor industrial devices. In *Proceedings of the XML Finland 2005: XML—the Enabling Technology for Integrating Business Processes*, Pori, Finland.

Terziyan, V., & Kononenko, O. (2003). Semantic Web enabled Web Services: State-of-art and industrial challenges. In M. Jeckle & L.-J. Zhang (Eds.), *Web Services: ICWS-Europe 2003* (LNCS 2853, pp. 183-197). Springer-Verlag.

Terziyan, V., & Zharko, A. (2004). Semantic Web and peer-to-peer: Integration and interoperability in industry. *International Journal of Computers, Systems and Signals, 4*(2), 33-46.

Teschke, T., & Ritter, J. (2001). Towards a foundation of component-oriented software reference models. In G. Butler & S. Jarzabek (Eds.), *Generative and component-based software engineering* (LNCS). Springer Verlag.

UDDI Spec Technical Committee Specification. (2004). Retrieved from http://www.uddi.org/specification.html

Web Service Description Language (WSDL) 1.1. (2001). Retrieved from http://www.w3.org/TR/wsdl

Web Services Modeling Ontology (WSMO). (2005). Retrieved from http://www.wsmo.org

XR homepage. (2004). *XML-to-RDF transformation format*. Retrieved October 19, 2004, from http://w3future.com/xr

Endnotes

[1]   Official Web site of the SmartResource project: http://www.cs.jyu.fi/ai/OntoGroup/SmartResource_details.htm

[2]   Official Web site of the Industrial Ontologies Group: http://www.cs.jyu.fi/ai/OntoGroup/

[3]   Official Web site of the Protégé tool: http://protege.stanford.edu/

[4]   Web pages of Deliverables 2 and 3 of the SmartResource I project: http://www.cs.jyu.fi/ai/OntoGroup/Deliverable2.htm, http://www.cs.jyu.fi/ai/OntoGroup/Deliverable3.htm.

[5]   MapForce homepage: http://www. altova.com/products_mapforce.html

[6]   Enterprise JavaBeans Technology : http://java.sun.com/products/ejb/

[7]   Description of the JBoss Application Server: http://www.jboss.org/products/jbossas

8   Java 2 Platform Enterprise Edition: http://java.sun.com/j2ee/

9   Eclipse Integrated Development Environment: http://www.eclipse.org/

10   Poseidon UML modeling tool: http://www.gentleware.com/

11   CVS (Concurrent Versions System) : https://www.cvshome.org/

12   Joseki RDF server: http://www.joseki.org/

13   Jena: A Semantic Web Framework for Java: http://jena.sourceforge.net/

14   Java Servlet Technology : http://java.sun.com/products/servlet/

15   JavaServer Pages Technology : http://java.sun.com/products/jsp/

16   Official Web page of Axis Apache: http://ws.apache.org/axis/

17   Lomboz ObjectLearn Eclipse plugin: http://www.objectlearn.com/index.jsp

18   JFreeChart (free Java class library for generating charts): http://www.jfree.org/jfreechart/

19   MapForce's homepage: http://www. altova.com/products_mapforce.html

20   Official Web site of the PaperIXI project: http://pim.vtt.fi/paperixi/

The chapter was previously published in the International Journal on Semantic Web & Information Systems, 1(3), 31-63, July-September 2005.

Chapter IV

A Survey on Ontology Creation Methodologies

Matteo Cristani, Università di Verona, Italy

Roberta Cuel, Università di Verona, Italy

Abstract

In the current literature of knowledge management and artificial intelligence, several different approaches to the problem have been carried out of developing domain ontologies from scratch. All these approaches deal fundamentally with three problems: (1) providing a collection of general terms describing classes and relations to be employed in the description of the domain itself; (2) organizing the terms into a taxonomy of the classes by the ISA relation; and (3) expressing in an explicit way the constraints that make the ISA pairs meaningful. Though a number of such approaches can be found, no systematic analysis of them exists which can be used to understand the inspiring motivation, the applicability context, and the structure of the approaches. In this paper, we provide a framework for analyzing the existing methodologies that compares them to a set of general criteria. In particular, we obtain a classification based upon the direction of ontology construction; bottom-up are those methodologies that start with some descriptions of the domain and obtain a classification, while top-down ones start with an abstract view of the domain itself, which is given a priori. The resulting classification is useful not only for theoretical purposes but also in the practice of deployment of ontologies in Information Systems, since it provides a framework for choosing the right methodology to be applied in the specific context, depending also on the needs of the application itself.

Introduction

In the recent past, complex markets have been characterized by a huge specialization of work, a high level of outsourcing processes, and a more open Porter's chain that develop and increase the needs of intra- and interorganizational networks. Both intraorganizational networks among strategic units, divisions, groups, and other even smaller substructures and interorganizational networks, such as industrial districts and knowledge networks (Hamel & Prahalad, 1990) are composed of a constellation of specialized units (Ashby; 1956; Numagami, Ohta, & Nonaka, 1989), which might not be controlled totally by a unique subject and might grow and differentiate their activities, their system of artifacts, and their view of the world in an autonomous way. Although every unit uses a different view of the world (i.e., different conceptualizations), they should coexist as in a biofunctional system (Maturana & Varela, 1980) and communicate, coordinate, and share knowledge in a networked environment. Furthermore, this continuous and unpredictable encountering of different views might enable the creation of an unexpected and innovative combination of processes and products (Chandler, 1962).

Most of these processes are based nowadays on the Web, and in this scenario, tools and technologies that sustain knowledge telecommunication, coordination, and sharing are increasing their importance. Therefore, both the scientific community on computer science and industries are interested in what is called the Semantic Web. The Semantic Web community has grown in terms of dimension and specialization, and different viewpoints of creating and managing semantic tools have been taken on the nature of the Web. In studies, an excellent role is being assumed by disciplines about development of systems and methodology that allow the combination of several different views (expressed through taxonomies, classifications, contexts, and ontologies) of the world. In particular, ontology can be considered as the boundary topic between the Semantic Web research and information systems that mostly deserves special attention to the methodological aspects. This is the argument that urged researchers all over the world to create outstanding projects that involve methodological research, and that urged industries to create ontology-based applications that express the units' points of view and, at the same time, allow knowledge exchange among different units and their perspectives (Bonifacio, Bouquet, & Cuel, 2002). In this work, we are interested especially in ontology, because that it is one of the most important systems and methods that allows an explicit representation of knowledge and expresses itself a view of the world. Even if implicitly, each organization, unit, or employee interconnected in a networked system uses a personal conceptual schema that could be shared or at least understood among them. Therefore, developing a good ontology seems to be one of the critical issues in this area. For this reason, this paper focuses on the methodologies in literature that provide frameworks for developing Formal Ontologies. Frameworks are provided by ontology creation tools, which explicitly or implicitly endow a series of steps that the developer should follow. For instance, some ontology development tools make available documentation that describe the better way in which an ontology developer might create an ontology; other ontology development tools implicitly force the developer to follow some specific steps during the process of ontology creation.

Background Theories

It is quite well established in recent investigations on information systems, that formal ontologies are a crucial problem to deal with, and, in fact, they received a lot of attention in several different communities (e.g., knowledge management, knowledge engineering, natural language processing, intelligent information integration, etc.) (Fensel, 2000). Ontologies have been developed in Artificial Intelligence to facilitate knowledge sharing and reuse, and now are applied and intended to be used in expert systems of almost all types of industries. The concept of ontology that is adopted in this paper is taken from the general considerations on the use of philosophical issues in artificial intelligence:

... the systematic, formal, axiomatic development of the logic of all forms and modes of being. (Cocchiarella, 1991, pp. 640, 647)

Another commonly accepted definition is that an ontology is an explicit specification of a shared conceptualization that holds in a particular context. The actual topic of ontology is one of those themes that epistemology dealt with in philosophical studies of Parmenides, Heraclitus, Plato, Aristotle, Kant, Leibnitz, Wittgenstein, and others. Ontologies define the kind of things that exist in the world and, possibly, in an application domain. In other words, an ontology provides an explicit conceptualization that describes semantics of data, providing a shared and common understanding of a domain. From an AI perspective we can say that:

... ontology is a formal explicit specification of a shared conceptualization. Conceptualization refers to an abstract model of phenomena in the world by having identified the relevant concepts of those phenomena. Explicit means that the type of concepts used, and the constraints on their use are explicitly defined. Formal refers to the fact that the ontology should be machine readable. Shared reflect that ontology should capture consensual knowledge accepted by the communities. (Gruber, 1993, p. 203)

... an ontology may take a variety of forms, but necessarily it will include a vocabulary of terms, and some specification of their meaning. This includes definition and an indication of how concepts are inter-related which collectively impose a structure on the domain and constrain the possible interpretation of terms. (Jasper & Uschold, 1999, p. 2)

The main idea is to develop an understandable, complete, and sharable system of categories, labels, and relations that represent the real world in an objective way. For instance, one of the interesting results achieved by Aristotle is the definition of general categories used to describe the main features of events, situations, and objects in the world: quality, quantity, activity, passivity, having, situated, spatial, temporal. Kant figured out only four macro categories used to describe the world: quantity, quality, relation, and modality. Nowadays, ontologies are not only an explicit and theoretical specification of a shared conceptualization or a common and abstract understanding of a domain, but they also are implied in projects as conceptual models that allow:

- Communication among people and heterogeneous and widely spread application systems
- Content-bases access on corporate knowledge memories, knowledge bases, archives
- Agent understanding through interaction, communication, and negotiation of meanings
- Understanding and agreement upon a piece of information structure

In other words, ontologies provide qualitatively new levels of services in several application domains such as the Semantic Web (Ding & Foo, 2002) or federated databases. Moreover, they enable reuse of domain knowledge, make domain assumption explicit, and separate domain knowledge from the operational knowledge.

Unfortunately, in the real world or in practical applications (i.e., information systems, knowledge management systems, portals, and other ICT applications), the general and universal categories (studied by philosophers for a long time) are not being used widely. In particular, two main problems come up in modern applications:

- It is difficult to implement a general ontology within specific domains.
- It is too expensive to create very complex, complete, and general ontologies.

Therefore, less complete, correct, and consistent ontologies have been used, and problems have arisen due to the fact that in the same project or domain, people might use different ontologies composed by various combinations of categories. This means that different ontologies might use different categories or systems of categories to describe the same kinds of entities; or even worse, they may use the same names or systems of category for different kinds of entities. Indeed, it might be that two entities with different definitions are intended to be the same, but the task of proving that they are, indeed, the same may be difficult, if not impossible (Sowa, 2000). The basic assumption of this behavior is that what we know cannot be viewed simply as a picture of the world, as it always presupposes some degree of interpretation. Different categories represent different perspectives, aims, and degrees of world interpretation. Indeed, depending on different interpretation schemas, people may use the same categories with different meanings or different words to mean the same thing. For example, two groups of people may observes the same phenomenon but still see different problems, different opportunities, and different challenges. This essential feature of knowledge was studied from different perspectives, and the interpretation schemas were given various names (e.g., paradigms [Kuhn, 1979], frames [Goffman, 1974], thought worlds [Dougherty, 1992], context [Ghidini & Giunchiglia, 2001], mental spaces [Fauconnier, 1985], cognitive path [Weick, 1979]). This view in which the explicit part of what we know gets its meaning from a typically implicit or taken-for-granted interpretation schema leads to some important consequences regarding the adoption and use of categories and ontologies.

Therefore, an ontology is not a neutral organization of categories, but rather it is the emergence of some interpretation schema, according to which it makes sense to organize and define things in that way. In short, an ontology is often the result of a sense-making process and always represents the point of view of those who took part in that process (see Benerecetti, Bouquet, & Ghidini [2000] for a in-depth discussion of the dimensions along which any representation — including an ontology — can vary, depending on contextual factors). The person who takes part in ontology creation and management can be an expert in ontology creation or a person who, through daily work, creates and manages his or her point of view represented by an ontology.

In computer science, several languages and tools exist for helping final users and system developers in creating good and effective ontologies. In particular, various tools help people create, either manually or semi-automatically, categories, partonomies, taxonomies, and other organization levels of ontologies. Some of the most important ontology editors and ontology manager are:

- **Protégé-2000:** http://protege.stanford.edu
- **SWOOP:** http://www.mindswap.org/2004/SWOOP
- **KAON:** http://kaon.semanticweb.org
- **WSMX:** Web services execution environment is a dynamic discovery system that allows selection, mediation, invocation, and interoperation of Semantic Web services. More information can be found at http://sourceforge.net/projects/wsmx.
- **OWL-S Editor:** A plug-in developed on Protégé. Its goal is to allow easy, intuitive OWL-S service development for users who are not experts in OWL-S. It's an open source software at http://owlseditor.projects.semwebcentral.org/.
- **OntoManager:** A workbench environment that facilitates the management of ontologies with respect to a user's needs. See http://ontoware.org/details/ontomanager.

Behind these tools and techniques, different domain-independent languages have been developed and spread using RDF(S), DAML+OIL, OWL and its specifications, KIF, and so forth. DAML+OIL has been developed as a language for specifying descriptions, in particular to serialize in XML description logics. The expressive power of DAML+OIL is, therefore, at syntactic level, equivalent to T-box of, for instance, SHIQ, the last evolution in KL-ONE family. Finally OWL (Web ontology language) is able to integrate the expressive power of DAML+OIL along with the specification of ISA relations in an explicit way.

A Framework for Methodology Analysis

In this work, we do not argue about correctness, completeness, and consistency of ontologies, and we do not point out special characteristics that specific development languages and systems should sustain. Moreover, in this paper, we will not focus upon the ontologies languages, even if these would be an interesting research topic. Although the evolution of languages is, indeed, a single stream and focuses upon expressive power and computational expressive, it is out of the scope of this chapter.

The first phase of the investigation documented in this chapter had the objective of reviewing the existing methodologies for the creation of a domain ontology from scratch. We discovered that in the existing methodologies, there is a core structure that is independent of both languages and tools; therefore, we analyze ways in which ontology developers can create their own ontology and practices that should be adopted by developers to create the most effective ontology. In particular, we want to measure what are the common elements that each methodology takes into account, in which way a methodology sustains the user in the ontology creation processes, and how non-expert people can adopt a methodology and create their own representations. Therefore, in the following section, some important methodologies will be described and analyzed. We tried to define:

- Names of the phases
- Elements and knowledge that should be in input in each phase
- Description of the processes and operations that are developed in each phase
- Expected output

Unfortunately, we do not have all the framework's elements for all of the following methodologies, because some of them are more research oriented and are not focused on the description of how users and developers can utilize them in the process of ontologies creation. Although these methodologies are not well described in existing papers, we decided to analyze them due to their importance in the Semantic Web community.

In Section 4, we survey the most relevant methodologies of recent investigations. We cannot be exhaustive for at least three reasons: (1) in the practice of Semantic Web applications and in several real cases of intelligent information systems, people developed their own methodologies, which makes almost impossible a complete review; (2) several methodologies have been developed as an illustration of the principles that inspired tools and languages but are essentially equivalent to other methodologies; and (3) several cases of implicit methodologies exist; in particular, in the specific context of languages or tools.

Some Relevant Methodologies

In computer science, knowledge management, knowledge representation, and other fields, several languages and tools have been developed with the aim of helping people and system developers to create good and effective ontologies. In particular, several tools help people create, either manually or semi-automatically, categories, partonomies, taxonomies, and so on. Indeed, behind these tools and techniques, different approaches, methods, and techniques are used to develop numerous of heterogeneous ontologies. In this section, we will describe some of them, and we will try to compare the more significant principles that are sustaining these approaches and that are all described in existing scientific papers.

DOLCE: Descriptive Ontology for Linguistic and Cognitive Engineering

The main authors' idea is to develop not a monolithic module, but rather a library of ontologies (WonderWeb Foundation Ontologies Library) that allows agents to understand one another despite forcing them to interoperate by adoption of a single ontology (Masolo et al., 2002). The authors intend the library to be:

- **Minimal:** The library is as general as possible, including only the most reusable and widely applicable upper-level categories.

- **Rigorous:** Ontologies are characterized by means of rich axiomatizations.

- **Extensively researched:** Modules in libraries are added only after careful evaluation by experts and after consultation with canonical works.

One of the first modules of their foundational ontologies library is a Descriptive Ontology for Linguistic Cognitive Engineering (DOLCE). DOLCE is an ontology of particulars and refers to cognitive artifacts that depend on human perception, cultural imprints, and social conventions. Their ontology derives from armchair research in particular (in other terms, it is the result of an intellectual speculation), referring to enduring and perduring entities from philosophical literature.

Finally, basic functions and relations (according to the methodology introduced by Gangemi, Pisanelli, & Steve [1998]) should be:

- General enough to apply to multiple domains
- Sufficiently intuitive and well studied in the philosophical literature
- Held as soon as their relata are given, without mediating additional entities

The methodology that sustain this type of ontologies is based on a few starting points for building new ontologies:

1. Determine what things there are in the domain to be modeled.
2. Develop easy and rigorous comparisons among different ontological approaches.
3. Analyze, harmonize, and integrate existing ontologies and meta-data standards.
4. Describe a foundational ontology on paper, using a full first-order logic with modality.
5. Isolate the part of the axiomatization that can be expressed in OWL and implement it.
6. Add the remaining part in the form of KIF comments attached to OWL concepts.

This methodology doesn't describe phases that a developer should follow in ontology creation, but rather focuses more on expressivity problems, on partial alignment to lower levels of WordNet, and on much more philosophical aspects of the ontology creation. Although it is not possible to complete our framework, we decided to add this methodology because we consider DOLCE as one of the most representative methodologies in the field.

Ontology Development 101

This methodology has been developed by the authors involved in ontology editing environment such as Protégé-2000, Ontolingua, and Chimaera (Noy & McGuinnes, 2001). They propose a very simple guide based on iterative design that helps developers, even the non-expert developer, to create an ontology using these tools. According to our framework, the sequence of steps to develop an ontology is described well in the Table 1.

OTK Methodology

The methodology developed within the On-To-Knowledge project is called OTK Methodology, and it is focused on application-driven development of ontology during the introduction of ontology-based knowledge management systems (Fensel et al., 2000; Lau & Sure, 2002; Sure et al., 2002; Sure, 2003). The main aim of this methodology is at sustaining a new process based on human issues, in which experts in industrial contexts are capable of creating and managing their own ontology, and ontology engineers are allowed to create effective ontologies. In other words, according to this methodology, strong efforts should be focused on physical presence

Table 1. Ontology development 101 methodology

Name of the Phase	Input	Phase Description	Output
Determine domain and scope of the ontology	Nothing. It is the first step	Definition of - what is the domain that the ontology will cover, - what ontology will be used, - what types of question the ontology should provide answers to (competency questions are very important in this domain; they allow the designer to understand when ontology contains enough information and when it achieves the right level of detail or representation), - who will use and maintain the ontology.	The resulting document may change during the whole process, but at any time, this documentation helps to limit the scope of the model.
Consider reusing existing ontologies	Documents with the domain and the scope of the ontology	Looking for other ontologies that are defining the domain. There are libraries of reusable ontologies on the Web and in literature (e.g., Ontolingua ontology library, DAML ontology library, UNSPSC, RosettaNet, and DMOZ)	One or more domain ontologies, or part of them with their description
Enumerate important terms in the ontology	Documents with the domain, the scope of the ontology, and libraries on the domain	Write a list of all terms used within the ontology, and describe the terms, their meanings, and their properties	Terms and important aspects to model in the ontology
Define the classes and the class hierarchy	Important terms in the ontology, domain, and scope description	There are several possible approaches in developing a class hierarchy: - top-down development process starts with the definition of the most general concepts in the domain and subsequent specialization of the concepts; - bottom-up development process goes in the opposite direction; - a combination development process is a combination of the top-down and bottom-up approaches	Classes and class hierarchy
Define the properties of classes-slot	The taxonomy, and the domain and scope description	Add all the necessary properties and information that allow the ontology to answer the competency questions	Classes, class hierarchy, and properties
Define the facets of the slots	Slots and classes	There are different facets describing the value type, allowed values, the number of the values, and other features of the values the slot can take: slot cardinality, slot-value type, domain, and range	Ontology
Create instances	The ontology	Create individual instances of classes in the hierarchy, which means choosing a class, creating an individual instance of that class, and filling in the slot values.	Ontology and the modeled domain

of engineering and industrial experts, brainstorming processes (in particular, during the early stages of ontology engineering, especially for domain experts not familiar with modelling), and advanced tools for supporting ontology creation. According to our framework analysis, the sequence of the steps to develop an ontology is described well in the Table 2.

Methontology

One of the most famous ontology design methodologies (supported by ontology engineering environment WebODE) is "Methontology." It tries to define the activities that people need to carry out when building an ontology (Fernández, Gòmez-Pérez, & Juristo, 1997). In other words, a flow of ontology development processes for three different processes: management, technical, and supporting.

The ontology development process is composed of the following steps:

- Project management activities include:
  - o **Planning:** it identifies which tasks are to be performed, how they will be arranged, how much time and what resources are needed for their completion;
  - o **Control:** it guarantees that planned tasks are completed in the manner in which they were intended to be performed;
  - o **Quality assurance:** it assures that the quality of each and every product output is satisfactory.
- Development oriented activities include:
  - o **Specification:** it states why the ontology is being built, what its intended uses are, and who are the end-users;
  - o **Conceptualization:** structures the domain knowledge as meaningful models at the knowledge level;
  - o **Formalization:** transforms the conceptual model into a formal or semi-computable model;
  - o **Implementation:** builds computable models in a computational language.
- Support activities include a series of activities performed at the same time as development-oriented activities:
  - o **Knowledge acquisition**;
  - o **Evaluation:** it makes a technical judgment of the ontologies, their associated software environment, and documentation with respect to a frame of reference;
  - o **Integration**;
  - o **Documentation**.

In Table 3, we provide a listing of the single phases of the previously mentioned methodology. It is also worth depicting one fundamental fact about methontology: its specific explicit avoidance to commit to the user's interest in the development of tools that automate all the phases.

Table 2. OTK methodology

Name of the Phase	Input	Phase Description	Output

Feasibility study: identify problem/opportunity areas and potential solutions, and put them into a wider organizational perspective. In general, a feasibility study serves as a decision support for economical, technical, and project feasibility in order to select the most promising focus area and target solution	Nothing. It is the first step	The process of studying the feasibility of the organization, the task, and the agent model proceeds in the following steps:
		- carry out a scoping and problem analysis study, consisting of two parts:
		  o identifying problem/opportunity areas and potential solutions and putting them into a wider organizational perspective;
		  o deciding about economic, technical, and project feasibility in order to select the most promising focus area and target solution;
		- carry out an impacts and improvements study for the selected target solution, again consisting of two parts:
		  o gathering insights into the interrelationships among the business task, actors involved, and use of knowledge for successful performance, and what improvements may be achieved here;
		  o deciding about organizational measures and task changes in order to ensure organizational acceptance and integration of a knowledge system solution.
			The resulting document may change during the whole process. Indication of the most promising area and target solutions and of measures and task changes in order to ensure organizational acceptance and integration of knowledge systems solutions. An ontology requirements specification document (ORDS) should be formed. The ORSD describes what an ontology should support, sketching the planned area of the ontology application and listing, for example, valuable knowledge sources for the gathering of the semi-formal description of the ontology.

Kick-off phase	It starts with an ORSD	The ORSD should guide an ontology engineer to decide about inclusion and exclusion of concepts and relations and the hierarchical structure of the ontology. In this early stage, one should look for already developed and potentially reusable ontologies.	The result will be a document containing: - goal, domain, and scope of the ontology; - design guidelines; - knowledge sources; - (potential) users and usage scenarios; - competency questions; supported applications.
Refinement phase	Specification given by the kick-off phase	The goal of the refinement phase is to produce a mature and application-oriented "target ontology" according to the specification given by the kick-off phase. This phase is divided into different subphases: - a knowledge elicitation process with domain experts based on the initial input from the kickoff phase. - a formalization phase to transfer the ontology into the target ontology expressed in formal representation language like DAML+OIL.	- The knowledge about the domain is captured from domain experts in the previously mentioned competency questions or by using brainstorming techniques; - To formalize the initial semi-formal description of the ontology, we first form a taxonomy out of the semi-formal description of the ontology and add relations other than the "is-a" relation, which forms the taxonomical structure.
Evaluation phase	The refinement results	The refinement phase is closely linked to the evaluation phase. If the analysis of the ontology in the evaluation phase shows gaps or misconceptions, the ontology engineer takes these results as an input for the refinement phase. It might be necessary to perform several (possibly tiny) iterative steps to reach a sufficient level of granularity and quality	It serves as a proof for the usefulness of developed ontologies and their associated software environment.
Application and evolution phases		Define strict rules for the update, insert and delete processes within ontologies	User guide for future application and evolution phases

Table 3. Methontology through our framework

Name of the Phase	Input	Description	Output
Planning	Nothing: first step	Plan the main tasks to be done, the way in which they will be arranged, the time and resources that are necessary to perform these tasks	A project plan
Specification	A series of question such as: "Why is this ontology being built and what are its intended uses and end-users?"	Identify ontology's goals	Ontology requirements specification document, specifying purposes and scopes. Its goal is to produce either an informal, semi-formal, or formal ontology specification document written in natural language, using a set of intermediate representations or using competency questions, respectively. The document has to provide at least the following information: the purpose of the ontology (including its intended uses, scenarios of use, end-users, etc.); the level of formality used to codify terms and meanings (highly informal, semi-informal, semi-formal, rigorously formal ontologies); the scope; its characteristics and granularity. Properties of this document are: concision, partial completeness, coverage of terms, the stopover problem and level of granularity of ache and every term, and consistency of all terms and their meanings.
Conceptualization	A good specification document	Conceptualize in a model that describes the problem and its solution. To identify and gather all the useful and potentially usable domain knowledge and its meanings	A complete glossary of terms (including concepts, instances, verbs, and properties). Then, a set of intermediate representations such as concepts classification trees, verb diagram, table of formulas, and table of rules. The aim is to allow the final user to ascertain whether or not an ontology is useful and to compare the scope and completeness of several ontologies, their reusability, and shareability.
Formalization	Conceptual model	Transform conceptual model into a formal or semi-compatible model, using frame-oriented or description logic representation systems	Formal conceptualization
Integration	Existing ontologies and the formal model	Processes of inclusion, polymorphic refinement, circular dependencies, and restriction. For example, select meta ontologies that better fit the conceptualisation	
Implementation	Formal model	Select target language	Create a computable ontology
Maintenance		Including, modifying definition in the ontology	Guidelines for maintaining ontologies
Acquisition		Searching and listing knowledge sources through non-structured interviews with experts, informal text analysis, formal text analysis, structured interviews with experts to have detailed information on concepts, terms, meanings, and so on	A list of the sources of knowledge and a rough description of how the process will be carried out and what techniques will be used.
Evaluation	Computable ontology	Technical judgment with respect to a frame of reference	A formal and correct ontology
Documentation			Specification document must have the property of concision

A Comprehensive Framework for Multilingual Domain Ontologies

The authors (Lauser et al., 2002) use the Methontology methodology defined by Fernández, Gòmez-Pérez, & Juristo (1997) and stress the specific actions for supporting the creation process for ontology-driven conceptual analysis.

The domain ontology is built using two different knowledge acquisition approaches (see Table 4):

- **Acquisition approach 1:** Creation of the core ontology. A small core ontology with the most important domain concepts and their relationships is created from scratch. This stage is comprised basically of the first three steps of Methontology development activities: requirement specification, conceptualization of domain knowledge, and formalization of the conceptual model in a formal language.
- **Acquisition approach 2:** deriving a domain ontology from thesaurus.

Table 4. Multilingual domain methodology

Name of the Phase	Input	Description	Output
Acquisition approach 1	Nothing: first step	The creation of the core ontology. A small core ontology with the most important domain concepts and their relationships is created from scratch.	The goal of this step is to define a list of frequent terms and a list of domain specific documents to analyze.
Acquisition approach 2	Nothing: first step	Deriving a domain ontology from thesaurus. A thesaurus consists of descriptive keywords linked by a basic set of relationships. The keywords are descriptive in terms of the domain in which they are used. The relationships either may describe a hierarchical relation or an interhierarchical relation.	The goal of this step is to refine an RDFS ontology model to develop a pruned ontology and a list of frequent terms.
Ontology merging	Manually created core ontology and thesaurus terms	Merging the manually created core ontology and the derived ontology using thesaurus terms.	A first version of the ontology
Ontology refinements and extension	The first version of the ontology	The frequent domain terms are used as possible candidate concepts or relationships for extending the ontology. These terms have to be assessed by subject specialists and checked for relevance to the ontology	The final ontology version

- **Ontology merging:** Merging the manually created core ontology and the derived ontology using thesaurus terms.

- **Ontology refinements and extension:** The frequent domain terms are used as possible candidate concepts or relationships for extending the ontology. These terms have to be assessed by subject specialists and checked for relevance to the ontology.

TOVE Methodology

Toronto virtual enterprise (TOVE) is a methodology for ontological engineering that allows the developer to build ontology following these steps:

- **Motivating scenarios:** The starting point is the definition of a set of problems encountered in a particular enterprise.

- **Informal competency questions:** Based on the motivating scenario, it is the definition of ontology requirements described as informal questions that an ontology must be able to answer.

- **Terminology specification:** The objects, attributes, and relations of the ontology are formally specified (usually first-order logic).

- **Formal competency question:** The requirements of the ontology are formalized in terms of the formally defined terminology.

- **Axiom specification:** Axioms that specify the definition of terms and constraints on their interpretations are given in first-order logic.

- **Completeness theorems:** An evaluation stage that assesses the competency of the ontology by defining the conditions under which the solutions to the competency question are complete.

The most distinctive aspect of TOVE is the focus on maintenance using formal techniques to address a limited number of maintenance issues (Gruninger, Atefi, & Fox, 2000; Kim, Fox, & Gruninger, 1999). According to our framework, this methodology can be summarized as shown in Table 5.

DILIGENT Methodology

The DILIGENT methodology (Tempich et al., 2004) aims at creating a set of effective ontologies that the user can share and, at the same time, expand for local use at their will and individual needs. The aim of this methodology is at overcoming the misunderstanding of ontologies that are created by a very small group of people

Table 5. TOVE methodology

Name of the Phase	Input	Description	Output
Motivating scenario	Nothing: first step	It's the starting point, the definition of a set of problems encountered in a particular enterprise	Identify intuitively possible applications and solutions.
Informal competency questions	The motivating scenario	It is the definition of ontology requirements described as informal questions that an ontology must be able to answer	Questions: terminology Answers: axioms and formal definitions
Terminology specification	Informal questions	The objects, attributes, and relations of the ontology are formally specified (usually first-order logic)	Objects: constants and variables Attributes and relations: functions and predicates
Formal competency question	Objects, attributes, and relations	The requirements of the ontology are formalized in terms of the formally defined terminology	Formally defined terminology
Axiom specification	Formally defined terminology	Axioms that specify the definition of terms and constraints on their interpretations are given in first-order logic;	First-order sentences, using predicates of ontology
Completeness theorems	First-order sentences	An evaluation stage that assesses the competency of the ontology by defining the conditions under which the solutions to the competency question are complete.	Conditions under which the solutions to the competency question are complete

(the ontology engineers and the domain experts who represent the users) but are utilized by a huge number of users. The authors postulate that:

Ontology engineering must take place in a Distributed evolvInG and Loosely-controlled setting. (Tempich et al., 2004, p. X)

With DILIGENT, the authors provide a process template for distributed engineering of knowledge structures and intend to extend it toward a fully worked out and multiply-tested methodology. Analyzing DILIGENT, we can say that it is based on dominating roles and five high-level phases that are described in Table 6. The key roles are several experts with different and complementary competencies, involved in collaboratively building the same ontology.

Business Object Ontology

The authors Izumy and Yamaguchi (2002) have used this methodology to develop an ontology for business coordination. They constructed the business activity repository by employing WordNet as a general lexical repository. They have constructed the business object ontology in the following ways:

- Concentrating the case-study models of e-business and extracting the taxonomy
- Counting the number of appearances of each noun concept
- Comparing the noun hierarchy of WordNEt and the taxonomy obtained and adding the number counted for the similar concepts
- Choosing the main concept with high scores as upper concepts and building upper ontologies by giving all the nouns the formal is-a relation
- Merging all the noun hierarchies extracted from the whole process

Although this methodology is quite general, it is important to notice that the continuous interdependencies among business people, industries, and case studies are the key factors in an effective ontology.

A Natural Language Interface Generator (GISE)

In Gatius and Rodríguez (1996), the authors developed three process steps to build a domain ontology:

- **First step:** building and maintenance of:
  - *The general linguistic knowledge:* It includes linguistic ontology that covers the syntactic and semantic information needed to generate the specific grammars and a general lexicon that includes functional, domain, and application independent lexical entries.
  - *The general conceptual knowledge:* It includes the domain and application-independent conceptual information as well as the meta-knowledge that will be needed in the following steps.
- **Second step:** Definition of the application in terms of the conceptual ontology. Both the domain description and the task structure description must be built and linked to the appropriate components of the conceptual ontology.

Table 6. DILIGENT methodology

Name of the Phase	Input	Description	Output
Build	Domain experts, users, knowledge engineers, and ontology engineers	The definition of an initial ontology. The team involved in building the initial ontology should be relatively small in order to find more easily a small and consensual first version of the shared ontology	Built an initial ontology. It is not required completeness of the initial shared ontology with respect to the domain.
Local adaptation	Core ontology	Users work in the core ontology and adapt it to their local needs, business, and system of artefacts.	Logging local adaptation, the control board collects change requests to the shared ontology
Analysis	Local ontologies and the local requests	The board analyzes the local ontologies and tries to identify similarities in users' ontologies. One of the crucial activities of the board is to decide which changes should be introduced in the shared ontology	A refined version of the shared ontology, users' changes and board evaluations.
Revision	Shared ontology and local ontologies. The board should have well-balanced and representative participation of the different kinds of participants involved in the process.	The board should regularly revise the shared and local ontologies. The board should evaluate the ontology, mostly from a technical and domain point of view. The board should assure some compatibility with previous versions.	Final revision of the shared ontology, which entails its evolution
Local update	New version of the shared ontology	Users can update their own local ontologies to better suit the new version of the shared ontology for their local needs.	New locally defined ontologies represent new concepts and criteria with new meaning. The locally defined ontologies constitute new versions of the locally shared ontology.

- **Third step:** definition of the control structure. It includes:

    o The meta-rules for mapping objects in the domain ontology with those in the task ontology

    o The meta-rules for mapping the conceptual ontology onto the linguistic ontology and those for allowing the generation of the specific interface knowledge sources, mainly the grammar and the lexicon

This methodology seems to be not specific enough to analyze it according to our framework. In any case, the most important point of this methodology is that it builds and maintains the general linguistic knowledge and conceptual ontology. This work is devoted to providing a mechanism based on the performance of a set of control rules relating general linguistic knowledge to the applications specifications in order to obtain automatically the natural language best suited for each application. The representation of the relevant knowledge in the process of generating an interface in separate data structures (conceptual ontology, linguistic ontology, general lexicon, and control rules) gives great flexibility in adapting linguistic resources to different applications and users.

Some Consideration Comparing These Methodologies

Although there are considerable differences between the methodologies previously described, a number of points clearly emerge:

- Many of the methodologies take a specific task as a starting point: choosing domains and categories that allow the correct representation. From one point of view, it focuses on the acquisition, provides the potential for evaluation, and provides a useful description of the capabilities of the ontology, expressed as the ability to answer well-defined competency questions. On the other hand, it seems to provide limitations to the reuse of the ontology and to the possible interactions among ontologies.

- There are two different types of methodology models: the stage-based models (represented, for example, by TOVE) and evolving prototype models (represented by Methontology). Both approaches have advantages and disadvantages: the first one seems more appropriate when purposes and requirements of the ontology are clear; the second one is more useful when the environment is dynamic and difficult to understand.

- Most of the time, there are both informal descriptions of the ontology and formal embodiment in an ontology language. These often are developed in separate stages, and this separation increases the gap between real world models and executable systems.

The common point in these methodologies is the starting point for creating an ontology that could arise from different situations (Uschold, 2000; Uschold & Gruninger, 1996):

- From scratch
- From existing ontologies (whether global or local)
- From corpus of information sources only
- A combination of the latter two approaches

Normally, methods to generate ontology could be summarized (Ding & Foo, 2002):

- **Bottom-up:** From specification to generalization
- **Top-down:** From generalization to specification such as KACTUS ontology
- **Middle-out:** From the most important concepts to generalization and specialization such as Enterprise ontology and Methondology

Figure 1 shows how different ontologies deal with both the top-down approach and the bottom-up approach.

As depicted in Figure 1, on one side, the Naïve approaches present a low level of quality in both approaches and are not taken into account in this analysis. Although different technology-driven methodologies are used, new methodologies and tools are needed for creating and managing local schemata. These methodologies and tools should allow both the creation of a schemata from scratch (analyzing documents, repeated occurrences within databases, etc.) and the management of sense-making processes on concepts. This framework is called in the figure "more sophisticated approaches." These should provide guidelines to assist the knowledge owner in making choices at different levels, from the high-level structure of the ontology to the fine detail of whether or not to include distinctions. These frameworks should

Figure 1. Methodologies according the top down and bottom up approach

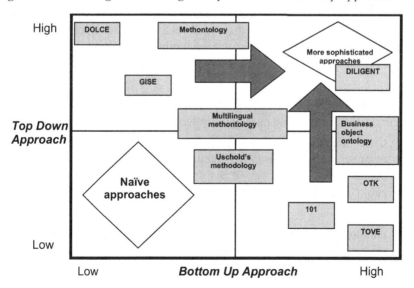

aim at satisfying all the knowledge the owner needs and merging two different requirements, a more adequate representation of a local domain and a very effective development of a top-level ontology. In this study, the authors would consider that manually constructed ontologies are time-consuming, labor intensive, and error-prone (Ding & Foo, 2002) but are necessary to define a domain in which the quality and general comprehension of the ontology are good.

There are also a number of general ontology design principles that are proposed:

• Guarino, Borgo, Masolo, Gangemi, and Oltramari (2002) proposed a methodology to design a formal ontology, in particular, defining domain, identifying a basic taxonomic structure, and pointing to a role.

• Uschold and Gruninger (1996) proposed a skeletal methodology for building ontologies via a purely manual process: identify purpose and scope, ontology capture (identification of key concepts and relationships and provision of definitions), ontology coding (committing to the basic terms for ontology), language, integrating existing ontologies, evaluation, documentation, guidelines.

• Other researchers separate the construction and definition of complex expression from its representation.

Other authors proposed a number of desirable criteria for the final generated ontology to be open and dynamic, scalable and interoperable, easily maintained, and context independent.

Finally, there is no one correct way to model a domain; there are always viable alternatives. Most of the time, the best solution depends on the application that the developer has in mind and the tools that the developer uses to develop the ontology. In particular, we can notice some emerging problems (Blázquez et al., 1998; Gómez-Pérez, 2001):

• Correspondence between existing methodologies for building ontologies and environments for building ontologies causes this consequences:
  o Conceptual models are implicit in the implementation codes, and a re-engineering process usually is required to make the conceptual models explicit.
  o Ontological commitments and design criteria are implicit in the ontology code.
  o Ontology developer preferences in a given language condition the implementation of the acquired knowledge. So when people code ontologies

directly in a target language, they are omitting the minimal encoding bias criterion defined by Gruber (1993).

- Most of the tools only give support for designing and implementing the ontologies, but they do not support all the activities of the ontology life-cycle.
- Ontology developers may find it difficult to understand implemented ontologies or even to build a new ontology.

Acknowledgments

The first author gratefully thanks the European Union under Grant GRD1-2001-40739 (the UPTUN Project) for supporting the investigation that we have documented in this paper.

The UPTUN-project, "Cost-effective, sustainable and innovative upgrading methods for fire safety in existing tunnels" is being carried out in the framework of the "Competitive and Sustainable Growth Programme" (project GRD1-2001-40739, Contract G1RD-CT-2002-0766), with a financial contribution of the European Community.

We also both gratefully thank Creative Consulting s.r.l. for the grant OASI (Ontologies of Artefacts and Services to Industry).

References

Ashby, W. R. (1956). *An introduction to cybernetics*. New York: John Wiley & Sons.

Benerecetti, M., Bouquet, P., & Ghidini, C. (2000). Contextual reasoning distilled. *Journal of Theoretical and Experimental Artificial Intelligence, 12*(3), 279-305.

Blázquez, M., Fernández, M., García-Pinar, J. M., & Gómez-Pérez, A. (1998). Building ontologies at the knowledge level using the ontology design environment. In *Proceedings of the KAW'98*, Banff, Canada.

Bonifacio, M., Bouquet, P., & Cuel, R. (2002). The role of classification(s) in distributed knowledge management. In *Proceedings of the 6th International Conference on Knowledge-Based Intelligent Information Engineering Systems & Allied Technologies (KES 2002)*, Podere d'Ombriano, Crema, Italy.

Chandler, A. D. (1962). *Strategy and structure: Chapters in the history of the industrial enterprise.* Cambridge, MA: MIT Press.

Cocchiarella, N. B. (1991). Formal ontology. In H. Burkhardt & B. Smith (Eds.), *Handbook of metaphysics and ontology.* Munich, Germany: Philosophia Verlag.

Ding, Y., & Foo, S. (2002). Ontology research and development, Part 1: A review of ontology generation. *Journal of Information Science, 3*(28), 123-136.

Dougherty, D. (1992). Interpretative barriers to successful product innovation in large firms. *Organization Science, 3*(2).

Fauconnier, G. (1985). *Mental spaces: Aspects of meaning construction in natural language.* MIT Press.

Fensel, D. (2000). *Ontologies: A silver bullet for knowledge management and electronic commerce.* Springer.

Fensel, D., van Harmelen, M., Klein, & Akkermans, H. (2000). On-to-knowledge: Ontology-based tools for knowledge management. In *Proceedings of eBusiness and eWork*, Madrid, Spain.

Fernández, M., Gòmez-Pérez, A., & Juristo, N. (1997). METHON-TOLOGY: From ontological art towards ontological engineering. In *Proceedings of the AAAI Spring Symposium on Ontological Engineering*, Stanford, CA.

Gangemi, A., Pisanelli, D. M., & Steve, G. (1998). Ontology integration: Experiences with medical terminologies. In N. Guarino (Ed.), *Formal ontology in information systems* (pp. 163-178). IOS Press.

Gatius, M., & Rodríguez, H. (1996). A domain-restricted task-guided natural language interface generator. In *Proceedings of the Second Edition of the Workshop Flexible Query Answering Systems (FQAS'96)*, Denmark.

Ghidini, C., & Giunchiglia, F. (2001). Local models semantics, or contextual reasoning = locality + compatibility. *Artificial Intelligence, 127*(2), 221-259.

Goffman, I. (1974). *Frame analysis.* New York: Harper & Row.

Gómez-Pérez, A. (2001). A proposal of infrastructural needs on the framework of the semantic Web for ontology construction and use. In *Proceedings of the FP6 Programme Consultation Meeting 9.*

Gruber, T. R. (1993). A translation approach to portable ontology specifications. *Knowledge Acquisition, 5*(2), 199-220.

Gruninger, M., Atefi, K., & Fox, M. S. (2000). Ontologies to support process integration in enterprise engineering. *Computational and Mathematical Organization Theory, 6*(4), 381-394.

Hamel, C., & Prahalad, G. (1990, May-June). *The core competences of the corporation.* Harvard Business Review.

Isumi, N., & Yamaguchi, T. (2002). Semantic coordination of Web services based on multi-layered repository. *PRICAI, 597*.

Jasper, R., & Ushold, M. (1999). A framework for understanding and classifying ontology applications. In *Proceedings of the 12ᵗʰ Workshop on Knowledge Acquisition, Modelling, and Management*, Ban®, Canada.

Kim, H. M., Fox, M. S., & Gruninger, M. (1999). An ontology for quality management — enabling quality problem identification and tracing. *BT Technology Journal, 17*(4), 131-140.

Kuhn, T. (1979). *The structure of scientific revolutions*. Chicago: University of Chicago Press.

Lau, T., & Sure, Y. (2002). Introducing ontology-based skills management at a language insurance company. *Modellierung*, 123-134.

Lauser, B., et al. (2002). A comprehensive framework for building multilingual domain ontologies: Creating a prototype biosecurity ontology. In *Proceedings of the Internatiional Conference on Dublin Core and Metadata for E-Communities*.

Masolo, C., Borgo, S., Gangemi, A., Guarino, N., & Oltramari, A. (2002). *Wonderweb deliverable d17* (Intermediate Report 2.0). ISTC-CNR.

Maturana, H. R., & Varala, F.J. (1980). *Autopoiesis and cognition: The realization of the living*. Dordrecht: D. Reidel.

Noy, N. F., & McGuinnes, D. L. (2001). *Ontology development 101: A guide to creating your first ontology*.

Numagami, T., Ohta, T., & Nonaka, I. (1989). *Self-renewal of corporate organizations: Equilibrium, self-sustaining, and self-renewing models* [working paper]. Berkeley: University of California at Berkeley.

Sowa, J. F. (2000). *Knowledge representation. Logical, philosophical and computational foundations*. Brooks/Cole.

Sure, Y. (2003). *Methodology, tools and case studies for ontology based knowledge management* [doctoral thesis]. University of Karlsruhe, Department of Economics and Business Engineering.

Sure, Y., Staab, S., & Angele, J. (2002). OntoEdit: Guiding ontology development by methodology and inferencing. *Proceedings of the Confederated International Conferences CoopIS, DOA and ODBASE 2002*, Irvine, CA.

Tempich, C., Pinto, S., Staab, S., & Sure, Y. (2004). A case study in supporting distributed, loosely-controlled and evolving engineering of ontologies (DILIGENT). In *Proceedings of the 4ᵗʰ International Conference on Knowledge Management (I-Know '04)*, Graz, Austria.

Uschold, M. (2000). Creating, integrating and maintaining local and global ontologies. In *Proceedings of the First Workshop on Ontology Learning (OL-2000)* *in conjunction with the 14th European Conference on Artificial Intelligence (ECAI 2000).*

Uschold, M., & Gruninger, M. (1996). Ontologies: Principles, methods, and applications. *Knowledge Engineering Review, 11*(2), 93-155.

Weick, E. K. (1979). *The social psychology of organizing.* McGraw-Hill.

The chapter was previously published in the International Journal on Semantic Web & Information Systems, 1(2), 49-69, April-June 2005.

Section III

Techniques and Tools

Chapter V

A Tool for Working with Web Ontologies

Aditya Kalyanpur, University of Maryland, USA

Bijan Parsia, University of Maryland, USA

James Hendler, University of Maryland, USA

Abstract

The task of building an open and scalable ontology browsing and editing tool based on OWL, the first standardized Web-oriented ontology language, requires the re-thinking of critical user interface and ontological engineering issues. In this article, we describe Swoop, a browser and editor specifically tailored to OWL ontologies. Taking a "Web view" of things has proven quite instructive, and we discuss some insights into Web ontologies that we gained through our experience with Swoop, including issues related to the display, navigation, editing, and collaborative an-notation of OWL ontological data.

Introduction

The Web ontology language, OWL (Dean & Schreiber, 2004), was approved in February 2004 as a World Wide Web Consortium (W3C) Recommendation for the publication of ontologies on the World Wide Web — creating a standard language for the publication and exchange of ontological models on the Web. OWL reflects almost 10 years of research, experimentation, and small-scale deployment of Web ontologies; a number of certain features in its design were made explicitly to help realize the ideal of Web-based ontologies, that is, of integrating knowledge representation with the open, global, and distributed hypermedia system of the Web, compatible with the principles of Web architecture design. In this article we discuss some insights into supporting the use of Web ontologies that we have gained in building Swoop,[1] an ontology browser and editor, designed specifically for use with OWL and directly supporting the use of Web-based "cultural metaphors" — that is, based on the way people are used to interacting with documents and data in current Web applications.

A Web (Ontology) Browser: OWL

OWL is a standard for representing knowledge on the Web, with a focus on both making these documents compatible with Web standards and on being useful for the modeling of knowledge using past research on ontologies and reasoning. OWL comes in three increasingly expressive sublanguages — OWL Lite, DL, and Full. The Lite and DL species of OWL are based on description logics, that is, decidable, class- and property-oriented subsets of first-order logic. OWL Full follows RDF schema in having a higher-order syntax (although first-order semantics) — OWL Full does not enforce a strict separation of classes, properties, individuals, datatypes, or data values. Any entity could be, for example, both a class and an individual. This design was motivated by the Web architecture dictum that "everything is a resource," thus an individual, and from the general modeling consideration that the choice between whether to represent some aspect of a domain as a class or an individual is not always clear. In a world where people are trying to reuse vocabulary and map between concepts, it seems quite natural to be able to express the dual view of certain domain objects as either classes or individuals, and sometimes both.

One characteristic of "Webized" languages, especially Semantic Web languages, is the systematic prevalence of universal resource indicators (URIs)[2] as names for most entities. In OWL, names for classes, properties, individuals, datatypes, and so forth are URIs. URIs have a number of useful properties, including:

1. For a number of URI schemes, notably http URIs, there is a well-developed set of mechanisms for avoiding name collisions, most notably the domain name system (DNS).

2. These mechanisms, especially the DNS, interact with various Internet protocols, notably HTTP, to make it very easy to publish and retrieve information associated with a URI.

3. URIs have various degrees of opacity. For example, HTTP imposes relatively few constraints on the semantics of the scheme specific part 1. A URI is a generalization of the more common URL, roughly composed of a naming scheme or protocol indicator (http, ftp, mailto, etc.), a unique indicator (a domain name space name for http, a mail address for mailto), and a "fragment id," which is a hash mark followed by a set of characters — thus, for example, an OWL class called "person" from an ontology on a university server might be named by the URI: http:/www.thisuniversity.edu/OntologyLib/csontology#person. The hierarchical structure seen in most http URIs can map directly into a file system (which is a very useful default behavior), but it can also map into queries on a relational database, the object structure of a long-running process, or any other Web resource.

4. URIs can work well for end users, who have developed a lot of expertise with using URIs when browsing or authoring. Web browsers are the ubiquitous way that people use URIs, and even in authoring tools, the primary mental model people have of URIs is derived from their use in browsers. In designing Swoop, we took the Web browser as our user interface (UI) paradigm, believing that URIs are central to the understanding and construction of Web ontologies. We contrast this to other ontology editors such as Protégé (Noy et al., 2001), OilED (Bechhofer, Horrocks, Goble, & Stevens, 2001), and OntoEdit (Sure et al., 2002), which either are or were influenced by traditional KR development tools and applications, and do not reflect this "Webiness" in their UI design. In particular, they do not fully support the use of hypertext to drive the exploration and editing of ontologies.

Hypertextual Navigation

In a Web browser, there are two primary modalities for URIs: manifest and hidden. The address bar is the central mechanism for manifest URIs. URIs must be typed into the address bar and are always visible there. Browser features such as history drop-downs and the use of name completion mean that users need not remember or enter entire URIs, while the address bar requires and abets interaction with raw URIs. The most prominent hidden use of URIs is the hyperlink wherein the URI address is the target of a clickable (in most browsers) region of text (or an image).

There are tight links between hidden and manifest URIs. The URIs hidden "in" hyperlinks appear in the address bar after one has followed a hyperlink or may be revealed by mousing over a hot region, retrieved by pop-up menu commands (i.e., copy hyperlink) or by viewing the actual HTML source.[3]

The ecology of Web pages depends on the ease of access to URIs, both hidden (there is no hypertext without hyperlinks!) and manifest. Much Web browsing starts with URIs discovered in non-Web media, from e-mail to billboards and buses. Writing Web pages requires, even in WYSIWIG HTML editors, familiarity with URIs and the ability to secure the right ones.

Bookmarks are another example of hidden URIs, at least in their most common form. Browsers typically have many ways to review bookmarked URIs. As the natural habitat of Web ontologies is the Web, Swoop allows the interactions with these, using the UI metaphors prevalent on the Web. For loading ontologies, Swoop presents the familiar address bar, and the URI for such an ontology can be secured by whatever means — e-mail, Google, or perhaps one day, a billboard or bus.

Views

It is worth considering the level of detail that needs to be displayed while rendering Web ontological information. While an OWL entity is represented by its URI, it is characterized in a specific context by the axioms dealing with the entity in that context (the document or ontology). Moreover, on the Semantic Web, we expect OWL entities to be characterized by axioms in remote documents. That is, we expect OWL documents and OWL ontologies to use Web links. When rendering the related axioms or definition of an OWL entity, we have taken care that the appropriate information is directly presented in an intelligible manner, and that all the known information is naturally accessible. We consider various levels of detail at which information related to an entity can be displayed:

1. Its definition and related axioms (within a single ontology)

2. Axioms relating it to imported entities (from an external ontology)

3. Inferred information (not explicitly stated in the ontology, but which is inferred from its definition using an OWL reasoner or otherwise)

4. Semantic consistency information (whether the concept is satisfiable or not, again using an OWL reasoner)

5. Provenance information (source location of a particular axiom, its author, creation date, etc.)

6. Entity annotations (human-readable comments made on the entity)

Figure 1. Web-browser UI reflected in Swoop

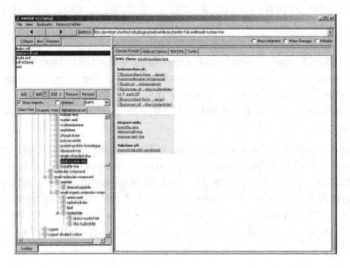

7.   Changes (a log of changes made to the entity definition)

8.   Usage of an entity (references in other Semantic Web documents)

Thus, there is an array of entity-related information that could be displayed as a single Web document that pertains to any OWL entity. Currently, Swoop supports all but the provenance information and usage views (#5,#8) listed above, making clear distinctions between the various view types displayed. For instance, inferred axioms are italicized, inconsistent classes have red icons, and changes pending are shown in green (see Figures 1 and 2). The other two open some complex research issues that are being explored by our research group and others.

Orthogonal to the above levels of detail is the syntax (format) used to render the ontology. Currently on the Semantic Web, a wide range of OWL presentation syntaxes exist — the raw RDF/XML serialization, the more triple-oriented Turtle language (Beckett, 2004), and the OWL Abstract Syntax (Patel-Schneider, Hayes, & Horrocks, 2004), to name a few. It is important to support as many as possible of these different syntaxes while designing an open, Semantic Web ontology engineering environment. One reason for this is that people tend to have strong biases toward different notations and simply prefer to work in one or another. A second is

Figure 2. Editing OWL entities in Swoop (concise format view)

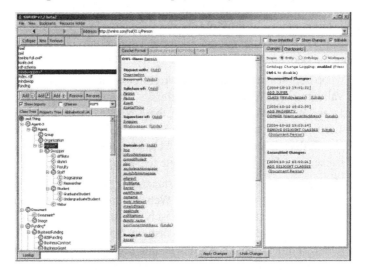

that some other tool might only consume one particular syntax (with the RDF/XML syntax being the most typical), but that syntax might not be an easy or natural one for a particular user.

A third is that it is important to support the "view source" effect, allowing cut-and-paste reuse into different tools, including text editors, markup tools, or other semantic Web tools. We have observed that the easy, direct data transformation between any two formats feels very powerful to the user, especially if they need to use more than one format for a particular task. The challenge here is that the formats should be treated as similarly as possible — that is, any task that can be done in one format should be allowed in any other so that people can stick with the syntax they prefer for both browsing and editing.

Swoop uses a plug-in-based mechanism for renderers. The architecture supports two types of renderers, a coarse-grained type for viewing the ontology as a whole (i.e., class/property tree, graphs, lists, etc.) and a fine-grained type for viewing the description of a single ontological entity (i.e., an OWL class, property, or individual). Other levels of granularity can be achieved by filtering out information from the above main types. All of these formats use URIs (and various URI abbreviations) throughout. Swoop renders those URIs as hyperlinks, allowing for essentially the same hypertext-based navigation, no matter what format is being used.

Also, the layout of the ontology and entity renderers resembles a familiar frame-based Web site viewed through a Web browser. As shown in Figure 1, a navigation sidebar on the left contains the multiple ontology list and class/property hierarchies for each ontology, and the center pane contains the various ontology/entity renderers for displaying the core content.

Currently, Swoop bundles in six renderers; two Ontology Renderers — Information and Species Validation; and four Entity Renderers — Concise Format, OWL Abstract Syntax, Turtle, and RDF/XML. Besides these, there exists a class/property hierarchy renderer for each ontology, along with an alphabetical list of entities present in the ontology. Here we discuss only the Concise Format renderer, since its motivation, design, and subsequent functionality is unique to Swoop.

The Concise Format entity renderer is a non-standard presentation syntax in Swoop (see Figure 2). The idea here is to generate a "Web document" that displays all information related to a particular OWL entity concisely in a single pane. Items are divided into logical groups and rendered in a linear fashion. So taking an OWL Class for example, its OWL enumerations if any, that is, intersectionOf, unionOf, and oneOf — are listed in one group, while the OWL properties related to it (through domain or range) are listed in another group. Standard description logic (DL) operators are used whenever they occur in class expressions to make the representation more concise. Here again, all entity references are made hyperlinks using their URIs as the identifiers. Thus, clicking on an OWL entity link in a particular document causes the view to shift directly to the linked entity's document. This is in keeping with the look and feel of traditional Web-like viewing and navigation of documents.

Editing

Editing OWL entities in a multiple ontology engineering environment can be challenging. Some of the issues that arise include:

1.   The scope of a change (should editing be restricted to the local ontology alone or can the imported ontology be [directly or indirectly] altered as well?).

2.   The types of changes allowed (i.e., atomic vs. composite change strategies as discussed in Bechhofer, Lord, & Volz, 2003).

3.   The level at which changes are made (in the abstract representations or directly in the source code).

4.   How to display the effects of changes before they are committed (direct vs. inferred effects on related entity definitions).

5.   The degree of rollback possible (for how long changes can be "undo"ne).

Issues 1 and 2 are dealt with in detail in subsequent sections; we consider the remaining here. All ontology editing in Swoop is done in line with the renderer pane. This way, context is maintained while editing a particular entity. Also, effects of change on any of the related entities can be easily observed (a single click away) by switching back and forth between the current entity and the related ones by following hyperlinks and use of the history buttons.

Swoop allows ontology editing either at the concise representation level or directly in the code (currently only RDF/XML code editing is supported). There are some fundamental differences between editing in these two modes. For instance, in the concise format, all information related to an entity is displayed in a single pane. As noted earlier, this information is further subdivided into various logical groups, each of which can be edited separately. The changes enacted in this mode are identifiable, and hence can be recorded and undone. Also, the axioms related to a particular entity may not be located in a single region of the code.

Thus, directly editing all references of a single entity in RDF/XML (for example) might be cumbersome. Moreover, given the arbitrary manner in which the RDF/XML code can be edited, it is not easy to capture and record changes easily. On the other hand, direct code editing can be faster and certain changes can be made easily, for example renaming all references of a single class in the entire ontology can be done using the find/replace functionality of an editor. Given the need for both types of changes, Swoop supports both forms of editing.

Another important consideration in Swoop is the manner in which changes are effected. Swoop provides two options for this: either a change can be applied immediately (upon enacting it), or a set of proposed changes can be set aside and collectively committed at a later stage. While the former approach gives immediate results, the latter has numerous advantages. It speeds up alteration of large ontologies, where enforcing multiple changes one at a time would take considerably more time. Additionally, it provides a composite change record that is especially useful for ontology versioning. Finally, it gives a basis for implementing Issue 4 noted above — displaying change effects before they are committed.[4]

Searching, Comparing, Reusing

In a distributed Web ontology setting, numerous engineering tasks — such as comparing entities with a view to understanding semantic differences, mapping entities to ensure semantic interoperability, or simply reusing entities to prevent reinventing the wheel — requires a search/browse process involving disparately located entities. The ontology engineering client can play a large role in making this process efficient.

We take inspiration from the hyperlink-based search and cross-referencing utility present in a programming IDE such as Eclipse (www.eclipse.org). All named entities in the code are identified, and one can easily obtain (and jump directly to) useful related information such as all its references.

During an extended search and browsing routine, the user of Swoop may come across numerous interesting results (OWL entities) that may need to be set aside and revisited. In Swoop we have a provision to store and compare OWL entities via a resource holder panel. Items can be added to this placeholder at any time and they remain static there until the user decides to remove or replace them at a later stage. Upon adding an entity, a time-stamped snapshot of it is saved (with hyperlinks and all), thus providing a reference point for future engineering tasks. These include, but are not limited to, tracking changes made to a particular entity; storing entities for reuse in another ontology; comparing differences in definitions of a set of entities; and determining semantic mappings between a specific pair of entities. We are working to further improve the resource holder by adding automatic dynamic tracking for selected entities, color coding diffs between different entity definitions, and providing support for the editing of mapping terms, such as "owl:equivalentTo" between terms in different resource panes.

Why Not a Web Site?

In principle, the entire Swoop interface and functionality could have been provided as a Web site, or on top of a more full fledged Web browser such as Mozilla. Indeed, a very common first question we get when we show people Swoop is, "Why not do it as a Web site?" There are several examples of current Web site-based ontology tools such as Ontosaurus (Farquhar, Fickas, & Rice, 1996) and WebODE (Arpírez, Corcho, Fernández-López, & Gómez-Pérez, 2001), and new ones are being developed such as pOWL (powl.sourceforge.net). However, we have found that using a standard Web-based server-client architecture for ontology engineering suffers from being slow (especially for large ontologies, and depending on network traffic), and cumbersome for maintaining consistency while editing (e.g., trapping input errors, changing/deleting objects but reloading from browser cache, etc.). In addition, such tools can be difficult to extend to new functionalities via plug-in architectures (such as the one used in Swoop). Finally, most Web site-based ontology editors use distinct HTML pages (perhaps dynamically generated) not just for each entity, but for each view of those entities. This indirection puts an uncomfortable distance between the user and the ontology itself. For these reasons, Swoop is developed as a separate Java application that attempts to provide the look and feel of a browser-based application, but with its specialized architecture designed to optimize OWL browsing and to be extensible via a plug-in architecture.

Multiple Ontologies: From Many, Many

OWL's Web-based features open up the Web ontology engineering environment to multiple ontologies which can, and often do, refer to each other in a number of ways or share terms. This has ramifications for a number of aspects of ontology-editing that have been largely ignored in many earlier AI-based ontology tools. Swoop assumes the use of multiple ontologies and supports this use in a number of ways.

Display and Navigation

Being an open multiple ontology engineering environment, Swoop has a no-holds-barred approach for pulling different Web ontologies into its model. Depending on the nature and context of the task being performed, ontologies are brought into Swoop seamlessly, that is, no additional user intervention is required and the UI treats all ontologies similarly. For example, consider the scenario in which the user is browsing a particular OWL class, say A, in a Web ontology that has an OWL class B related to it by an axiom (say rdfs:subClassOf). Also, B is not defined in the same ontology; instead it has a separate physical Web location and has a number of URIs that share no common prefix with the rest of A's URIs. Clicking on the class B hyperlink causes Swoop to directly load the external ontology referenced and select class B in it. Thus, no distinction is made in terms of UI between navigation across entities in a single ontology or those present in multiple ontologies. Also, the back and next buttons can be used to jump between OWL entities in different ontologies on a single click, ensuring the familiar Web browser experience.

Besides the aforementioned scenario, there are various other situations that can drive Swoop to load more than one ontology. For example, multiple ontologies can be loaded at any point by entering their Web location URLs in the address bar. Alternately, the bookmarks feature can be used to store, categorize, and reload ontologies directly. Finally, if a particular OWL ontology has imported ontologies (defined using owl:imports), loading it causes all its imports under transitive closure to be loaded into Swoop directly.

Living with Imports

The use of owl:imports reveals numerous open issues in Web ontology engineering. Two interrelated issues are considered here — UI issues in distinguishing between the definitions and semantics of imported OWL axioms, and editing support for axioms defined in the importing ontology. Consider the case when an OWL class A is related by an axiom (say owl:disjointWith) to another class B. Suppose A and B have been defined in different ontologies, OA and OB respectively, and moreover, OA imports OB. (In OWL, an entity reference is defined in an ontology using rdf: ID, and it can be further referenced in the same or any other ontology using rdf: about — thus allowing cross-referencing of terms between ontologies.)

Now, the owl:disjointWith axiom can be defined in either ontology OA or ontology OB (or both!). Either way, the semantics of owl:imports, and the fact that OA imports OB, ensures the axiom is present in ontology OA. Yet, it is important to display to the user the exact source of axiom definition. This is especially important when the user wishes to delete this axiom. Obviously, the axiom cannot be deleted in the importing ontology; instead, the user must delete the axiom at the location at which it is originally defined (i.e., imported ontology). Hence, in our case, if the axiom is defined in OB, even though it is displayed in OA as well, it can only be deleted in OB. Swoop needs to make these distinctions since it does viewing and editing axioms inline. Currently, this is accomplished by italicizing all imported axioms (but if an axiom is also local, that overrides).

Also, given that we use the URI of a class as its identifier in a hyperlink, there is an ambiguity of a URI when the class is referenced in different ontologies in terms of what class definition needs to be displayed when the hyperlink is clicked. So consider the above case involving classes A and B, but here the owl:disjointWith axiom is present in OA and not OB. Now, if the user is viewing the axiomatic definitions of class A and clicks on the hyperlink corresponding to class B, there are two possibilities:

1.   Swoop jumps to the class definition B in ontology OB (imported ontology), and here the disjointWith axiom is neither defined nor displayed.

2.   Swoop jumps to the class definition B in ontology OA itself (importing ontology), and here all imported axioms from OB are displayed along with the owl: disjointWith axiom.

Note how the two views hold different semantics and rightly so, reiterating the point that the meaning of an OWL entity is defined in a specific context (ontology). To solve the URI ambiguity problem, Swoop provides labels next to the hyperlinks as an indicator to the jump location.

Beyond Imports?

Current research makes it clear that owl:imports is not the last word in combining (or referencing) Web-based ontologies; in fact, problems with the use of this mechanism were pointed out as part of the OWL documents as an important area for future standardization. Recent work, for example, has been looking at using concepts from foreign ontologies without resorting to the all or nothing approach that owl:imports demands (Borgida & Serafini, 2003; Kutz, Lutz, Wolter, & Zakharyaschev, 2003; Cuenca-Grau, Parsia, & Sirin, 2004). We have discovered in Swoop that the problem of "where to go" when following a URI in an OWL document is not unique to owl: imports and arises in many different contexts during the editing of multiple, linked ontologies. Different collections of axioms seem to define (or characterize) different concepts. The RDF(S)/OWL Full view of concepts (or properties) as entities which may have varying definitions (and extensions) associated with them in different contexts — even in situations where there is no disagreement, but mere normal use — is helpful, especially when coupled with some explicit identification mechanism for various definitions. In our work we have observed that the OWL Full view is more helpful at the Web infrastructure level than, as far as we can currently see, at the logic level. Classes as instances can be a USEFUL Ontological modeling tool (Noy, 2004), but it might be that in the Semantic Web context, much of their value lies outside their use in characterizing a domain. For this reason, Swoop supports OWL Full, and the concise view displays both the class and instance properties of an entity in the same panel. However, these are separated visually to allow the user to more easily identify cases where this occurs.

Annotations

When browsing or building ontologies that live on the Web, it is almost as important to have information about the ontologies as it is to have the ontologies themselves. OWL allows for the associating of variously structured information with its core entities (e.g., classes and properties).

Swoop supports the editing and display of textual or HTML-formatted comments, and of photos and other multimedia (both via HTML and independently) as part of ontologies (see Figure 3). Since OWL ontologies can reference and import other ontologies, one can separate annotations about ontologies from the core ontologies themselves. The Annotea framework (Kahan, Koivunen, Prud'Hommeaux, & Swick, 2001) takes this idea and provides both a specific RDF-based, extensible annotation vocabulary, and a protocol for publishing and finding out-of-band annotations. Swoop uses the Annotea framework as the basis of collaborative ontology development.

Annotea support in Swoop is provided via a simple plug-in whose implementation is based on the standard W3C Annotea protocols (Swick, Prud'Hommeaux, Koivunen, & Kahan, 2001) and uses the default Annotea RDF schema to specify annotations. Any public Annotea server can then be used to publish and distribute the annotations created in Swoop. The default annotation types (comment, advice, example, etc.)

Figure 3. Annotating OWL entities — "Prototypical Illustration" of classes

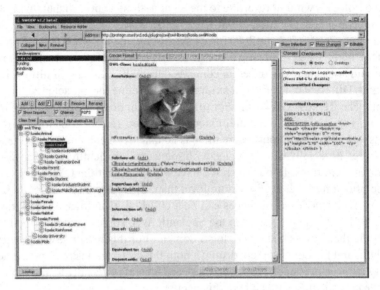

seem an adequate base for human-oriented ontology annotations. One extension we have begun experimenting with is "Prototypical Illustration," that is, a photo or drawing that represents a typical or canonical instance of the class.

Change Annotations

We have extended the Annotea Schema with the addition of an OWL ontology for a new class of annotations — ontology changes (similar to Klein & Noy, 2003). The "Change" annotation defined by the Annotea projected was designed to indicate a proposed change to the annotated document, with the proposal described in HTML-marked-up natural language. In our extended ontology, change individuals correspond to specific, undoable changes made in Swoop during editing.

Swoop uses the OWL API (Bechhofer et al., 2003) to model ontologies and their associated entities, benefiting from its extensive and clean support for changes. The OWL API separates the representation of changes from the application of changes. Each possible change type has a corresponding Java class in the API which is subsequently applied to the ontology (essentially, the Command design pattern). These classes allow for the rich representation changes, including metadata about the changes.

The Swoop change annotations can be published and retrieved by Annotea servers or any other annotation distribution mechanism. The retrieved annotations can then be browsed, filtered, endorsed, recommended, and selectively accepted. It is thus possible to define "virtual versions" of an ontology, by specifying a base ontology and a set of changes to apply to it. This is a fairly new addition to Swoop, and we are just beginning to explore the implications of change tracking, coupled with annotations for the development of large, curated ontologies by collaborative groups of scientists or other ontology definers.

Conclusion

We have built a Web (ontology) browser and editor, Swoop, which takes the standard Web browser as the UI paradigm, believing that URIs are central to the understanding and construction of Semantic Web ontologies. The familiar look and feel of a browser emphasized by the address bar and history buttons, navigation side bar, bookmarks, hypertextual navigation, and so forth are all supported for Web ontologies, corresponding with the mental model people have of URI-based Web tools based on their current Web browsers.

All design decisions are in keeping with the OWL nature and specifications. Thus, multiple ontologies are supported easily, various OWL presentation syntaxes are used to render ontologies, and an OWL reasoner can be integrated for consistency checking. A key point in our work is that the hypermedia basis of the UI is exposed in virtually every aspect of ontology engineering—easy navigation of OWL entities, comparing and editing related entities, search and cross-referencing, multimedia support for annotation, and so forth — thus allowing the Swoop user to take advantage of the Web-based features of OWL significantly more easily than the user of other ontology-editing tools.

In this chapter, we discuss some of the key issues that our work in Swoop has identified as being important in Web ontology tools. Topics we are currently exploring, not yet implemented in Swoop, are dealing with the ad hoc modification of ontologies by one or more users working on the ontology over time. These are issues exploring the editing of imported ontology data, and the use of annotated ontology change sets for ontology versioning as described. Currently, we have preliminary solutions for these issues implemented in Swoop, but we are investigating alternate approaches that may be more powerful and better integrated with emerging Web standards. For example, one such approach is the use of the XPointer framework (DeRose, Maler, & Daniel, 2002) to enable efficient syntactic filtering of ontological code, in order to reduce ontology modification time and effort.

References

Arpírez, J., Corcho, O., Fernández-López, M., & Gómez-Pérez, A. (2001). We-bODE: A scalable ontological engineering workbench. In *Proceedings of the 1st International Conference on Knowledge Capture (K-CAP)*.

Bechhofer, S., Horrocks, I., Goble, C., & Stevens, R. (2001). OilEd: A reason-able ontology editor for the Semantic Web. In *Proceedings of KI2001, Joint German/Austrian Conference on Artificial Intelligence*.

Bechhofer, S., Lord, P., & Volz, R. (2003). Cooking the Semantic Web with the OWL API. In *Proceedings of the International Semantic Web Conference*.

Beckett, D. (2004). *Turtle — Terse RDF Triple Language*. Retrieved from www.ilrt.bris.ac.uk/discovery/2004/01/turtle/.

Borgida, A., & Serafini, L. (2003). Distributed description logics: Assimilating information from peer sources. *Journal of Data Semantics*.

Cuenca-Grau, B., Parsia, B., & Sirin, E. (2004). Working with multiple ontologies on the Semantic Web. To appear in *Proceedings of the 3rd International Semantic Web Conference (ISWC)*.

Dean, M., & Schreiber, G. (2004). *OWL Web Ontology Language Reference* (W3C Recommendation). Retrieved from www.w3.org/tr/owl-ref/.

DeRose, S., Maler, E., & Daniel Jr., R. (2002). *XPointer xpointer() Scheme* (W3C Working Draft). Retrieved from www.w3.org/tr/xptr-xpointer/.

Farquhar, A., Fickas, R., & Rice, J. (1996). The Ontolingua server: A tool for collaborative ontology construction. In *Proceedings of the 10th Banff Knowledge Acquisition for Knowledge-Based System Workshop (KAW95)*.

Kahan, J., Koivunen, M. R., Prud'Hommeaux, E., & Swick, R. (2001). Annotea: An open RDF infrastructure for shared Web annotations. In *Proceedings of the WWW10 International Conference*.

Klein, M., & Noy, N. (2003). A component-based framework for ontology evolution. In *Proceedings of the Workshop on Ontologies and Distributed Systems at IJCAI*.

Kutz, O., Lutz, C., Wolter, F., & Zakharyaschev, M. (2003). E-connections of description logics. In *Proceedings of the 2003 International Workshop on Description Logics*.

Noy, N. (2004). *Representing classes as property values on the Semantic Web* (W3C Working Draft). Retrieved from www.w3.org/tr/2004/wd-swbp-classes-as-values-20040721/

Noy, N., Sintek, M., Decker, S., Crubezy, M., Fergerson, R., & Musen, M. (2001). *Creating Semantic Web contents with Protégé-2000*. IEEE Intelligent Systems.

Patel-Schneider, P., Hayes, P., & Horrocks, I. (2004). *OWL Web Ontology Language semantics and abstract syntax* (W3C Recommendation). Retrieved from www.w3.org/tr/2004/rec-owl-semantics-20040210/

Stojanovic, L., Maedche, A., Motik, B., & Stojanovic, N. (2002). User-driven ontology evolution management. In *Proceedings of the 13ᵗʰ International Conference on Knowledge Engineering and Knowledge Management. Ontologies and the Semantic Web.*

Sure, Y., Erdmann, M., Angele, J., Staff, S., Studer, R., & Wenke, D. (2002). OntoEdit: Collaborative ontology development for the Semantic Web. In *Proceedings of the International Semantic Web Conference (ISWC).*

Swick, R., Prud'Hommeaux, E., Koivunen, M.R., & Kahan, J. (2001). *Annotea protocols*. Retrieved from www.w3.org /2001/Annotea/User/Protocol.html

Endnotes

[1]   Visit the SWOOP Web site at http://www.mindswap.org/2004/SWOOP to obtain the latest information on the tool, to download a free copy of the source code or binary release, and/or to try out the online demo.

[2]   A URI is a generalization of the more common URL, roughly composed of a naming scheme or protocol indicator (http, ftp, mailto, etc.) a unique indicator (a domain space name for http, a mail address for mailto) and a "fragment id" which is a hash mark followed by a set of characters — thus, for example, an owl class called "person" from an ontology on a University server might be named by the URI http://www.thisuniversity.edu/OntologyLib/csontology#person.

[3]   Bookmarks are another example of hidden URIs, at least in their most common form. Browsers typically have many ways to review bookmarked URIs.

[4]   We plan to extend our ontology evolution/versioning framework based on related work such as Stojanovic, Maedche, Motik, and Stojanovic (2002) in a specific project or working set. This practice is highly beneficial in understanding and debugging code.

The chapter was previously published in the International Journal on Semantic Web & Information Systems, 1(1), 36-49, January-March 2005.

Chapter VI

An Ontology-Based Multimedia Annotator for the Semantic Web of Language Engineering

Artem Chebotko, Wayne State University, USA

Yu Deng, Wayne State University, USA

Shiyong Lu, Wayne State University, USA

Farshad Fotouhi, Wayne State University, USA

Anthony Aristar, Wayne State University, USA

Abstract

The development of the Semantic Web, the next-generation Web, greatly relies on the availability of ontologies and powerful annotation tools. However, there is a lack of ontology-based annotation tools for linguistic multimedia data. Existing tools either lack ontology support or provide limited support for multimedia. To fill the gap, we present an ontology-based linguistic multimedia annotation tool, On-toELAN, which features: (1) the support for OWL ontologies; (2) the management of language profiles, which allow the user to choose a subset of ontological terms for annotation; (3) the management of ontological tiers, which can be annotated with language profile terms and, therefore, corresponding ontological terms; and (4) storing OntoELAN annotation documents in XML format based on multimedia and domain ontologies. To our best knowledge, OntoELAN is the first audio/video annotation tool in the linguistic domain that provides support for ontology-based annotation. It is expected that the availability of such a tool will greatly facilitate the creation of linguistic multimedia repositories as islands of the Semantic Web of language engineering.

Introduction

The Semantic Web (Lu, Dong, & Fotouhi, 2002; Berners-Lee, Hendler, & Lassila, 2001) is the next-generation Web, in which information is structured with well-defined semantics, enabling better cooperation of machine and human effort. The Semantic Web is not a replacement, but an extension of the current Web, and its development greatly relies on the availability of ontologies and powerful annotation tools.

Ontology development and annotation management are two challenges of the development of the Semantic Web, as we discussed in Chebotko, Lu, and Fotouhi (2004). In this chapter, although we use our developed general multimedia ontology as the framework and the GOLD ontology developed at the University of Arizona as an ontology example for ontology-based annotation of linguistic multimedia data, our focus will be on addressing the second challenge — the development of an ontology-based multimedia annotator OntoELAN for the Semantic Web of language engineering.

Recently, there is an increasing interest and effort for preserving and documenting endangered languages (Lu et al., 2004; The National Science Foundation, 2004). Many languages are in serious danger of being lost, and if nothing is done to prevent it, half of the world's approximately 6,500 languages will disappear in the next 100 years. The death of a language entails the loss of a community's traditional culture, for the language is a unique vehicle for its traditions and culture.

In the linguistic domain, many language data are collected as audio and video recordings, which impose a challenge to document indexing and retrieval. Annotation of multimedia data provides an opportunity for making the semantics explicit and facilitates the searching of multimedia documents. However, different annotators might use different vocabulary to annotate multimedia, which causes low recall and precision in search and retrieval. In this article, we propose an ontology-based annotation approach, in which a linguistic ontology is used so that the terms and their relationships are formally defined. In this way, annotators will use the same vocabulary to annotate multimedia, so that ontology-driven search engines will retrieve multimedia data with greater recall and precision. We believe that even though in a particular domain, it can be very difficult to enforce a uniform ontology that is agreed on by the whole community, ontology-driven annotation will benefit the community once ontology-aware federated retrieval systems are developed based on ontology techniques such as ontology mapping, alignment, and merging (Klein, 2001).

In this article, we present an ontology-based linguistic multimedia annotation tool, OntoELAN — a successor of EUDICO Linguistic Annotator (ELAN) (Hellwig & Uytvanck, 2004), developed at the Max Planck Institute for Psycholinguistics, Nijmegen, The Netherlands, with the aim to provide a sound technological basis for the annotation and exploitation of multimedia recordings. Although ELAN is designed specifically for linguistic domain (analysis of language, sign language, and gesture), it can be used for annotation, analysis, and documentation purposes in other multimedia domains. We briefly describe the features of ELAN in the section, "An Overview of OntoELAN," and refer the reader to Hellwig and Uytvanck (2004) for details. OntoELAN inherits all ELAN's features and extends the tool with an ontology-based annotation approach. In particular, our main contributions are:

- OntoELAN can open and display ontologies, specified in OWL Web Ontology Language (Bechhofer et al., 2004).
- OntoELAN allows the creation of a language profile, which enables a user to choose a subset of terms from a linguistic ontology and conveniently rename them if needed.
- OntoELAN allows the creation of ontological tiers, which can be annotated with profile terms and, therefore, their corresponding ontological terms.
- OntoELAN saves annotations in XML (Bray, Paoli, Sperberg-McQueen, Maler, & Yergeau, 2004) format as class instances of the general multimedia ontology, which is designed based on the XML Schema (Fallside, 2001) for ELAN annotation files.
- OntoELAN, while annotating ontological tiers, creates class instances of corresponding ontologies linked to annotation tiers and relates them to instances of the general multimedia ontology classes.

This chapter extends the presentation of OntoELAN in Chebotko et al. (in press), with more details on ontological and architectural aspects of OntoELAN and with a premier on OWL. Since OntoELAN is developed to fulfill annotation requirements for the linguistic domain, it is natural that, in this article, we use linguistic annotation examples and link the general ontology for linguistic description (GOLD) (Farrar & Langendoen, 2003) to an ontological tier. To our best knowledge, OntoELAN is the first audio/video annotation tool in the linguistic domain that provides support for ontology-based annotation. It is expected that the availability of such a tool will greatly facilitate the creation of linguistic multimedia repositories as islands of the Semantic Web of language engineering.

Related Work

In the following, first we identify the requirements for linguistic multimedia annotation, then we review existing annotation tools with respect to these requirements. We conclude that these tools do not fully satisfy our requirements, and this motivates our development of OntoELAN.

Linguistic domain places some minimum requirements on multimedia annotation tools. While semantics-based contents such as speeches, gestures, signs, and scenes are important, color and shape are not of interest. To annotate semantics-based content, a tool should provide a time axis and the capability of its subdivision into time slots/segments, multiple tiers for different semantic content. Obviously, there should be some multimedia resource metadata such as title, authors, date, and time. Additionally, a tool should provide ontology-based annotation features to enable the same annotation vocabulary for a particular domain.

As related work, we give a brief description of the following tools: Protégé (Stanford University, 2004), IBM MPEG-7 Annotation Tool (International Business Machines Corporation, 2004), and ELAN (Hellwig & Uytvanck, 2004).

Protégé is a popular ontology construction and annotation tool developed at Stanford University. Protégé supports the Web Ontology Language through the OWL plug-in, which allows a user to load OWL ontologies, annotate data, and save annotation markup. Unfortunately, Protégé provides only simple multimedia support through the Media Slot Widget. The Media Slot Widget allows the inclusion and display of video and audio files in Protégé, which may be enough for general description of multimedia files like metadata entries, but not sufficient for annotation of a speech, where the multimedia time axis and its subdivision into segments are crucial.

The IBM MPEG-7 Annotation Tool was developed by IBM to assist annotating video sequences with MPEG-7 (Martínez, 2003) metadata based on the shots of the video. It does not support any ontology language and uses an editable lexicon from which a user can choose keywords to annotate shots. A shot is defined as a time period in video in which the frames have similar scenes. Annotations are saved based on MPEG-7 XML Schema (Martínez, 2003). Although the IBM MPEG-7 Annotation Tool was specially designed to annotate video, shot and lexicon-based annotation does not provide enough flexibility for linguistic multimedia annotation. In particular, the shot approach is good for the annotation of content-based features like color and texture, but not for time alignment and time segmentation required for semantics-based content annotation.

ELAN (EUDICO Linguistic Annotator), developed at the Max Planck Institute for Psycholinguistics, Nijmegen, The Netherlands, is designed specifically for linguistic domain (analysis of language, sign language, and gesture) to provide a sound technological basis for the annotation and exploitation of multimedia recordings. ELAN provides many important features for linguistic data annotation such as time segmentation and multiple annotation layers, but not the support of an ontology. Annotation files are saved in the XML format based on ELAN XML Schema.

As a summary, existing annotation tools such as Protégé and the IBM MPEG-7 Annotation Tool are not suitable for our purpose since they do not support many multimedia annotation operations such as multiple tiers, time transcription, and translation of linguistic audio and video data. ELAN is the best candidate for becoming a widely accepted linguistic multimedia annotator, and it is already used by linguists throughout the world. ELAN provides most of the required features for linguistic multimedia annotation, which motivates us to use it as the basis for the development of OntoELAN to add ontology-based annotation features such as the support of an ontology and a language profile.

An Overview of OntoELAN

OntoELAN is an ontology-based linguistic multimedia annotator, developed on the top of ELAN annotator. It was partially sponsored and developed as a part of Electronic Metastructure for Endangered Languages Data (E-MELD) project. Currently, OntoELAN source code contains more than 60,000 lines of Java code and has several years of development history started by the Max Planck Institute for Psycholinguistics team and continued by the Wayne State University team. Both development teams will continue their collaboration on ELAN and OntoELAN.

OntoELAN has a long list of detailed descriptions of all its technical features, including the following features that are inherited from ELAN:

- Display a speech and/or video signals, together with their annotations
- Time linking of annotations to media streams
- Linking of annotations to other annotations
- Unlimited number of annotation tiers as defined by a user
- Different character sets
- Basic search facilities

OntoELAN implements the following additional features:

- Loading of OWL ontologies
- Language profile creation
- Ontology-based annotation
- Storing annotations in the XML format based on the General Multimedia Ontology and domain ontologies

The main window of OntoELAN is shown in Figure 1. OntoELAN has the video viewer, the annotation density viewer, the waveform viewer, the grid viewer, the subtitle viewer, the text viewer, the timeline viewer, the interlinear viewer, and associated with them controls and menus. All viewers are synchronized so that whenever a user accesses a point in time in one viewer, all the other viewers move to the corresponding point in time automatically. The video viewer displays video in "mpg" and "mov" formats, and can be resized or detached to play video in a separate window. The annotation density viewer is useful for navigation through the media file and analysis of annotations concentration. The waveform viewer displays the waveform of the audio file in "wav" format; in case of video files, there should be an additional "wav" file present to display waveform. The grid viewer displays annotations and associated time segments for a selected annotation tier. The subtitle viewer displays annotations on selected annotation tiers at the current point in time. The text viewer displays annotations of a selected annotation tier as a continuous text. The timeline viewer and the interlinear viewer are interchangeable, and both display all tiers and all their annotations; only one viewer can be used at a time. In this article, we will mostly work with the timeline viewer (see Figure 1), which allows a user to perform of operations on tiers and annotations. Because a significant part of the OntoELAN interface is inherited from ELAN, the reader can refer to Hellwig and Uytvanck (2004) for detailed description.

OntoELAN uses and manages several data sources:

- **General multimedia ontology (OWL):** ontological terms for multimedia annotations.
- **Linguistic domain ontologies (OWL):** ontological terms for linguistic annotations.
- **Language profiles (XML):** a selected subset of domain ontology terms for linguistic annotations.
- **OntoELAN annotation documents (XML):** storage for linguistic multimedia annotations.

Figure 1. A snapshot of the OntoELAN main window

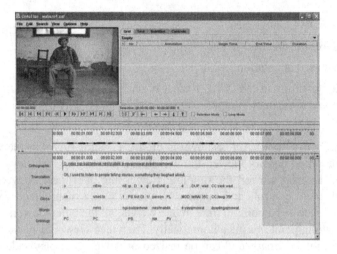

Figure 2. OntoELAN data flow diagram

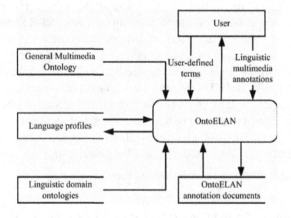

A data flow diagram for OntoELAN is shown in Figure 2. We do not specify names of most data flows, as they are too general to give any additional information. Two data flows from a user are user-defined terms for language profiles and linguistic multimedia annotations.

In the following sections, we will give more details on OntoELAN data sources and data flows. We focus more on the description of features that make OntoELAN an ontology-based multimedia annotator, like OWL support, linguistic domain ontology and the General Multimedia Ontology, a language profile, ontological annotation tiers, and so forth.

Support of OWL

OWL Web ontology language (Bechhofer et al., 2004) is recently recommended as the semantic markup language for publishing and sharing ontologies on the World Wide Web. It is developed as a revision of DAML+OIL language and has more expressive power than XML, RDF, and RDF Schema (RDF-S). OWL provides constructs to define ontologies, classes, properties, individuals, data types, and their relationships. In the following, we present a brief overview of the major constructs and refer the reader to Bechhofer et al. (2004) for more details.

Classes

A class defines a group of individuals that share some properties. A class is defined by owl:Class, and different classes can be related by rdfs:subClassOf into a class hierarchy. Other relationships between classes can be specified by owl:equivalent-Class, owl:disjointWith, and so forth. The extension of a class can be specified by owl:oneOf with a list of class members or by owl:intersectionOf, owl:unionOf and owl:complementOf with a list of other classes.

Properties

A property states relationships between individuals or from individuals to data values. The former is called ObjectProperty and specified by owl:ObjectProperty. The latter is called DatatypeProperty and specified by owl:DatatypeProperty. Similarly to classes, different properties can be related by rdfs:subPropertyOf into a property hierarchy. The domain and range of a property are specified by rdfs:domain and rdfs:range, respectively. Two properties might be asserted to be equivalent by owl:equivalentProperty. In addition, different characteristics of a property can be specified by owl:FunctionalProperty, owl:InverseFunctionalProperty, owl:TransitiveProperty, and owl: SymmetricProperty.

Property Restrictions

A property restriction is a special kind of a class description. It defines an anonymous class, namely the set of individuals that satisfy the restriction. There are two kinds of property restrictions: value constraints and cardinality constraints. Value constraints restrict the values that a property can take within a particular class, and they are specified by owl:allValuesFrom, owl:someValuesFrom, and owl:hasValue. Cardinality constraints restrict the number of values that a property can take within a particular class, and they are specified by owl:minCardinality, owl:maxCardinality, owl:cardinality, and so forth.

OWL is subdivided into three species (in increasingly-expressive order): OWL Lite, OWL DL, and OWL Full. OWL Lite places some limitations on the usage of constructs and is primarily suitable for expressing taxonomies. For example, owl:unionOf and owl:complementOf are not part of OWL Lite, and cardinality constraints may only have a 0 or 1 value. OWL DL provides more expressivity and still guarantees computational completeness and decidability. In particular, OWL DL supports all OWL constructs, but places some restrictions (e.g., class cannot be treated as an individual). Finally, OWL Full gives maximum expressiveness, but not computational guarantee.

OntoELAN uses the Jena 2 (Hewlett-Packard Labs, 2004) Java framework for writing Semantic Web applications to provide OWL DL support. On the language profile creation stage, OntoELAN basically uses class hierarchy information based on rdfs: subClassOf construct. However, while annotating data with ontological terms (by means of a language profile), OntoELAN generates dynamic interface for creating instances, assigning property values, and so forth.

Linguistic Domain Ontology

As a linguistic domain ontology example, we use the General Ontology for Linguistic Description (GOLD) (Farrar & Langendoen, 2003). To make things clear from the beginning, OntoELAN does not have GOLD as a component; both are independent. The user can load any other linguistic domain ontology, therefore OntoELAN can be used as a multimedia annotator in other domains that require similar features. Moreover, the user can load several different ontologies for distinct annotation tiers to provide multi-ontological or even multi-domain annotation approaches. For example, a gesture ontology can be used for linguistic multimedia annotation, as a speaker's gestures help the audience understand the meaning of a speech better.

Therefore, linguists can use GOLD in one tier and the gesture ontology in another tier to capture more semantics.

The General Ontology for Linguistic Description is an ongoing research effort led by the University of Arizona to define linguistic domain-specific terms using OWL. GOLD is constantly under revision, and the ontology changes with introduction of new classes, properties, and relations; its structure also changes. Current information about GOLD is available at www.emeld.org, and the ontology is also downloadable from www.u.arizona.edu/~farrar/gold.owl. We briefly describe GOLD content in the next few paragraphs and refer the reader to Farrar and Langendoen (2003) and also to Farrar (2004) for more details.

GOLD provides a semantic framework for the representation of linguistic knowledge and organizes knowledge into four major categories:

- **Expressions:** Physically accessible aspects of a language. Linguistic expressions include the actual printed words or sounds produced when someone speaks. For example, Orthographic Expression, Utterance, Signed Expression, Word, WordPart, Prefix.

- **Grammar:** The abstract properties and relations of a language. For example, Tense, Number, Agreement, PartOf Speech.

- **Data structures:** Constructs that are used by linguists to analyze language data. A linguistic data structure can be viewed as a structuring mechanism for linguistic data content. For example, a lexical entry is a data structure used to organize lexical content. Other examples are a phoneme table and a syntactic tree.

- **Metaconcepts:** The most basic concepts of linguistic analysis. The example of a metaconcept is a language itself.

Through the article we will use only simple GOLD concepts like Noun, Verb, Participle, Preverb. They are subclasses of PartOfSpeech, and their meaning is easy to understand without special training. Additionally, we will use the concepts Animate (living things, including humans, animals, spirits, trees, and most plants) and Inanimate (non-living things, such as objects of manufacture and natural "non-living" things), which are two grammatical genders or classes of nouns.

General Multimedia Ontology

Although OntoELAN is an ontology-based annotator, a user may not use ontological terms for annotation. In fact, for linguistic multimedia annotation there should usually be several annotation tiers whose annotation is not based on ontological terms. For example, a speech transcription and a speech translation into another language do not use an ontology. Consequently, OntoELAN needs to save not only instances of classes created for ontology-based annotations, but also other text data created without ontologies. One solution is to use XML Schema definitions to save an annotation file in the XML format — this is what ELAN does. Being consistent in using an ontological approach and, therefore, building the Semantic Web, we provide another solution — the multimedia ontology.

We have developed the multimedia ontology that we called General Multimedia Ontology and that serves as a semantic framework for multimedia annotation. In contrast to domain ontologies, the General Multimedia Ontology is a crucial component of the system. OntoELAN saves its annotations in the XML format as class instances of the General Multimedia Ontology and class instances of linguistic domain ontologies that are used in ontological tiers.

The General Multimedia Ontology is expressed in Web Ontology Language and is designed based on ELAN XML Schema for annotation. The General Multimedia Ontology contains the following classes:

- AnnotationDocument, which represents the whole annotation document.

- Tier, which represents a single annotation tier/layer. There are several types of tiers that a user can choose.

- TimeSlot, which represents a concept of a time segment that may subdivide tiers.

- Annotation, which can be either AlignableAnnotation or Referring Annotation.

- AlignableAnnotation, which links directly to a time slot.

- ReferringAnnotation, which can reference an existing Alignable Annotation.

- AnnotationValue, which has two subclasses StringAnnotation and Ontology Annotation that represent two different ways of annotating.

- MediaDescriptor, TimeUnit and others.

Relationships among some important General Multimedia Ontology classes are presented in Figure 3. In general, AnnotationDocument may have zero or many Tiers, which, in turn, may have zero or many Annotations. Annotation can be either AlignableAnnotation or ReferringAnnotation, where Alignable Annotation can be divided by TimeSlots, and ReferringAnnotation can refer to another annotation. ReferringAnnotation may refer to AlignableAnnotation, as well as to ReferringAnnotation, but the root of the referenced annotations must be an AlignableAnnotation. Each Annotation has one AnnotationValue, which can be either a StringAnnotation

Figure 3. Relationships among some General Multimedia Ontology classes (UML class diagram)

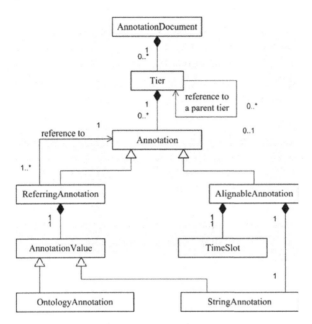

or an OntologyAnnotation. StringAnnotation represents any string that a user can input as an annotation value, but values, represented by OntologyAnnotation, come from a language profile and, consequently, from an ontology. Note that the General Multimedia Ontology allows Ontology Annotation to be used only with ReferringAnnotation. In other words, tiers with AlignableAnnotations do not support an ontology-based approach. This limitation is due to software development issues — OntoELAN does not support annotation with ontological terms in alignable tiers. We intentionally emphasize this constraint in the ontology, although conceptually it should not be the case.

Among our contributions is the introduction of the OWL class OntologyAnnotation, which serves as an annotation unit for an ontology-based annotation. OntologyAnnotation has restrictions on the following properties:

- hasOntAnnotationId: The ID of the annotation. The property cardinality equals one (owl:cardinality = 1).

- hasUserDefinedTerm, which relates OntologyAnnotation to a term in a language profile (described in the next section). The property cardinality equals one (owl:cardinality = 1).

- hasInstances, which relates Ontology Annotation to a term (represented as an instance) in an ontology used for annotation. The property cardinality is greater than zero (owl:minCardinality = 1).

- hasOntAnnotationDescription: Descriptions/comments on the annotation. The property cardinality is not restricted.

The General Multimedia Ontology is available at database.cs.wayne.edu/proj/OntoELAN/multimedia.owl. We will add new concepts to the ontology in case if OntoELAN needs them for annotation. We have developed the General Multimedia Ontology especially for OntoELAN and have not included most concepts in multimedia domain. In particular, we did not include multimedia concepts such as those related to shapes, colors, motions, audio spectrum, and so forth. Our small ontology focuses on high-level multimedia annotation features and can be used for similar annotation tasks.

Language Profile

A language profile is a subset of ontological terms, possibly renamed, that are used in the annotation of a particular multimedia resource. The idea of a language profile comes from the following practical issues related to an ontology-based annotation.

A domain ontology defines all terms related to a particular domain, and the number of terms is usually considerably large. However, to annotate a concrete data resource, an annotator usually does not need all terms from an ontology. Moreover, an experienced annotator can identify a subset of ontological terms that will be useful for a given resource. Speaking in terms of a linguistic domain, an annotator will only use a subset of GOLD to annotate a particular language and may need a different subset for another language.

Linguists have been annotating multimedia data for years without standardized terms from an ontology. They have their individual sets of terms that they are accustomed to using for annotation. It will be difficult to come to a consensus about class names in GOLD so that every linguist is satisfied with it. Additionally, linguists widely use abbreviations like "n" for "noun" which is concise and convenient. Finally, linguists whose native language is, for example, Ukrainian may prefer to use annotation terms in Ukrainian rather than in English.

More formally, a language profile is defined as a quadruple: ontological terms; user-defined terms; a mapping between ontological terms and user-defined terms; and a reference to an ontology, which contains the structural information about terms (like subclass relationship). In summary, a language profile in OntoELAN provides convenience and flexibility for a user to:

•   Select a subset of ontological terms useful for a particular resource annotation

•   Rename ontological terms, for example, use another language, give an abbreviation or a synonym

•   Combine the meaning of two or many ontological terms in one user-defined term (e.g., ontological terms "Inanimate" and "Noun" may be conveniently renamed as "NI")

OntoELAN allows ontology-based annotation by means of a language profile. A user opens an ontology, creates a profile, and links it to an ontological tier. Annotation values for an ontological tier can only be selected from a language profile.

A language profile in OntoELAN is represented as a simple XML document (see Figure 4) with a specified schema, which basically maps ontological terms to user-defined terms, and has a link to the original ontology and some metadata. A user can easily create, open, edit, and save profiles with OntoELAN.

Figure 4 presents an example language profile, created by the author Artem and linked to GOLD ontology at URI www.u.arizona.edu/~farrar/gold.owl. In this example, there is only one user-defined term "NI" that maps to ontological terms "Noun" and "Inanimate." This is a one-to-many mapping, but a mapping can be many-to-many as well. For example, we can add another user-defined term "IN" that maps to the same ontological terms "Noun" and "Inanimate." In general, a mapping can be one-to-one, one-to-many, many-to-one, or many-to-many.

Figure 4. An example of the language profile XML document

```
<?xml version="1.0" encoding="UTF-8"?>
<PROFILE AUTHOR="Artem" DESCRIPTION="" VERSION="1.0"
SOURCE= "http://www.u.arizona.edu/~farrar/gold.owl">
<USER_DEFINED_TERM DESCRIPTION="" NAME="NI">
   <ONTOLOGY_TERM NAME="Noun"/>
   <ONTOLOGY_TERM NAME="Inanimate"/>
</USER_DEFINED_TERM>
</PROFILE>
```

Annotation Tiers and Linguistic Types

OntoELAN allows a user to create an unlimited number of annotation tiers. Multiple-tier feature is a must for linguistic multimedia annotation. For example, while annotating an audio monolog, a linguist may choose separate tiers to write a monolog transcription, a translation, a part of speech annotation, a phonetic transcription, and so forth.

An annotation tier can be either alignable or referring. Alignable tiers are directly linked to the time axis of an audio/video clip and can be divided into segments (time slots); referring tiers contain annotations that are linked to annotation on another tier, which is also called a parent tier and can be alignable or referring. Thus, tiers form a hierarchy, where its root must be an alignable tier. Following the previous example, the speech transcription could be an independent time-alignable tier that is divided into time slots of the speaker's utterances. On the other hand, the translation-referring tier could refer to the transcription tier, so that the translation tier inherits its time alignment from the transcription tier.

After a tier hierarchy is established, changes in one tier may influence other tiers. Deletion of a parent tier is cascaded: all its child tiers are automatically deleted. Similarly, this is true about annotations on a tier: deletion of an annotation on a parent tier causes the deletion of all corresponding annotations on its child tiers. Alteration of the time slot on a parent tier influences all child tiers as well.

Each annotation tier has associated with it linguistic type. There are five predefined linguistic types in OntoELAN which put some constraints on tiers assigned to them. The first four of them are described in Hellwig and Uytvanck (2004), and we also give their definitions here:

- **None:** The annotation on the tier is linked directly to the time axis. This is the only type that alignable tiers can have.

- **Time subdivision:** The annotation on the parent tier can be subdivided into smaller units, which, in turn, can be linked to time slots. They differ from annotations on alignable tiers in that they are assigned to a slot that is contained within the slot of their parent annotation.

- **Symbolic subdivision:** Similar to the previous type, but the smaller units cannot be linked to the time slots.

- **Symbolic association:** The annotation on the parent tier cannot be subdivided further, so there is a one-to-one correspondence between the parent annotation and its referring annotation.

- **Ontological type:** The annotation on such a tier is linked to a language profile. This is not an independent type, as it can be used only in combination with

Figure 5. A snapshot of creating a language profile

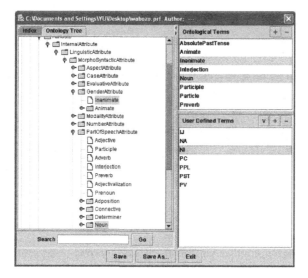

referring tier types such as Time Subdivision, Symbolic Subdivision, or Symbolic Association. To emphasize that a referring tier allows ontology-based annotation, we call it an ontological tier.

Only ontological tiers allow annotation based on language profile terms; other types of tiers allow annotation with any string value.

Linguistic Multimedia Annotation with OntoELAN

In this section, we describe an annotation process in OntoELAN using a linguistic multimedia resource annotation example. In general, an annotation process in OntoELAN consists of three major steps: (1) language profile creation, (2) creation of tiers, and (3) creation of annotations. The first step is unnecessary if ontological tiers will not be defined. The second step can be completed partially for non-ontological tiers before the creation of a language profile. It is also possible to have multiple

Figure 6. A snapshot of annotation tiers in the OntoELAN main window

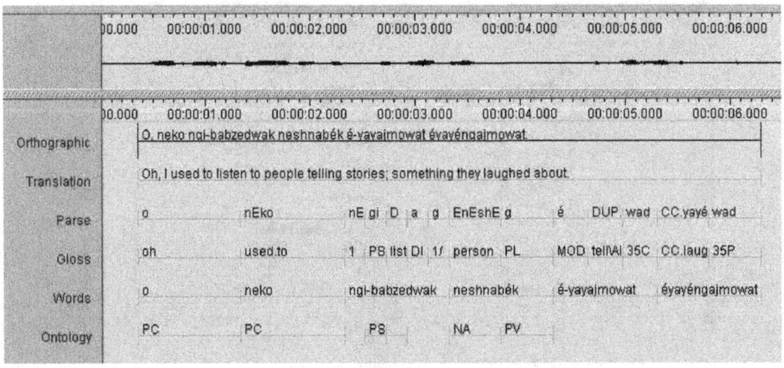

profiles for multiple ontological tiers, but there is always one-to-one correspondence between a profile and an ontological tier.

As an example, we annotate the audio file, which contains a sentence in Potawatomi, one of the North American native languages.

We first load GOLD ontology and create the Potawatomi language profile. Figure 5 presents a snapshot of the profile creation window. The tabs "Index" and "Ontology Tree" on the left provide two views of an ontology: a list view, which displays all the terms of an ontology alphabetically as a list, and a hierarchical view, which displays all the terms of an ontology in a hierarchical fashion to illustrate parent-child relationships between terms. From any of these two views, a user can select required terms and add them to the "Ontological Terms" list, and rename ontological terms as shown in the "User-Defined Terms" list. In Figure 5, we selected the ontological terms "Inanimate" and "Noun" and combine them under one user-defined term "NI."

After the language profile is ready, we define six tiers in the OntoELAN main window (see Figure 6):

- Orthographic of type "None" (linked to the time axis)
- Translation of type "Symbolic Association" (referring to Orthographic)
- Words of type "Symbolic Subdivision" (referring to Orthographic)
- Parse of type "Symbolic Subdivision" (referring to Words)
- Gloss of type "Symbolic Association" (referring to Parse)

Figure 7. A snapshot of the tier hierarchy

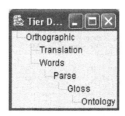

- Ontology of type "Symbolic Association" and "Ontological Type" (referring to Gloss)

The created tier hierarchy is shown in Figure 7.

Finally, we specify annotation values on all six tiers (see Figure 6). We annotate the Orthographic tier first, because it is the root of the tier hierarchy, and its time alignment is inherited by other tiers. We do not divide the Orthographic tier into time slots, and its time axis contains the whole sentence in Potawatomi. The Translation tier inherits time alignment from its parent and cannot subdivide it any further (type "Symbolic Association"). The Words tier also inherits Orthographic time alignment, but in this case we subdivide it into segments that correspond to words in the sentence. Similarly, we subdivide the Parse tier alignment inherited from Words. The Gloss tier inherits alignment from Parse, and the Ontology tier inherits alignment from Gloss; both Gloss and Ontology do not allow further subdivision. Correct alignment inheritance is important, because there is a semantic correspondence between segments of different tiers. For example, if we look at a Potawatomi word "neko" in the Words tier, we can find its gloss "used to" in the Gloss tier and part of speech "PC" (maps to GOLD Participle concept) in the Ontology tier.

Except for the annotations on the Ontology tier, which is defined as an ontological tier, all the annotations are annotated by a string value. Unlike the text annotation, the user annotates the ontological tier by selecting a user-defined term from the profile. Once the term is selected, the next step is creating individuals of the corresponding ontological term(s). The user needs to do nothing if the ontological term is defined as an instance in the ontology, to input an instance name if the ontological term is defined as a class with no restrictions, or to provide all information based on the definition of the ontological class, properties, and so forth.

The annotation is saved in the XML format as instances of the General Multimedia Ontology and, in our case, GOLD. The example of the XML markup for the Ontology tier instance and referring annotation instance with ID "a42" on that tier is shown in Figure 8. For the Ontology tier, several properties are defined such as ID, parent tier,

Figure 8. An example of the XML markup for the OntoELAN annotation

```
...
<media:Tier rdf:ID="Ontology">
  <media:hasTierID>Ontology</media:hasTierID>
  <media:hasParent rdf:resource="file:///C:/wabozo4.eaf#Gloss"/>
  <media:hasProfile>C:\wabozo.prf</media:hasProfile>
  <media:hasLinguisticType>
    <media:LinguisticType rdf:ID="ontology">
      <media:hasTimeAlignable>false</media:hasTimeAlignable>
      <media:hasLinguisticTypeID>ontology</media:hasLinguisticTypeID>
      <media:hasConstraint rdf:resource="file:///C:/wabozo4.eaf#Symbolic_Association"/>
      <media:hasGraphicRef>false</media:hasGraphicRef>
    </media:LinguisticType>
  </media:hasLinguisticType>
  ...
</media:Tier>
  ...
<media:RefAnnotation rdf:ID="a42">
  <media:hasAnnotationID>a42</media:hasAnnotationID>
  <media:hasAnnotationRef rdf:resource="file:///C:/wabozo4.eaf#a31"/>
  <media:hasAnnotationValue>
    <media:OntologyAnnotation rdf:ID="a42Value">
      <media:hasUserDefinedTerm>PV</media:hasUserDefinedTerm>
      <media:hasInstances
            rdf:resource="http://www.u.arizona.edu/~farrar/gold.owl#Preverb"/>
      <media:hasOntAnnotationDescription>comments</media:hasOntAnnotationDescription>
      <media:hasOntAnnotationId>e</media:hasOntAnnotationId>
    </media:OntologyAnnotation>
  </media:hasAnnotationValue>
</media:RefAnnotation>
  ...
```

profile, linguistic type, and so forth. For the referring annotation, OntoELAN has defined ID, reference to another annotation, and annotation value that includes an OntologyAnnotation class instance with ID, user-defined term "PV," and reference to GOLD concept Preverb, which is defined as an instance. The markup in Figure 8 is based on the General Multimedia Ontology, except the reference to a GOLD instance mentioned above.

Conclusion and Future Work

In this article, we address the challenge of annotation management for the Semantic Web of language engineering. Our contribution is the development of OntoELAN, a linguistic multimedia annotation tool that features an ontology-based annotation approach. OntoELAN is the first attempt at annotating linguistic multimedia data with a linguistic ontology. Meanwhile, the ontological annotations share the data on the linguistic ontologies. Future work will improve the system and provide more channels for sharing data on the Web, such as the multimedia descriptions, the language words, and so forth. Also, a future version will improve the current searching system, which supports text searching and retrieval in one annotation document, to search, retrieve, and compare the linguistic multimedia annotation data on the Web. Additionally, we plan to integrate a text document annotation into OntoELAN and include semi-automatic annotation support, similar to Shoebox (SIL International, 2000).

Acknowledgments

Developers of ELAN from Max Planck Institute for Psycholinguistics, Hennie Brugman, Alexander Klassmann, Han Sloetjes, Albert Russel, and Peter Wittenburg, provided us with ELAN's source code and documentation. Also, we would like to thank Dr. Laura Buszard-Welcher and Andrea Berez from the E-MELD (Electronic Metastructure for Endangered Languages Data) project for their constructive comments on OntoELAN.

References

Bechhofer, S., Harmelen, F., Hendler, J., Horrocks, I., McGuinness, D., Patel-Schneider, et al. (2004). *OWL Web Ontology Language reference* (W3C Recommendation). Retrieved from www.w3.org/TR/owl-ref/

Berners-Lee, T., Hendler, J., & Lassila, O. (2001). The Semantic Web. *Scientific American.* Retrieved from www.sciam.com/article.cfm?articleID=00048144-10D2-1C70-84A9809EC588EF21

Bray, T., Paoli, J., Sperberg-McQueen, C., Maler, E., & Yergeau, F. (2004). *Extensible Markup Language (XML) 1.0* (3rd edition, W3C Recommendation). Retrieved from www.w3.org/TR/REC-xml/

Chebotko, A., Deng, Y., Lu, S., Fotouhi, F., Aristar, A., Brugman, H., et al. (in press). OntoELAN: An ontology-based linguistic multimedia annotator. In *Proceedings of the IEEE 6th International Symposium on Multimedia Software Engineering (IEEE-MSE 2004),* Miami, FL.

Chebotko, A., Lu, S., & Fotouhi, F. (2004, April). Challenges for information systems towards the Semantic Web. *AIS SIGSEMIS Semantic Web and Information Systems Newsletter,* 1. Retrieved from www.sigsemis.org/newsletter/newsletter/April2004/FINAL_AIS_SIGSEMIS_Bulletin_1_1_04_1_.pdf

Fallside, D.C. (2001). *XML Schema part 0: Primer* (W3C Recommendation). Retrieved from www.w3.org/TR/xmlschema-0/

Farrar, S. (2004). *GOLD: A progress report.* Retrieved from www.u.arizona.edu/~farrar/gold-status-report.pdf

Farrar, S., & Langendoen, D. T. (2003). A linguistic ontology for the Semantic Web. *GLOT International, 7*(3), 97-100.

Hellwig, B., & Uytvanck, D. (2004). *EUDICO Linguistic Annotator (ELAN) Version 2.0.2 manual* [software manual]. Retrieved from www.mpi.nl/tools/ELAN/ELAN _Manual-04-04-08.pdf

Hewlett-Packard Labs. (2004). *Jena 2 — a Semantic Web framework* [computer software]. Retrieved from www.hpl.hp.com/semWeb/jena2.htm

International Business Machines Corporation. (2004). *IBM MPEG-7 Annotation Tool* [computer software]. Retrieved from www.alphaworks.ibm.com/tech/videoannex

Klein, M. (2001). Combining and relating ontologies: An analysis of problems and solutions. In *Proceedings of the IJCAI-2001 Workshop on Ontologies and Information Sharing,* Seattle, WA.

Lu, S., Dong, M., & Fotouhi, F. (2002). The Semantic Web: Opportunities and challenges for next-generation Web applications. *International Journal of Information Research, 7*(4). Retrieved from InformationR.net/ir/7-4/paper 134.html

Lu, S., Liu, D., Fotouhi, F., Dong, M., Reynolds, R., Aristar, A., et al. (2004). Language engineering for the Semantic Web: A digital library for endangered languages. *International Journal of Information Research, 9*(3). Retrieved from InformationR.net/ir/9-3/paper 176.html

Martínez, J. M. (2003). MPEG-7 overview (version 9). *International Organisation for Standardisation.* Retrieved from www.chiariglione.org/mpeg/standards/mpeg-7/mpeg-7.htm

National Science Foundation, The. (2004). *Documenting endangered languages (DEL)* (NSF 04-605). Retrieved from www.nsf.gov/pubs/2004/nsf04605/nsf04605.htm

SIL International. (2000). *The linguist's Shoebox: Tutorial and user's guide* [software manual]. Retrieved from www.sil.org/computing/shoebox/ShTUG.pdf

Stanford University. (2004). *The Protégé Project* [computer software]. Retrieved from protege.stanford.edu.

The chapter was previously published in the International Journal on Semantic Web & Information Systems, 1(1), 50-67, January-March 2005.

Chapter VII

A Layered Model for Building Ontology Translation Systems

Oscar Corcho, Intelligent Software Components, Spain*

Asunción Gómez-Pérez, Universidad de Madrid, Spain

Abstract

In this chapter we present a model for building ontology translation systems between ontology languages and/or ontology tools, where translation decisions are defined at four different layers: lexical, syntax, semantic, and pragmatic. This layered approach provides a major contribution to the current state of the art in ontology translation, since it makes ontology translation systems easier to build and understand and, consequently, to maintain and reuse. As part of this model, we propose a method that guides in the process of developing ontology translation systems according to this approach. The method identifies four main activities: feasibility study, analysis of source, and target formats, design, and implementation of the translation system, with their decomposition in tasks, and recommends the techniques to be used inside each of them.

Introduction

An ontology is defined as a "formal explicit specification of a shared conceptualization" (Studer et al., 1998); that is, an ontology must be machine readable (it is formal), all its components must be described clearly (it is explicit), it describes an abstract model of a domain (it is a conceptualization), and it is the product of a consensus (it is shared).

Ontologies can be implemented in varied ontology languages, which are usually divided in two groups: classical and ontology markup languages. Among the classical languages used for ontology construction, we can cite (in alphabetical order): CycL (Lenat & Guha, 1990), FLogic (Kifer et al., 1995), KIF (Genesereth & Fikes, 1992), LOOM (MacGregor, 1991), OCML (Motta, 1999), and Ontolingua (Gruber, 1992). Among the ontology markup languages used in the context of the Semantic Web, we can cite (in alphabetical order): DAML+OIL (Horrocks & van Harmelen, 2001), OIL (Horrocks et al., 2000), OWL (Dean & Schreiber, 2004), RDF (Lassila & Swick, 1999), RDF Schema (Brickley & Guha, 2004), SHOE (Luke & Hefflin, 2000), and XOL (Karp et al., 1999). Each of these languages has its own syntax, its own expressiveness, and its own reasoning capabilities provided by different inference engines. Languages also are based on different knowledge representation paradigms and combinations of them (frames, first order logic, description logic, semantic networks, topic maps, conceptual graphs, etc.).

A similar situation applies to ontology tools: several ontology editors and ontology management systems can be used to develop ontologies. Among them, we can cite (in alphabetical order): KAON (Maedche et al., 2003), OilEd (Bechhofer et al., 2001), OntoEdit (Sure et al., 2002), the Ontolingua Server (Farquhar et al., 1997), OntoSaurus (Swartout et al., 1997), Protégé-2000 (Noy et al., 2000), WebODE (Arpírez et al., 2003), and WebOnto (Domingue, 1998). As in the case of languages, the knowledge models underlying these tools have their own expressiveness and reasoning capabilities, since they are also based on different knowledge representation paradigms and combinations of them. Besides, ontology tools usually export ontologies to one or several ontology languages and import ontologies coded in different ontology languages.

There are important connections and implications between the knowledge modeling components used to build an ontology in such languages and tools, and the knowledge representation paradigms used to represent formally such components. With frames and first order logic, the knowledge components commonly used to build ontologies are (Gruber, 1993) classes, relations, functions, formal axioms, and instances; with description logics, they are usually (Baader et al., 2003) concepts, roles, and individuals; with semantic networks, they are: nodes and arcs between nodes; etc.

The ontology translation problem (Gruber, 1993) appears when we decide to reuse an ontology (or part of an ontology) with a tool or language that is different from those where the ontology is available. If we force each ontology-based system developer to commit individually to the task of translating and incorporating the necessary ontologies to the developer's system, the developer will need a lot of effort and time to achieve his or her objectives (Swartout et al., 1997). Therefore, ontology reuse in different contexts will be boosted highly, as long as we provide ontology translation services among those languages and/or tools.

Many ontology translation systems can be found in the current ontology technology. They are aimed mainly at importing ontologies implemented in a specific ontology language to an ontology tool, or at exporting ontologies modeled with an ontology tool to an ontology language. A smaller number of ontology translation systems is aimed at transforming ontologies between ontology languages or between ontology tools.

Since ontology tools and languages have different expressiveness and reasoning capabilities, translations between them are neither straightforward nor easily reusable. They normally require many decisions at different levels, which range from low layers (i.e., how to transform a concept name identifier from one format to the other) to higher layers (i.e., how to transform a ternary relation among concepts to a format that only allows representing binary relations between concepts).

Current ontology translation systems usually do not take into account such a layered structure of translation decisions. Besides, in these systems, translation decisions usually are hidden inside their programming code. Both aspects make it difficult to understand how ontology translation systems work.

To ameliorate this problem, in this chapter we propose a new model for building and maintaining ontology translation systems, which identifies four layers where ontology translation decisions can be made: lexical, syntax, semantic, and pragmatic. This layered architecture is based on existing work in formal languages and the theory of signs (Morris, 1938).

The following section describes the four layers where ontology translation problems may appear, with examples of how transformations have to be made at each layer; then we describe an ontology translation method based on the previous layers, which is divided into four main activities; finally, we present the main conclusions of our work and related work.

Ontology Translation Layers

As discussed previously, our ontology translation model proposes to structure translation decisions in four different layers. The selection of layers is based on existing

Figure 1. Classifications of semantic interoperability problems and relationships between them

[Morris, 1938]	*[Chalupsky, 2000]*	*[Klein, 2001]*	*[Euzenat, 2001]*
Pragmatic			Semiotic
Semantic	Expressivity	Language expressivity Semantics of primitives Logical representation	Semantic
Syntax	Syntax	Syntax	Syntax Lexical Encoding

work on formal languages and the theory of signs (Morris, 1938), which consider the existence of several levels in the definition of a language: syntax (related to how the language symbols are structured), semantics (related to the meaning of those structured symbols), and pragmatics (related to the intended meaning of the symbols; that is, how symbols are interpreted or used).

In the context of semantic interoperability, some authors have proposed classifications of the problems to be faced when managing different ontologies in possibly different formats. We will enumerate only the ones that are due to differences between the source and target formats.[1] Euzenat (2001) distinguishes the following non-strict levels of language interoperability: encoding, lexical, syntactic, semantic, and semiotic. Chalupsky (2000) distinguishes two layers: syntax and expressivity (aka semantics). Klein (2001) distinguishes four levels: syntax, logical representation, semantics of primitives, and language expressivity; the last three levels correspond to the semantic layer identified in the other classifications. Figure 1 shows the relationship between these layers.

The layers proposed in our model are based mainly on Euzenat, the only one in the context of semantic interoperability who deals with pragmatics (although he uses the term semiotics for it). However, we consider it unnecessary to split the lexical and encoding layers when dealing with ontologies and consider them as a unique layer, called lexical.

In the next sections we describe the types of translation problems that usually can be found in each of these layers and will show some examples of common transformations performed in each of them.

Lexical Layer

The lexical layer deals with the ability to segment the representation in characters and words (or symbols) (Euzenat, 2001). Different languages and tools normally use different character sets and grammars for generating their terminal symbols (i.e., ontology component identifiers, natural language descriptions of ontology components, and attribute values). This translation layer deals with the problems that may arise in these symbol transformations.

Therefore, in this layer, we deal with the following types of transformations:

- **Transformations of ontology component identifiers:** For instance, the source and target formats use different sets of characters for creating identifiers; the source and target format use different naming conventions for their component identifiers, or their components have different scopes; hence, some component identifiers cannot overlap with the identifiers of other components.

- **Transformations of pieces of text used for natural language documentation purposes:** For instance, specific characters in the natural language documentation of a component must be escaped since the target format does not allow them as part of the documentation.

- **Transformations of values:** For instance, numbers must be represented as character strings in the target format, or dates must be transformed according to the date formulation rules of the target format.

From a lexical point of view, among the most representative ontology languages and tools we can distinguish three groups of formats:

- **ASCII-based formats:** Among these formats, we can cite the following classical languages: KIF, Ontolingua, CycL, LOOM, OCML, and FLogic. Also in this group, we can include the ontology tools related to some of these languages (Ontolingua Server, OntoSaurus, and WebOnto). These languages are based on ASCII encodings, and hence, the range of characters allowed for creating ontology component identifiers and for representing natural language texts and values is restricted to most of the characters allowed in this encoding.

- **UNICODE-based formats:** Among these formats, we can cite the following ontology tools: OntoEdit, Protégé-2000, and WebODE. These formats are based on the UNICODE encoding, which is an extension of the ASCII encoding and, thus, allows using more varied characters (including Asian and Arabic characters, more punctuation signs, etc.).

- **UNICODE&XML-based formats:** Among these formats we can refer to the ontology markup languages: SHOE, XOL, RDF, RDFS, OIL, DAML+OIL, and OWL, and some of the tools that are related to them, such as KAON and OilEd. These formats are characterized not only for being UNICODE compliant, as the previous ones, but also for restricting the use of some characters and groups of characters in the component identifiers and in the natural language documentation and values, such as the use of tag-style pieces of text (e.g., <example>) inside documentation tags. An important restriction is the compulsory use of qualified names (QNames) as identifiers of ontology concepts and properties, since they are used to construct tags when dealing with instances.

The easiest lexical transformations are usually those to be done from the first and third group of formats to the second one, which is the most unrestricted one. In other cases, the specific features of each format do not allow us to generalize the types of transformations to be done, which mainly consist in replacing non-allowed characters with others that are allowed, or in replacing identifiers that are reserved keywords in a format with other identifiers that are not. Obviously, there are also differences among the languages and tools inside each group, although the transformations needed in those cases are minimal.

Special attention deserves the problem related to the scope of the ontology component identifiers in the source and target formats, and to the restrictions related to overlapping identifiers. These problems appear when, in the source format, a component is defined inside the scope of another and, thus, its identifier is local to the latter, while the correspondent component has a global scope in the target format. As a consequence, there could be clashes of identifiers if two different components have the same identifier in the source format.

Table 1 shows examples of how some ontology component identifiers can be transformed from WebODE to Ontolingua, RDF(S), OWL and Protégé-2000, taking into account the rules for generating identifiers in each format and the constraints about the scope and possible overlap of some ontology component identifiers.

As previously expressed, inside this layer, we also deal with the different naming conventions that exist in different formats.[2] For instance, in Lisp-based languages and tools such as Ontolingua, LOOM, OCML, and their corresponding ontology tools, compound names usually are joined together using hyphens (e.g., Travel-Agency). In tools like OntoEdit, Protégé, and WebODE, words are separated with blank spaces (e.g., Travel Agency). In ontology markup languages, the convention used for class identifiers is to write all the words together, with no blank spaces or hyphens, and with the first capital letter for each word (e.g., TravelAgency).

Syntactic Layer

This layer deals with the ability to structure the representation in structured sentences, formulas or assertions (Euzenat, 2001). Ontology components in each language or tool are defined with different grammars. Hence, the syntactic layer deals with the

Table 1. Examples of transformations at the lexical layer

WebODE Identifier	Target	Result	Reasons for Transformation
Business Trip	Ontolingua	Business-Trip	Blank spaces in identifiers are not allowed in Ontolingua
1StarHotel	RDF(S)	OneStarHotel	Identifiers cannot start with a digit in RDF(S). They do not form valid QNames
Concepts Name and Name	Ontolingua	classes Name and Name_1	Ontolingua is not case sensitive
Concept Room attribute fare Concept Flight attribute fare	OWL	classes Room, Flight datatypeProperty roomFare datatypeProperty flightFare	WebODE attributes are local to concepts. OWL datatype properties are not defined in the scope of OWL classes, but globally
Concept Name attribute Name	Protégé-2000	class Name; slot name	The identifiers of classes and slots cannot overlap in Protégé-2000

Figure 2. Examples of transformations at the syntactic layer

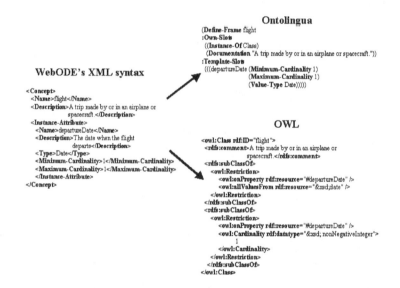

problems related to how the symbols are structured in the source and target formats, taking into account the derivation rules for ontology components in each of them.

In this layer, the following types of transformations are included:

- **Transformations of ontology component definitions according to the grammars of the source and target formats:** For instance, the grammar to define a concept in Ontolingua is different than that in OCML.

- **Transformations of datatypes:** For instance, the datatype date in WebODE must be transformed to the datatype &xsd;date in OWL.

Figure 2 shows an example of how a WebODE concept definition (expressed in XML) is transformed into Ontolingua and OWL. In this example, both types of translation problems are dealt with.

Among the most representative ontology languages and tools, we can distinguish the following (overlapping) groups of formats:

- **Lisp-based formats:** The syntax of several classical ontology languages are based on the Lisp language; namely, KIF and Ontolingua, LOOM, and OCML, together with their corresponding ontology tools (Ontolingua Server, OntoSaurus, and WebOnto, respectively).

- **XML-based formats:** Ontology markup languages are characterized by being represented in XML syntax. Among them, we can cite SHOE, XOL, RDF, RDFS, OIL, DAML+OIL, and OWL. In addition, ontology tools such as OntoEdit, Protégé-2000, and WebODE also provide ad hoc XML backends to implement their ontologies.

- **Ad hoc text formats:** There are other ontology languages that do not provide any of the previous syntaxes, but they provide their own ad hoc formats. These languages are F-Logic, the ASCII syntax of OIL, and the Notation-3 (N3) syntax used to represent ontologies in RDF, RDFS, and OWL. Except for F-Logic, these syntaxes are alternative and mainly intended for human consumption.

- **Ontology management APIs:** Finally, several ontology languages and tools provide ontology management APIs. These APIs are included here because they can be considered as another form of syntax; the expressions used to access, create, and modify ontology components in the programming language in which these APIs are available have to be created according to the specification provided by the API. Among the languages with an ontology management API, we have all the ontology markup languages, where ontologies can be created using available XML Java APIs such as DOM, SAX, and so forth; and, more specifically, RDF, RDFS, DAML+OIL, and OWL, for which there are specific

APIs that resemble the knowledge models of the ontology languages, such as Jena, the OWL API, and so forth. Among the tools, we have KAON, OntoEdit, Protégé-2000, and WebODE.

There are other aspects to be considered in this layer, such as the fact that some ontology languages and tools allow defining the same component with different syntaxes. For example, Ontolingua provides at least four different ways to define concepts using KIF, using the Frame Ontology or using the OKBC-Ontology exclusively, or embedding KIF expressions inside definitions that use the Frame Ontology. This variety adds complexity both for the generation of such a format (we must decide what kind of expression to use[3]) and for its processing (we have to take into account all the possible syntactic variants for the same piece of knowledge).

Inside this layer, we also must take into account how the different formats represent datatypes. Two groups can be distinguished:

- **Formats with their own internal datatypes:** Among these formats, we can refer to most of the ontology languages except RDF, RDFS, and OWL, and most of the ontology tools.
- **Formats with XML Schema datatypes:** These datatypes have been defined with the aim of providing datatype standardization in Web contexts (e.g., in Web services). They can be used in the ontology languages RDF, RDFS, and OWL, and in the ontology tool WebODE, which allows using both types of datatypes (internal and XML Schema).

Therefore, with regard to datatypes, the problems to be solved will consist mainly of finding the relationships between the internal datatypes of the source and target formats (not all the formats have the same group of datatypes) or finding relationships between the internal datatypes of a format and the XML Schema datatypes, and vice versa.

Semantic Layer

This layer deals with the ability to construct the propositional meaning of the representation (Euzenat, 2001). Different ontology languages and tools can be based on different KR paradigms (frames, semantic networks, first order logic, conceptual graphs, etc.) or on combinations of them. These KR paradigms do not always allow expressing the same type of knowledge, and sometimes the languages and tools based on these KR paradigms allow expressing the same knowledge in different ways.

Therefore, in this layer, we deal not only with simple transformations (e.g., WebODE concepts are transformed into Ontolingua and OWL classes), but also with complex transformations of expressions that usually are related to the fact that the source and target formats are based on different KR paradigms (e.g., WebODE disjoint decompositions are transformed into subclass-of relationships and PAL[4] constraints in Protégé-2000, WebODE instance attributes attached to a class are transformed into datatype properties in OWL and unnamed property restrictions for the class).

As an example, Figure 3 shows how to represent a concept partition in different ontology languages and tools. In WebODE and LOOM, there are specific built-in primitives for representing partitions. In OWL the partition must be represented by defining the rdfs:subClassOf relationship between each class in the partition and the parent class, by stating that every possible pair of classes in the decomposition is disjoint, and by defining the parent class as the union of all the classes in the partition. In Protégé-2000, the partition is represented like in OWL, with subclass-of relationships between all the classes in the partition and the parent class, with several PAL constraints that represent disjointness between all the classes in the partition, and with the statement that the parent class is abstract (that is, it cannot have direct instances).

Figure 3. Examples of transformations at the semantic layer

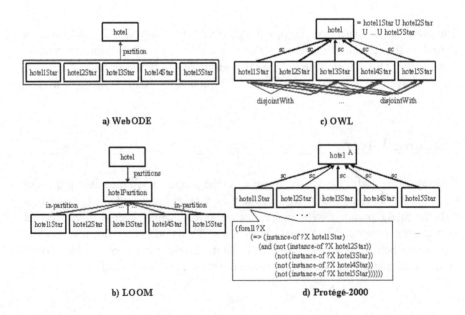

Most of the work on ontology translation done so far has been devoted to solving the problems that arise in this layer. For example, in the literature, we can find several formal, semi-formal, and informal methods for comparing ontology languages and ontology tools' knowledge models (Baader, 1996; Borgida, 1996; Corcho & Gómez-Pérez, 2000; Euzenat & Stuckenschmidt, 2003; Knublauch, 2003), which aim at helping to decide whether two formats have the same expressiveness or not, so that knowledge can be preserved in the transformation. Some of these approaches also can be used to decide whether the reasoning mechanisms present in both formats will allow inferring the same knowledge in the target format.

Basically, these studies allow analyzing the expressiveness (and, in some cases, the reasoning mechanisms) of the source and target formats, so that we can know which types of components can be translated directly from a format to another, which types of components can be expressed using other types of components from the target format, which types of components cannot be expressed in the target format, and which types of components can be expressed, although losing part of the knowledge represented in the source format.

Therefore, the catalogue of problems that can be found in this layer are related mainly to the different KR formalisms in which the source and target formats are based. This does not mean that translating between two formats based on the same KR formalism is straightforward, since there might be differences in the types of ontology components that can be represented in each of them. This is specially important in the case of DL languages, since many different combinations of primitives can be used in each language, and, hence, many possibilities exist in the transformations between them, as shown in Euzenat and Stuckenschmidt (2003). However, the most interesting results appear when the source and target KR formalisms are different.

Pragmatic Layer

This layer deals with the ability to construct the pragmatic meaning of the representation (or its meaning in context). Therefore, in this layer we deal with the transformations to be made in the ontology resulting from the lexical, syntactic, and semantic transformations, so that both human users and ontology-based applications will notice as few differences as possible with respect to the ontology in the original format, either in one-direction transformations or in cyclic transformations.

Therefore, transformations in this layer will require the following: adding special labels to ontology components in order to preserve their original identifier in the source format; transforming sets of expressions into more legible syntactic constructs in the target format; hiding completely or partially some ontology components not defined in the source ontology but that have been created as part of the transformations (such as the anonymous classes discussed previously); and so forth.

Figure 4 shows two transformations of the OWL functional object property usesTransportMean to WebODE. The object property domain is the class flight, and its range is the class airTransportMean. The figure shows two of the possible semantically equivalent sets of expressions that can be obtained when transforming that definition. In the first one, the object property is transformed into the ad hoc relation usesTransportMean that holds between the concepts flight and airTransportMean, with its maximum cardinality set to one. In the second one, the object property is transformed into the ad hoc relation usesTransportMean, whose domain and range is the concept Thing (the root of the ontology concept taxonomy), with no restrictions on its cardinality, plus three formal axioms expressed in first-order logic, the first one stating that the relation domain is flight, the second one that its range is airTransportMean, and the third one imposing the maximum cardinality constraint.[5]

Figure 4. Examples of transformations at the pragmatic layer

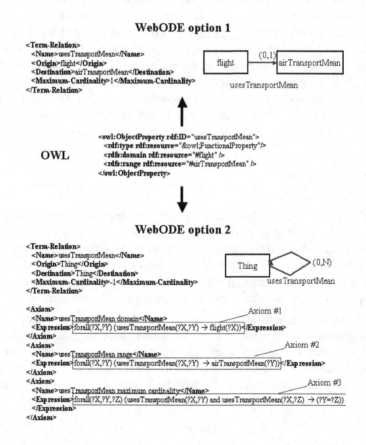

From a human user's point of view, the first WebODE definition is more legible; at first glance, the user can see that the relation usesTransportMean is defined between the concepts flight and airTransportMean, and that its maximum cardinality is one. In the second case, the user must find and interpret the four components (the ad hoc relation definition and the three formal axioms) to reach the same conclusion.

A similar conclusion can be obtained from an application point of view. Let us suppose that we want to populate the ontology with an annotation tool. The behavior of the annotation tool is different for both definitions. With the first definition, the annotation tool will easily understand that its user interface cannot give users the possibility of adding more than one instance of the relation, and that the drop-down lists used for selecting the domain and range of a relation instance will show only direct or indirect instances of the concepts flight and airTransportMean, respectively. With the second definition, the annotation tool will allow creating more than one relation instance from the same instance and will display all the ontology instances in the drop-down lists instead of just presenting instances of flight and airTransport-Mean, respectively. After that, the annotation tool will have to run the consistency checker to detect inconsistencies in the ontology.

Relationships Between Ontology Translation Layers

Figure 5 shows an example of a transformation from the ontology platform We-bODE to the language OWL DL. In this example, we have to transform two ad hoc relations with the same name (usesTransportMean) and with different domains and ranges (a flight uses an airTransportMean, and a cityBus uses a bus). In OWL DL, the scope of an object property is global to the ontology, and thus we cannot define two different object properties with the same name. In this example, we show that translation decisions have to be taken at all layers, and we also show how the decision taken at one layer can influence the decisions to be made at the others, hence showing the complexity of this task.

Option 1 is driven by semantics; to preserve semantics in the transformation, two different object properties with different identifiers are defined. Option 2 is driven by pragmatics; only one object property is defined from both ad hoc relations, since we assume that they refer to the same meaning, but some knowledge is lost in the transformation (the one related to the object property domain and range). Finally, Option 3 also is driven by pragmatics, with more care on the semantics; again, only one object property is defined, and its domain and range is more restricted than in Option 2, although we still lose the exact correspondence between each domain and range.

Figure 5. Example of translation decisions to be taken at several layers

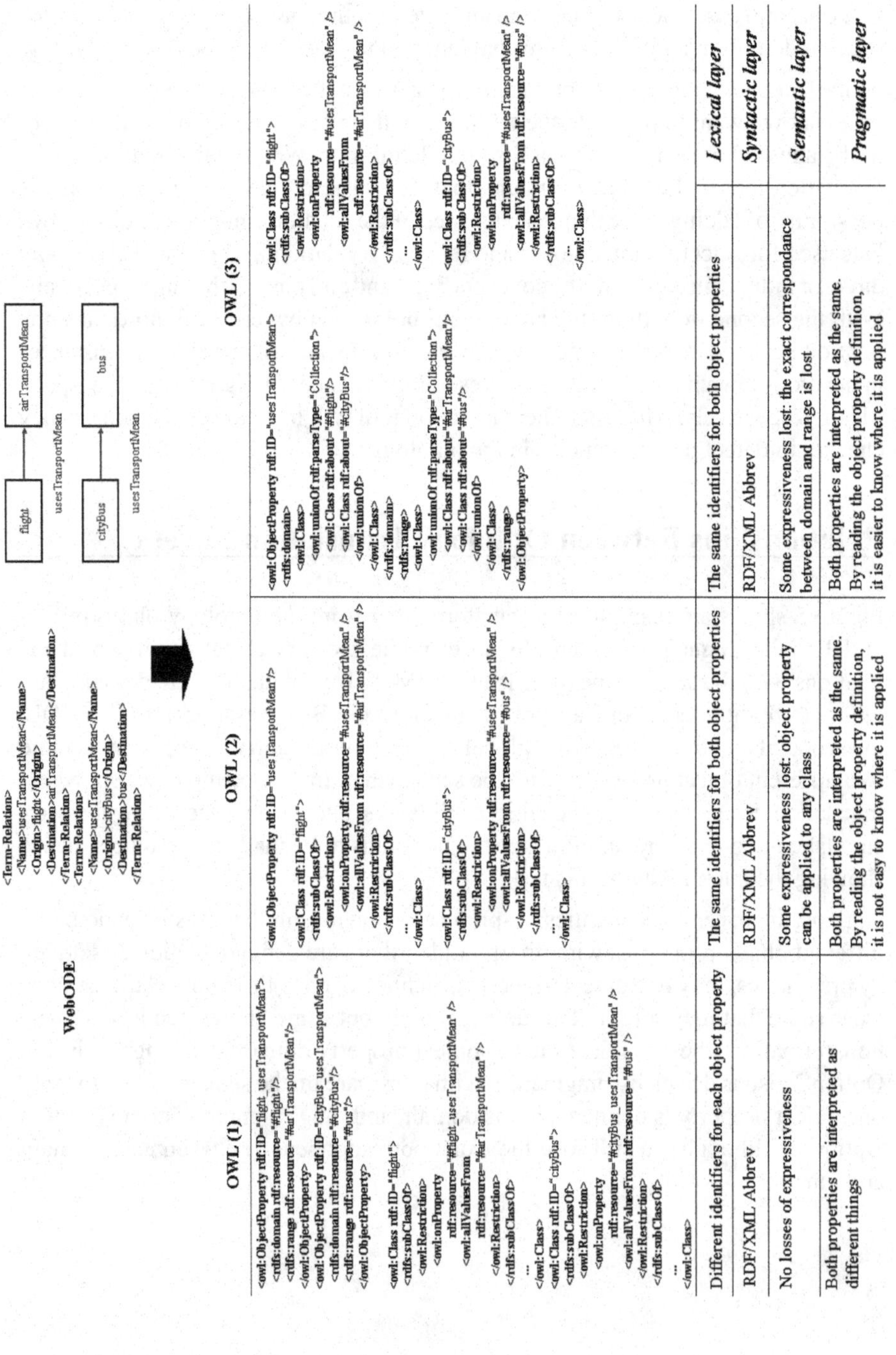

	OWL (1)	OWL (2)	OWL (3)	
Different identifiers for each object property		The same identifiers for both object properties	The same identifiers for both object properties	*Lexical layer*
RDF/XML Abbrev		RDF/XML Abbrev	RDF/XML Abbrev	*Syntactic layer*
No losses of expressiveness		Some expressiveness lost: object property can be applied to any class	Some expressiveness lost: the exact correspondance between domain and range is lost	*Semantic layer*
Both properties are interpreted as different things		Both properties are interpreted as the same. By reading the object property definition, it is not easy to know where it is applied	Both properties are interpreted as the same. By reading the object property definition, it is easier to know where it is applied	*Pragmatic layer*

A Layered Ontology Translation Method

Once we have described the four layers where ontology translation decisions have to be made, we will present our method for building ontology translation systems, based on these layers. This method consists of four activities: feasibility study, analysis of source and target formats, design and implementation of the translation system. As we will describe later, these activities are divided into tasks, which can be performed by different sets of people and with different techniques.

Ontology translation systems are difficult to create, since many different types of problems have to be dealt with. Consequently, this method recommends developing ontology translation systems following an iterative life cycle. It proposes identifying a first set of expressions that can be translated easily from one format to another, so that the first version of the ontology translation system can be developed and tested quickly; then, it proposes refining the transformations performed to analyze more complex expressions and to design and implement their transformations, and so forth. The reason for such a recommendation is that developing an ontology translation system is usually a complex task that requires taking into account too many aspects of the source and target formats, and many different types of decisions on how to perform specific translations. In this sense, an iterative life cycle ensures that complex translation problems are tackled once the developers have a

Figure 6. Proposed development process of ontology translation system

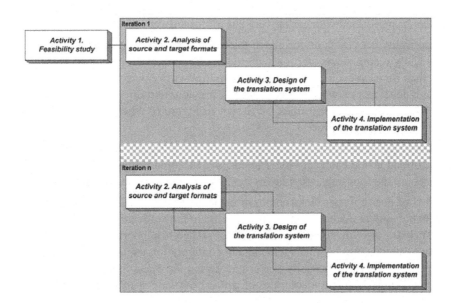

Table 2. List of activities and tasks of the method for developing ontology translation systems

Activity	Task
1. Feasibility study	1.1. Identify ontology translation system scope 1.2. Analysis of current ontology translation systems 1.3. Ontology translation system requirement definition 1.4. Feasibility decision-making and recommendation
2. Analysis of source and target formats	2.1. Describe source and target formats 2.2. Determine expressiveness of source and target formats 2.3. Compare knowledge models of source and target formats 2.4. Describe and compare additional features of source and target formats 2.5. Determine the scope of translation decisions 2.6. Specify test plan
3. Design of the translation system	3.1. Find and reuse similar translation systems 3.2. Propose transformations at the pragmatic level 3.3. Propose transformations at the semantic level 3.4. Propose transformations at the syntax level 3.5. Propose transformations at the lexical level 3.6. Propose additional transformations
4. Implementation of the translation system	4.1. Find translation functions to be reused 4.2. Implement transformations in the pragmatic level 4.3. Implement transformations in the semantic level 4.4. Implement transformations in the syntax level 4.5. Implement transformations in the lexical level 4.6. Implement additional transformations 4.7. Declarative specification processing and integration 4.8. Test suite execution

better knowledge of the source and target formats and once they have tested simpler translations performed with earlier versions of the software produced.

The feasibility activity is performed at the beginning of the development project. If this study recommends starting with the ontology translation system development, then for each cycle, the other three activities will be performed sequentially, although developers always can go back to a previous activity using the feedback provided by the subsequent ones, as shown in Figure 6, which summarizes the proposed development process.

As a summary, Table 2 lists the activities that the method proposes and the tasks to be performed inside each activity. The design and implementation activities take into account the four translation layers described in the previous section.

The method does not put special emphasis on other activities that usually are related to software system development, either specific to the software development process, such as deployment and maintenance, or related to support activities, such as quality assurance, project management, and configuration management. Nor does it emphasize other tasks usually performed during the feasibility study, analysis, design, and implementation activities of general software system development. It only describes those tasks that are specifically related to the development of ontology translation systems and recommends performing such additional activities and tasks that will be beneficial to their development.

In the following sections, we will describe briefly the objective of each of these activities, the techniques that can be used to perform them, and their inputs and outputs.

Feasibility Study

The objective of this activity is to analyze the ontology translation needs, so that the proposed solution takes into account not only the technical restrictions (technical feasibility), but also other restrictions related to the business objectives of an organization (business feasibility) and to the project actions that can be undertaken successfully (project feasibility). As a result of this activity, the main requisites to be satisfied by the ontology translation system are obtained, and the main costs, benefits, and risks are identified. The most important aspect of this feasibility study regards the technical restrictions, which can determine whether it is recommended or not to proceed with the ontology translation system development.

The techniques (and documents) used in the execution of these tasks are inspired by knowledge engineering approaches (Gómez-Pérez et al., 1997; Schreiber et al., 1999) and based mainly on the CommonKADS worksheets.

As shown in Figure 7, we first propose to determine the scope of the ontology translation system that will be implemented, its expected outcome, the context where it will be used, and so forth. We then propose to analyze current translation systems that are available between the source and target formats and determine the requisites of the new system. Finally, we propose to fill in a checklist where the three dimensions identified are considered (technical, business, and project feasibility), allowing us to make a decision on the feasibility of the system and to propose a set of actions and recommendations to be followed.

Figure 7. Task decomposition of activity 1 (feasibility study)

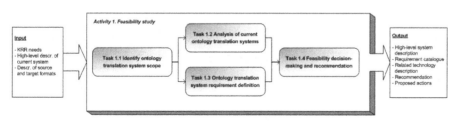

Consequently, the input in this activity consists of some preliminary high-level information about current systems, the KRR needs, and the source and target formats. The results consist in a deeper description of the current ontology translation systems available for the origin and target formats, a preliminary catalogue of requisites for the system to be developed, and the recommendation about its feasibility, including the main costs, benefits, and risks involved.

Analysis of the Source and Target Formats

The objective of this activity is to obtain a thorough description and comparison of the source and target formats of the ontology translation system. We assume that this will allow us to gain a better understanding of the similarities and differences in expressiveness, which will be useful in designing and implementing the translation decisions in the subsequent activities. Moreover, in this activity we refine the catalogue of requirements already obtained as a result of the feasibility study, and we identify the test suite that will be used to test the translation system validity after each iteration in its development process. A summary of the tasks to be performed and the input and outputs of this activity is shown in Figure 8.

Many techniques can be used to describe the source and target formats of the translation system. Among them, the method recommends describing their KR ontologies (as shown in Broekstra et al., 2000 or Gómez-Pérez et al., 2003), which provide a good overview of the ontology components that can be used to represent ontologies with them.

For the comparison tasks, we can use either formal, semi-formal, or informal approaches, such as the ones identified in Section 2.3, which show good examples of the results that should be obtained. Once the two formats have been described, evaluated, and compared, we recommend focusing on other additional features that might be needed in the translation process. They may include reasoning mechanisms or any other specific details that could be interesting for the task of translation.

Figure 8. Task decomposition of activity 2 (analysis of source and target formats)

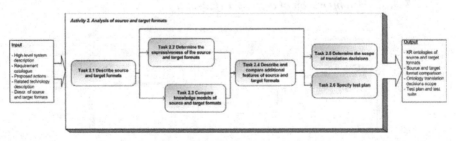

The information gathered in the previous tasks is used to determine the scope of the translation decisions to be made; that is, which components map to each other, which components of the source format must be represented by means of others in the target format, which components cannot be represented in the target format, and so forth. As a result, we obtain a refinement of the requirement catalogue obtained during the feasibility study, which serves as the basis for the next activities (design and implementation of the translation system).

Finally, we propose to define the test plan, which consists of a set of unitary tests that the translation system must pass in order to be considered valid. The test suite must consider all of the possible translation situations that the translation system must cover. These ontologies will be available in the source format and in the target format, which should be the output of the translation process. The test execution will consist of comparing the output obtained and the output expected. For each iteration of the software development process, we will define different sets of ontologies.

This activity receives as an input all the results of the feasibility study, together with the description of the source and target formats (also used as an input for that activity). It outputs a comparison of both formats; the scope of the translation decisions to be performed, with a refined requirements catalogue, and a test plan with its corresponding test suite.

Design of the Translation System

The design activity aims at providing a detailed specification of the transformations to be performed by the ontology translation system. From this specification, we will be able to generate the implementation of the translation decisions at each layer, which will be used in its turn to generate the final ontology translation system. The tasks, inputs, and outputs of this activity are shown in Figure 9.

The objective of the first task is to analyze similar ontology translation systems and to detect which of their translation decisions actually can be reused. We assume that by reusing existing translation decisions, we will be able to minimize the sources of errors in our translation proposals. Furthermore, we will benefit from work already known, for which we already know its properties (namely, how they preserve semantics and pragmatics). We must remember that the potential reusable systems were already identified and catalogued during the feasibility study.

The second group of tasks deals with the four layers of translation problems described in Section 2. We propose to design transformations at different interrelated levels, using different techniques for each layer. All these tasks should be performed mainly in parallel, and the decisions taken at one task provide feedback for the others, as shown in the figure. We propose to start with the translation decisions at

Figure 9. Task decomposition of activity 3 (design of the ontology translation system)

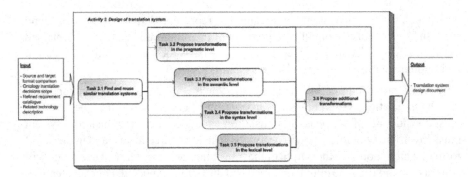

the pragmatic and semantic levels, leaving the syntax and lexical transformations for the last steps. The pragmatic and semantic translation decisions are proposed mainly by knowledge engineers, while the syntax and lexical transformations can be proposed jointly by knowledge and software engineers, since they have more to do with general programming aspects rather than with the complexity of transforming knowledge. The method proposes to represent these translation decisions mainly with tables and diagrams, such as the ones proposed in Table 3 and Figure 10 for transformations between WebODE and OWL DL.

Finally, the objective of the last task is to propose any additional transformations or design issues that have not been covered by the previous tasks, because they could not be catalogued as lexical, syntax, semantic, or pragmatic transformations, which are necessary for the correct functioning of the ontology translation system. These transformations include design issues such as the initialization and setting up of parameters in the source and target formats, any foreseen integration needs of the generated system in the case of transformations where ontology tools or specific libraries are used, and so forth.

As shown in Figure 9, we may need to come back to the second group of activities after proposing some additional transformations. This is a cyclic process until we have determined all the transformation to be performed in the corresponding development iteration. All the output results obtained from the tasks in this activity are integrated in a single document called "translation system design document," as shown in the figure.

Table 3. Semantic transformation of WebODE partitions to OWL DL

WebODE	OWL DL
Partition (C, {C1,C2,…,Cn})	$C \equiv C1 \cup C2 \cup \ldots \cup Cn$ $Ci \subseteq C \quad \forall\ Ci \in \{C1,C2,\ldots,Cn\}$ $Ci \cap Cj \subseteq \perp \quad \forall\ Ci \neq Cj,,\ Ci,Cj \in \{C1,C2,\ldots,Cn\}$

Figure 10. Pragmatic transformations with regard to the scope of WebODE ad hoc relations

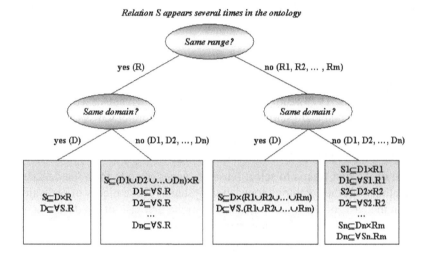

Implementation of the Translation System

The objective of the implementation activity is to create the declarative specifications of the transformations to be performed by the ontology translation system, which will be used to generate its final code. The method proposes to implement these translations using three different formal languages — ODELex, ODESyntax, and ODESem — which correspond to the lexical, syntax, and semantic/pragmatic ontology translation layers, respectively. The same language (ODESem) is used for implementing semantic and pragmatic transformations, because the translation decisions at both layers are similar. The description of these languages is out of the scope of this chapter and can be found in Corcho and Gómez-Pérez (2004) and Corcho (2005). We can say that the ODELex and ODESyntax languages are simi-

Figure 11. Task decomposition of activity 4 (implementation of the ontology translation system)

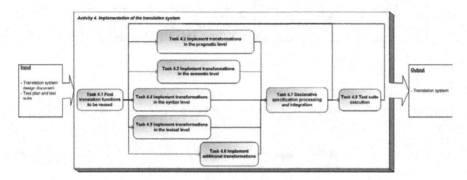

lar to the lex (Lesk, 1975) and yacc (Johnson, 1975) languages used for compiler construction, and that ODESem is based on common rule-based systems.

As in the design activity, the tasks inside this implementation activity are divided in groups — four, in this case — as shown in Figure 11.

The goal of the first task is to select reusable pieces of code from the declarative specifications of other ontology translation systems. These pieces of code are selected on the basis of the results obtained from the first task of the design activity and can be related to any of the four translation layers.

The next five tasks are grouped together and should be performed almost in parallel, as shown in the figure. In these tasks, software and knowledge engineers actually must implement the transformations at the four layers — lexical, syntax, semantic, and pragmatic — and the additional transformations described in task 3.6. Unlike in the design activity, we propose to start with the low-level transformations (those at the lexical and syntax layers) and continue with the more abstract (and difficult) ones. The reason for the task ordering suggested is that the semantic and pragmatic transformation implementations usually need to take into account the specific implementations at the lexical and syntax layers. We are currently developing automatic tools that transform the declarative specifications in ODELex, ODESyntax, and ODESem into Java code.

In task 4.7 — declarative specification processing and integration — the software engineer is in charge of transforming the previous declarative implementations at all levels, plus the additional transformations, into actual running code, which will perform the translations as specified in the previous code. In addition, the software engineer has to integrate the resulting ontology translation system into another information system (e.g., an ontology tool), if required. Given that most of the transformations have been implemented in formal languages, most of the processes involved in this task can be automated. If problems are detected during this task, the method recommends going back to the implementation activities in order to solve them.

Finally, the method proposes to execute the test suite that was defined during the analysis activity, which is considered the system tests for our system. This does not prevent us from defining and executing other kinds of tests (from unitary tests to integration tests) at any point during the development. This task consists of inputting the ontologies in the test suite to the resulting ontology translation system and checking whether the output corresponds to the one expected. Note that in most cases, this check will consist of comparing whether the output file(s) and the expected file(s) are identical, but there are cases where this kind of comparison will not be possible, since the results can come in any order (e.g., in RDF and OWL ontologies). If any of the test fails, we must go back to the previous implementation activities to detect the problems. Furthermore, we must consider that the method allows moving to previous activities if problems are detected at any point of our development.

Conclusion

This chapter presents two important contributions to the current state of the art on ontology translation. First, it proposes to consider that ontology translation problems can appear at four different layers, which are interrelated, and can describe the most common problems that may appear at each of those layers. Some existing approaches have identified similar layers in ontology translation. However, these and other approaches have focused mainly on the problems related to the semantic layer and have not considered the other ones, which are also important for building systems that make good quality translations. The low quality of some translation systems has been shown recently in the interoperability experiment performed for the ISWC2003 workshop on Evaluation of Ontology Tools.[6] The results obtained in this workshop showed that making good translation decisions at the lexical, syntax, and pragmatic levels is also as important as making good translation decisions at the semantic level.

The second main contribution of this chapter is related to the fact that it is the first approach that gives an integrated support for the complex task of building ontology translation systems. As we commented in the introduction, ontology translation systems are not easy to create and are difficult to maintain, as well. Most of the translation systems currently available have been developed ad hoc; the translation decisions that they implement are usually difficult to understand and hidden in the source code of the systems; and, in addition, it is neither clear nor documented how much knowledge is lost in the transformations that they perform. There are many complex decisions that have to be implemented, and these decisions are usually taken at the low implementation level instead of performing a detailed analysis and design of the different translation choices available and taking a decision based on the actual ontology translation requirements. The method proposed in this chapter helps in this task by identifying clearly the activities to be performed, the tasks in which each activity is decomposed, how these tasks have to be performed, the inputs and outputs of the activities, and the set of techniques that can be used to perform them. Moreover, a set of declarative languages is proposed, although not described in this chapter, to help in the implementation of translation decisions.

This method has been derived from our long experience in the generation of ontology translation systems from the ontology engineering platform WebODE to different ontology languages and tools, and vice versa (12 systems), and has been used for building other six ontology translation systems. These systems have been built successfully by different people with backgrounds in knowledge and software engineering, following the method proposed in this chapter and the techniques identified for each task.

Related Work

Although there are no other integrated methods for building ontology translation systems available, we can find some technology that allows creating them. Specifically, we can cite two tools: Transmorpher and OntoMorph:

- Transmorpher[7] (Euzenat & Tardif, 2001) is a tool that facilitates the definition and processing of complex transformations of XML documents. Among other domains, this tool has been used in the context of ontologies, using a set of XSLT documents that is able to transform from one DL language to another, expressed in DLML.[8] This tool is aimed at supporting the "family of ontology languages" approach for ontology translation described in Euzenat and Stuckenschmidt (2003). The main limitation of this approach is that it only deals with problems in the semantic layer and does not focus on other problems related to the lexical, syntax, and pragmatic layers.

- OntoMorph (Chalupsky, 2000) is a tool that allows creating translators declaratively. Transformations between the source and target formats are specified by means of pattern-based transformation rules and are performed in two phases: syntactic rewriting and semantic rewriting. The last one needs the ontology or part of it translated into PowerLoom, so that this KR system can be used for certain kinds of reasoning, such as discovering whether a class is a subclass of another, whether a relation can be applied to a concept or not, and so forth. Since this tool is based on PowerLoom (and consequently on Lisp), it cannot handle easily all the problems that may appear in the lexical and syntax layers.

Although these tools do not give an integrated support for the task of building ontology translation systems, this does not mean that they cannot be used as a technological support for the method proposed in this chapter, especially for the implementation activity.

Acknowledgments

This work has been supported by the IST project Esperonto (IST-2001-34373). Part of this chapter is based on Section 3.4 of the book A Layered Declarative Approach to Ontology Translation with Knowledge Preservation, (Corcho, 2005).

References

Arpírez, J. C., Corcho, O., Fernández-López, M., & Gómez-Pérez, A. (2003). WebODE in a nutshell. *AI Magazine, 24*(3),37-48.

Baader, F. (1996). A formal definition for the expressive power of terminological knowledge representation languages. *Journal of Logic and Computation, 6*(1), 33-54.

Baader, F., McGuinness, D., Nardi, D., & Patel-Schneider, P. (2003). *The description logic handbook: Theory, implementation and applications.* Cambridge, UK: Cambridge University Press.

Bechhofer, S., Horrocks, I., Goble, C., & Stevens, R. (2001). OilEd: A reasonable ontology editor for the Semantic Web. In *Proceedings of the Joint German/ Austrian conference on Artificial Intelligence (KI'01),* Vienna, Austria.

Borgida, A. (1996). On the relative expressiveness of description logics and predicate logics. *Artificial Intelligence, 82*(1-2), 353-367.

Brickley, D., & Guha, R. V. (2004). *RDF vocabulary description language 1.0: RDF Schema.* W3C. Retrieved from http://www.w3.org/TR/PR-rdf-schema

Chalupsky, H. (2000). OntoMorph: A translation system for symbolic knowledge. In *Proceedings of the 7th International Conference on Knowledge Representation and Reasoning (KR'00).* Breckenridge, CO.

Corcho, O. (2005). *A layered declarative approach to ontology translation with knowledge preservation*. Frontiers in Artificial Intelligence and its Applications. Dissertations in Artificial Intelligence. IOS Press

Corcho, O., & Gómez-Pérez, A. (2000). A roadmap to ontology specification languages. In *Proceedings of the 12th International Conference in Knowledge Engineering and Knowledge Management (EKAW'00)*, Berlin, Germany.

Corcho, O., & Gómez-Pérez, A. (2004). ODEDialect: A set of declarative languages for implementing ontology translation systems. In *Proceedings of the ECAI2004 Workshop on Semantic Intelligent Middleware for the Web and the Grid*, Valencia, Spain.

Dean, M., & Schreiber, G. (2004). *OWL Web ontology language reference*. W3C. Retrieved from http://www.w3.org/TR/owl-ref/

Domingue, J. (1998). Tadzebao and WebOnto: Discussing, browsing, and editing ontologies on the Web. In *Proceedings of the 11th International Workshop on Knowledge Acquisition, Modeling and Management (KAW'98)*, Banff, Canada.

Euzenat, J. (2001). Towards a principled approach to semantic interoperability. In *Proceedings of the IJCAI 2001 Workshop on Ontologies and Information Sharing*, Seattle, WA.

Euzenat, J., & Stuckenschmidt, H. (2003). The "family of languages" approach to semantic interoperability. In B. Omelayenko & M. Klein (Eds.), *Knowledge transformation for theSemantic Web* (pp. 49-63). Amsterdam, The Netherlands: IOS Press.

Euzenat, J., & Tardif, L. (2001). XML transformation flow processing. *Markup Languages: Theory and Practice, 3*(3), 285-311.

Farquhar, A., Fikes, R., & Rice, J. (1997). The ontolingua server: A tool for collaborative ontology construction. *International Journal of Human Computer Studies, 46*(6), 707-727.

Genesereth, M. R., & Fikes, R. E. (1992). *Knowledge Interchange Format. Version 3.0. Reference Manual* (Tech. Rep. No. Logic-92-1). Retrieved from http://meta2.stanford.edu/kif/Hypertext/kif-manual.html

Gómez-Pérez, A., Fernández-López, M., & Corcho, O. (2003). *Ontological engineering: With examples from the areas of knowledge management, e-commerce and the Semantic Web*. New York: Springer-Verlag.

Gómez-Pérez, A., Juristo, N., Montes, C., & Pazos, J. (1997). *Ingeniería del conocimiento*. Centro de Estudios Ramón Areces

Gruber, T. R. (1992). *Ontolingua: A mechanism to support portable ontologies* (Tech. Rep. No. KSL-91-66). Retrieved from ftp://ftp.ksl. stanford.edu/pub/ KSL_Reports/KSL-91-66.ps

Gruber, T. R. (1993). A translation approach to portable ontology specification. *Knowledge Acquisition, 5*(2), 199-220.

Horrocks, I., Fensel, D., Harmelen, F., Decker, S., Erdmann, M., & Klein, M. (2000). OIL in a Nutshell. In *Proceedings of the 12th International Conference in Knowledge Engineering and Knowledge Management (EKAW'00)*. Juan-Les-Pins, France.

Horrocks, I., & van Harmelen, F. (Eds.) (2001). *Reference description of the DAML+OIL (March 2001) ontology markup language* (Technical report). Retrieved from http://www.daml.org/2001/03/reference.html

Johnson, S. C. (1975). *Yacc: Yet another compiler compiler. Computing science technical report no. 32*. Murray Hill, NJ: Bell Laboratories.

Karp, P. D., Chaudhri, V., & Thomere, J. (1999). *XOL: An XML-based ontology exchange language*. Retrieved from http://www.ai.sri.com/~pkarp/xol/xol.html

Kifer, M., Lausen, G., & Wu, J. (1995). Logical foundations of object-oriented and frame-based languages. *Journal of the ACM, 42*(4), 741-843.

Klein, M. (2001). Combining and relating ontologies: An analysis of problems and solutions. In *Proceedings of the Workshop on Ontologies and Information Sharing*, Seattle, WA.

Knublauch, H. (2003). Editing semantic Web content with Protégé: The OWL pPlugin. In *Proceedings of the 6th Protégé Workshop*. Manchester, UK.

Lassila, O., & Swick, R. (1999). *Resource description framework (RDF) model and syntax specification*. W3C. Retrieved from http://www.w3.org/TR/REC-rdf-syntax/

Lenat, D. B., & Guha, R.V. (1990). *Building large knowledge-based systems: Representation and inference in the cyc project*. Boston: Addison-Wesley.

Lesk, M. E. (1975). *Lex — A lexical analyzer generator* (Computing Science Tech. Rep. No. 39). Murray Hill, NJ: Bell Laboratories.

Luke, S., & Heflin, J. (2000). *SHOE 1.01. Proposed specification* (Technical report). Parallel Understanding Systems Group. Retrieved from http://www.cs.umd.edu/projects/plus/SHOE/spec1.01.htm

MacGregor, R. (2001). Inside the LOOM classifier. *SIGART Bulletin, 2*(3), 88-92.

Maedche, A., Motik, B., Stojanovic, L., Studer, R., & Volz, R. (2003). Ontologies for enterprise knowledge management. *IEEE Intelligent Systems, 18*(2), 26-33.

Morris, C. W. (1938). Foundations of the theory of signs. In O. Neurath, R. Carnap, & C. W. Morris (Eds.), *International encyclopedia of unified science*. Chicago: Chicago University Press.

Motta, E. (1999). *Reusable components for knowledge modelling: Principles and case studies in parametric design.* Amsterdam, The Netherlands: IOS Press.

Noy, N. F., Fergerson, R. W., & Musen, M. A. (2000). The knowledge model of Protege-2000: Combining interoperability and flexibility. In *Proceedings of the 12ᵗʰ International Conference in Knowledge Engineering and Knowledge Management (EKAW'00)*, Juan-Les-Pins, France.

Schreiber, G., et al. (1999). *Knowledge engineering and management. The commonKADS methodology.* Cambridge, MA: MIT Press.

Studer, R., Benjamins, V. R., & Fensel, D. (1998). Knowledge engineering: Principles and methods. *IEEE Transactions on Data and Knowledge Engineering, 25*(1-2), 161-197.

Sure, Y., Staab, S., & Angele, J. (2002). OntoEdit: Guiding ontology development by methodology and inferencing. In *Proceedings of the Confederated International Conferences CoopIS, DOA and ODBASE 2002*, Berlin, Germany.

Swartout, B., Ramesh, P., Knight, K., & Russ, T. (1997). Toward distributed use of large-scale ontologies. In *Proceedings of the Spring Symposium on Ontological Engineering*, Stanford, CA.

Endnotes

[*]   The current affiliation of the author is Intelligent Software Components, Spain. The work presented was performed at Universidad Politécnica de Madrid.

[1]   The problems that may appear in the context of semantic interoperability are due not only to the fact that ontologies are available in different formats, but they are also related to the content of ontologies, their ontological commitments, and so forth. We only focus on the problems related exclusively to the differences between ontology languages and/or tools.

[2]   These types of problems also may be related to the pragmatic layer, as we will describe later in this section. We also will see that the limits of each translation layer are not strict; hence, we can find transformation problems that are in the middle of several layers.

[3]   As with naming conventions, this decision also will be related to the pragmatic translation layer.

[4]   Protégé Axiom Language

[5]   We must note that this second option may be obtained because expressions in OWL ontologies may appear in any order in an OWL file and, hence, may be processed independently.

[6]   http://km.aifb.uni-karlsruhe.de/ws/eon2003/

[7]   http://transmorpher.inrialpes.fr/

[8]   Description Logic Markup Language. http://co4.inrialpes.fr/xml/dlml/

The chapter was previously published in the International Journal on Semantic Web & Information Systems, 1(2), 22-48, April-June 2005.

Chapter VIII

Querying the Web Reconsidered:
Design Principles for Versatile Web Query Languages

François Bry, University of Munich, Germany

Christoph Koch, Vienna University of Technology, Austria

Tim Furche, University of Munich, Germany

Sebastian Schaffert, University of Munich, Germany

Liviu Badea,
Nat. Inst. for Research & Development Informatics, Bucharest, Romania

Sacha Berger, University of Munich, Germany

Abstract

A decade of experience with research proposals as well as standardized query languages for the conventional Web and the recent emergence of query languages for the Semantic Web call for a reconsideration of design principles for Web and Semantic Web query languages. This chapter first argues that a new generation of versatile Web query languages is needed for solving the challenges posed by the changing Web: We call versatile those query languages able to cope with both Web and Semantic Web data expressed in any (Web or Semantic Web) markup language. This chapter further suggests that well-known referential transparency and novel answer-closedness are essential features of versatile query languages. Indeed, they allow queries to be considered like forms and answers like form-fillings in the spirit of the query-by-example paradigm. This chapter finally suggests that the decentralized and heterogeneous nature of the Web requires incomplete data specifications (or incomplete queries) and incomplete data selections (or incomplete answers); the form-like query can be specified without precise knowledge of the queried data, and answers can be restricted to contain only an excerpt of the queried data.

Introduction

After a decade of experience with research proposals as well as standardized query languages for the conventional Web, and following the recent emergence of query languages for the Semantic Web a reconsideration of design principles for Web and Semantic Web query languages is called for.

The Semantic Web is an endeavor widely publicized in 2001 by an influential but also controversial article from Tim Berners-Lee, James Hendler, and Ora Lassila (Berners-Lee et al., 2001). The Semantic Web vision is that of the current Web which consists of (X)HTML and documents in other XML formats extended by metadata specifying the meaning of these documents in forms usable by both humans and computers.

One might see the Semantic Web metadata added to today's Web documents as semantic indices similar to encyclopedias. A considerable advantage over paper-printed encyclopedias is that the relationships expressed by Semantic Web metadata can be followed by computers, very much like hyperlinks, and be used for drawing conclusions using automated reasoning methods:

For the Semantic Web to function, computers must have access to structured collections of information and sets of inference rules that they can use to conduct automated reasoning. (Berners-Lee et al., 2001)

A number of formalisms have been proposed in recent years for representing Semantic Web metadata (e.g., RDF [Klyne et al., 2004], Topic Maps [ISO, 1999], and OWL [Bechhofer et al., 2004]). Whereas RDF and Topic Maps provide merely a syntax for representing assertions on relationships like "a text T is authored by person P," schema or ontology languages such as RDFS (Brickley et al., 2004) and OWL allow one to state properties of the terms used in such assertions (e.g., that no person can be a text). Building upon descriptions of resources and their schemas, as detailed in the architectural road map for the Semantic Web (Berners-Lee, 1998), rules expressed in SWRL (Horrocks et al., 2004) or RuleML (Boley et al., 2002), for example, allow the specification of actions to be taken, knowledge to be derived, or constraints to be enforced.

Essential for realizing this vision is the integrated access to all kinds of data represented in any of these representation formalisms or even in standard Web languages such as (X)HTML, SVG. Considering the large amount and the distributed storage of data already available on the Web, the efficient and convenient access to such data becomes the enabling requirement for the Semantic Web vision. It has been recognized that reasonably high-level, declarative query languages are needed for such efficient and convenient access, as they allow separation of the actual data storage from the view of the data that a query programmer operates on. This chapter presents a novel position on design principles for guiding the development of query languages that allow access to both standard and Semantic Web data. The authors believe that it is worthwhile to reconsider principles that have been stated almost a decade ago for query languages such as XML-QL (Deutsch et al., 1998) and XQuery (Boag et al., 2004), then agnostic of the challenges imposed by the emerging Semantic Web.

Three principles are at the core of this chapter:

- As discussed above, the same query language should provide convenient and efficient access to any kind of data expected to be found on the Semantic Web (e.g., to documents written in (X)HTML, to RDF descriptions of these documents, and even to ontologies). Only by intertwining data from all the different layers of the Semantic Web can vision be realized in its full potential.

- Convenience for the user of the query language requires the reuse of knowledge obtained in another context. Therefore, the query language should be based upon the principles of referential transparency and answer-closedness (see Section 2.4) realized by rules and patterns. Together, these principles allow for (1) querying existing and constructing new data by a form-filling approach (similar to but arguably more expressive than the query-by-example paradigm [Zloof, 1975]); and (2) basic reasoning capabilities including the provision of different views of the same data even represented in different Web formalisms.

- The decentralized and heterogeneous nature of the Web requires query languages that allow queries and answers to be incomplete: In queries, only known parts of the requested information are specified, similar to a form, leaving other parts incomplete. Conversely, the answer to a query may leave out uninteresting parts of the matching data.

It is worth noting that these core principles and the more detailed discussion of the design principles in Section 2 are describing general principles of query languages rather than specific issues of an implementation or storage system. Therefore, implementation issues, such as processing model (in-memory vs. database vs. data stream) or distributed query evaluation, are not discussed in this chapter. Rather, the language requirements are considered independently of such issues but allow for further extensions or restrictions of the language, if necessary, for a particular setting or application.

These design principles result in large part from experience in the design of Web query languages by the authors, in particular from the experience in designing the Web query language Xcerpt (Schaffert & Bry, 2004).

Design Principles

The rest of this chapter is organized around 13 design principles deemed essential for versatile Web query languages, starting with principles concerning the dual use of a query language for both Web and Semantic Web data (Section 2.1), the specific requirements on how to specify data selection (Section 2.2), the makeup of an answer (Section 2.3), further principles regarding declarativity and structuring of query programs (Section 2.4), reasoning support (Section 2.5), and finally, those regarding the relation of querying and evolution (Section 2.6) are outlined.

Versatility: Data, Syntax, and Interface

A Query Language for the Standard Web and Semantic Web

A hypothesis of this chapter is that a common query language for both conventional Web and Semantic Web applications is desirable (this requirement for a Web query language also has been expressed by other authors (e.g., Olken & McCarthy, 1998). There are two reasons for this hypothesis:

First, in many cases, data is not inherently conventional Web data or Semantic Web data. Instead, it is the usage that gives data a conventional Web or Semantic Web status. Consider, for example, a computer science encyclopedia. It can be queried like any other Web document using a Web query language. If its encyclopedia relationships (i.e., formalizing expressions such as "see," "see also," or "use instead," commonly used in traditional encyclopedia) are marked up using, for example, XLink or any other ad hoc or generic formalism, as one might expect from an online encyclopedia, then the encyclopedia also can be used as Semantic Web data (i.e., metadata) in retrieving computer science texts (e.g., the encyclopedia could relate a query referring to Linux to Web content referring to "operating systems of the 90s") or enhance the rendering of Web contents (e.g., adding hypertext links from some words to their definitions in the encyclopedia).

Second, Semantic Web applications most likely will combine and intertwine queries to Web data and to metadata (or Semantic Web data) in all possible manners. There is no reason to assume that Semantic Web applications will rely only on metadata or that querying of conventional Web data and Semantic Web data will take place in two (or several) successive querying phases, referring each to data of one single kind. Consider again the computer science encyclopedia example. Instead of one single encyclopedia, one might use several encyclopedias that might be listed in a (conventional Web) document. Retrieving the encyclopedias requires a conventional Web query. Merging the encyclopedias is likely to call for specific features of a Semantic Web query language. Enhancing the rendering of a conventional Web document using the resulting (merged) encyclopedia is likely to require (a) conventional Web queries (for retrieving conventional Web documents and the addresses of the relevant encyclopedias), (b) Semantic Web queries (for merging the encyclopedias), or (c) mixed conventional and Semantic Web queries (for adding hypertext links from words defined in the merged encyclopedia).

Integrated View of Standard and Semantic Web Data: Graph Data

Both XML and semi-structured data in general, as predominantly used on the (standard) Web, and RDF, the envisioned standard for representing Semantic Web data, can be represented in a graph data model. Although XML is often seen as a tree model only (see XML Information Set [Cowan & Tobin, 2004] and the XQuery data model [Fernandez et al., 2004]), it does provide nonhierarchical relations (e.g., by using ID/IDREF links or XLink [DeRose et al., 2001]).

Similar to the proposal for an integrated data model and (model-theoretic) Semantics of XML and RDF presented in Patel-Schneider and Simeon (2002), a query language for both standard and Semantic Web must be able to query any such data in a natural way. In particular, an abstraction of the various linking mechanisms is desirable for easy query formulation; one approach is the automatic dereferencing of ID/IDREF-links in XML data, and another is the unified treatment of typed relations provided both in RDF and XLink.

The restriction to hierarchical (i.e., acyclic) relations is not realistic beyond the simplest Semantic Web use cases. Even if each relation for itself is acyclic, inference based not only on relations of a single type must be able to cope with cycles. Therefore, a (rooted) graph data model is called for.

Three Syntaxes: XML, Compact Human-Readable, and Visual

While it is desirable that a query language for the (conventional and/or Semantic) Web has an XML syntax, because it makes it easier to exchange query programs on the Web and to manipulate them using the query language, a second, more compact syntax easier for humans to read and write is desirable. Therefore, two textual syntaxes should be provided: a purely term-oriented XML syntax and another one that combines term expressions with non-term expressions like most programming languages. This other syntax should be more compact than the XML syntax and better readable for human beings. Both syntaxes should be interchangeable (the translation being a low cost process).

Third, a visual syntax can greatly increase the accessibility of the language, in particular for non-experts. This visual syntax should be a mere rendering of the textual language, a novel approach to developing a visual language with several advantages. It results in a visual language tightly connected to the textual language; namely, it is a rendering of the textual language. This tight connection makes it possible to use both the visual and the textual language in the development of applications. Last, but not least, a visual query language conceived as a hypertext application is especially accessible for Web and Semantic Web application developers.

Modeling, Verbalizing, and Visualizing

- **Authoring and modeling:** Authoring correct and consistent queries often requires considerable effort from the query programmer. Therefore, semi-automated or fully automated tool support both for authoring and for reading and understanding queries is essential.

- **Verbalization:** For verbalizing queries, as well as their input and output, some form of controlled natural language processing is promising and can provide an interface to the query language for untrained users. The importance of such a seemingly free-form "natural" interface for the Web is demonstrated by the widespread success of Web search engines.

- **Visualization:** As already discussed, a visualization based on styling of queries is highly advantageous in a Semantic Web setting. As demonstrated in Berger et al. (2003], it also can serve as a foundation for interactive features such as authoring of queries. On this foundation, more advanced authoring tools (e.g., for verification and validation of queries) can be implemented.

Data Selection: Pattern-Based, Incomplete

Every query language has to define means for accessing or selecting data. This section discusses principles for data selection in a Web context.

Pattern Queries

Patterns, as used in Xcerpt (Schaffert & Bry, 2004) and XML-QL (Deutsch et al., 1998), for example, provide an expressive and yet easy-to-use mechanism for specifying the characteristics of data sought. In contrast to path expressions, as used in XPath (Clark & DeRose, 1999) and languages building upon it, for example, they allow an easy realization of answer-closedness in the spirit of "query by example" query languages. Query patterns are especially well suited for a visual language, because they give queries a structure very close to that of possible answers. One might say that query patterns are like forms and answers are like form fillings.

Incomplete Query Specifications

Incomplete queries specify only part of the data to retrieve (i.e., only some of the children of an XML element (referring to the tree representation of XML data called "incompleteness in breadth") or an element at unspecified nesting depth (referring to the tree representation of XML data called "incompleteness in depth"). Such queries are important on the conventional Web because of its heterogeneity; one often knows only part of the structure of the XML documents to retrieve.

Incomplete queries specifying only part of the data to retrieve are also important on the Semantic Web. There are three reasons for this: first, Semantic Web data such as RDF or Topic Map data might be found in different (XML) formats that, in general, are easier to compare in terms of only some salient features. Second, the merging of Semantic Web data is often done in terms of components common to distinct data items. Third, most Semantic Web data standards allow data items with optional components. In addition, query languages for the conventional and Semantic Web should ease retrieving only parts of (completely or incompletely specified) data items.

Incomplete Data Selections

Because Web data is heterogeneous in its structure, one is often interested in "incomplete answers." Two kinds of incomplete answers can be considered. First, one might not be interested in some of the children of an XML (sub-) document retrieved by a query. Second, one might be interested in some child elements if they are available, but would accept answers without such elements.

An example of the first case would be a query against a list of students asking for the name of students having an e-mail address but specifying that the e-mail address should not be delivered with the answer.

An example of the second case would be a query against an address book asking for names, e-mail addresses, and, if available, cellular phone numbers.

But the limitation of an answer to "interesting" parts of the selected data is helpful not only for XML data. A common desire when querying descriptions of Web sites, documents, or other resources stored in RDF is to query a description of a resource (i.e., everything related to the resource helping to understand or identify it). In this case, for example, one might want to retrieve only data related by, at most, n relations to the original resource and also avoid following certain relation types not helpful in identifying a resource.

Polynomial Core

The design principles discussed in this chapter point toward a general-purpose, and due to general recursion, most likely Turing-complete, database programming language. However, it is essential that for the most frequently used queries, small upper bounds on the resources taken to evaluate queries (i.e., main memory and query evaluation time) can be guaranteed. As a consequence, it is desirable to identify an interesting and useful fragment of a query language for which termination can be guaranteed and which can be evaluated efficiently.

When studying the complexity of database query languages, one distinguishes between at least three complexity measures: data complexity, where the database is considered to be the input and the query is assumed fixed; query complexity, where the database is assumed fixed and the query is the input; and combined complexity, which takes both the database and the query as input and expresses the complexity of query evaluation for the language in terms of the sizes of both (Vardi, 1982).

For a given language, query and combined complexity are usually much higher than data complexity. In most relational query languages are by one exponential factor harder (e.g., in PSPACE vs. LOGSPACE-complete for first-order queries and EXPTIME-complete vs. PTIME-complete for Datalog, cf. [Abiteboul et al., 1995]). On the other hand, since data sizes are usually much larger than query sizes, the data complexity of a query language is the dominating measure of the hardness of queries.

One complexity class that is usually identified with efficiently solvable problems (or queries) is that of all problems solvable in polynomial time. PTIME queries still can be rather inefficient on large databases. Another even more desirable class of queries would thus be that of those queries solvable in linear time in the size of the data.

Database theory provides us with a number of negative results on the complexity of query languages that suggest that neither polynomial-time query complexity nor linear-time data complexity are feasible for data-transformation languages that construct complex structures as the result. For example, even conjunctive relational queries are NP-complete with respect to query complexity (Chandra & Merlin, 1977). Conjunctive queries only can apply selection, projection, and joins to the input data, all features that are among the requirements for query languages for the Semantic Web. There are a number of structural classes of tractable (polynomial-time) conjunctive queries, such as those of so-called "bounded tree-width" (Flum et al., 2002) or "bounded hypertree-width" (Gottlob et al., 2002), but these restrictions are not transparent or easy to grasp by users. Moreover, even if such restrictions are made, general data transformation queries only need very basic features (i.e., joins or pairing) to produce query results that are of super-linear size. That is, just writing the results of such queries is not feasible in linear time.

If one considers more restrictive queries that view data as graphs or, more precisely, as trees, and which only select nodes of these trees, there are a number of positive results. The most important is the one that monadic (i.e., node-selecting) queries in monadic second-order logic on trees are in linear time with respect to data complexity (Courcelle, 1990) but have non-elementary query complexity (Grohe & Schweikardt, 2003). Reasoning on the Semantic Web naturally happens on graph data, and results for trees remain relevant because many graphs are trees. However, the linear time results already fail, if very simple comparisons of data values in the trees are permitted.

Thus, the best we can hope for in a data transformation query language fragment for reasoning on the Semantic Web is PTIME data complexity. This is usually rather easy to achieve in query languages by controlling the expressiveness of higher-order quantification and recursion. In particular, the latter is relevant in the context of the design principles laid out here. A PTIME upper bound on the data complexity of recursive query languages is achieved either by disallowing recursion or by imposing an appropriate monotonicity requirement (i.e., those that form the basis of PTIME data complexity in standard Datalog or Datalog with inflationary fix-point semantics (Abiteboul et al., 1995).

Finding a large fragment of a database programming language and determining its precise complexity is an important first step. However, even more important than worst-case complexity bounds is the efficiency of query evaluation in practice. This leads to the problem of query optimization. Optimization also is usually best done on restricted query language fragments, in particular if such fragments exhibit alternative algebraic, logical, or game-theoretic characterizations.

Answers: Arbitrary XML, Ranked

Answers as Arbitrary XML Data

XML is the lingua franca of data interchange on the Web. As a consequence, answers should be expressible in every possible XML application. This includes both text without markup and freely chosen markup and structure. This requirement is obvious and widely accepted for conventional Web query languages. Semantic Web query languages also should be capable of delivering answers in every possible XML application in order to make it possible, for instance, to mediate between RDF and XTM (an XML serialization of Topic Maps [Pepper & Moore, 2001]) data or to translate RDF data from one RDF syntax into another RDF syntax.

Answer Ranking and Top-k Answers

In contrast to queries posed to most databases, queries posed to the conventional and Semantic Web might have a rather unpredictable number of answers. As a consequence, it is often desirable to rank answers according to some application-dependent criteria. It is desirable that Web and Semantic Web query languages offer (a) basic means for specifying ranking criteria and, (b) for efficiency reasons, evaluation methods computing only the top-k answers (i.e., a given number k of best-ranked answers according to a user-specified ranking criterion).

Query Programs: Declarative, Rule based

The following design principles concern the design of query programs beyond the data selection facilities discussed in Section 2.2.

Referential Transparency

This property means that within a definition scope, all occurrences of an expression have the same value (i.e., denote the same data). Referential transparency is an essential, precisely-defined trait of the rather vague notion of "declarativity."

Referential transparency is a typical feature of modern functional programming languages. For example, evaluating the expression f 5 in the language Haskell will always yield the same value (assuming the same definition of f is used). Contrasting with languages like C or Java: the expression f(5) might yield different results every time it is called because its definition depends on constantly changing state information.

Referentially transparent programs are easier to understand and, therefore, easier to develop, maintain, and optimize as referential transparency allows query optimizers to dynamically rearrange the evaluation order of (sub-) expressions (e.g., for evaluating in a "lazy manner" or computing an optimal query evaluation plan). Therefore, referential transparency surely is one of the essential properties a query language for the Web should satisfy.

Answer-Closedness

We call a query language "answer-closed" if replacing a sub-query in a compound query by a possible (not necessarily actual) single answer always yields a syntactically valid query. Answer-closed query languages ensure in particular that every data item (i.e., every possible answer to some query) is a syntactically valid query. Functional programs can but are not required to be answer-closed. Logic programming languages are answer-closed, but SQL is not (e.g., the answer person(a) to the Datalog query person(X) is itself a possible query, while the answer "name = 'a' " to the SQL query SELECT name FROM person cannot (without significant syntactical changes) be used as a query. Answer-closedness is the distinguishing property of the "query by example" paradigm (Zloof, 1975), even though it is called differently there, separating it from previous approaches for query languages. Answer-closedness eases the specification of queries because it keeps limited the unavoidable shift in syntax from the data sought for and the query specifying these data.

To illustrate the importance of answer-closedness in the Web context, assume an XML document containing a list of books with titles, authors, and prices (e.g., the XML Query Use Case XMP [Chamberlain et al., 2003]). The XPath (Clark and DeRose, 1999) query:

/bib/book/title/text()

selects the (text of) titles of books, while a similar query in the (answer-closed) language Xcerpt ([Schaffert and Bry, 2004) is:

bib {{ book {{ title { var T } }} }}.

XPath does not allow to substitution (e.g., the string "Data on the Web" for the query is thus not answer-closed). In Xcerpt, on the other hand, the following is both an answer to the query and a perfectly valid query in itself:

bib {{ book {{ title { "Data on the Web" } }} }}

Answer-closedness is useful (e.g., when joining several documents). For instance, a query first could select book titles in a person's favorite book list and then substitute these titles in the previous query:

and {
my-favorite-books {{ title { var T } }},
bib {{ book {{ title { var T } }} }}
}

Rule-Based, Chaining, and Recursion

- **Rule-based:** Rules are understood here as means to specify novel, maybe virtual, data in terms of queries (i.e., what is called "views" in (relational) databases, regardless of whether this data is materialized or not). Views (i.e., rule-defined data) are desirable for both conventional and Semantic Web applications. There are three reasons for this:
  - o First, view definitions or rules are a means for achieving the so-called "separation of concerns" in query programs (i.e., the stepwise specifications of data to retrieve and/or to construct). In other words, rules and view definitions are a means for "procedural abstraction" (i.e., rules [view definitions, resp.] are the Prolog and Datalog (SQL, resp.) counterpart of functions and/or procedures.
  - o Second, rules and view definitions give rise to easily specifying inference methods needed (e.g., by Semantic Web applications).
  - o Third, rules and view definitions are means for "data mediation." Data mediation means translating data to a common format from different sources. Data mediation is needed both on today's Web and on the emerging Semantic Web because of their heterogeneity.
- **Backward and forward chaining:** On the Web, backward chaining (i.e., computing answers starting from rule heads) is, in general, preferable to forward chaining (i.e., computing answers from rule's bodies). While forward chaining is, in general, considered to be more efficient then backward chaining, there are many situations where backward chaining is necessary, in particular when dealing with Web data. For example, a query might dynamically query Web pages depending on the results of previous queries and, thus, unknown in advance. Thus, a forward chaining evaluation would require considering the whole Web, which is clearly unfeasible.

- **Recursion:** On the Web, recursion is needed at least for:
    - Traversing arbitrary-length paths in the data structure
    - Querying on the standard Web when complex transformations are needed
    - Querying on the Semantic Web when inference rules are involved

    Note that a free recursion is often desirable and that recursive traversals of XML documents as offered by the recursive computation model of XSLT 1.0 are not sufficient.

Separation of Queries and Constructions

Two standard and symmetrical approaches are widespread, as far as query and programming languages for the Web are concerned:

- Queries or programs are embedded in a Web page or Web page skeleton giving the structure of answers or data returned by calls to the programs.
- Parts of a Web page specifying the structure of the data returned to a query or program evaluation are embedded in the queries or programs.

It is a hypothesis of this chapter that both approaches to queries or programs are hard to read and, therefore, hard to write and maintain.

Instead of either approach, a strict separation of queries and "constructions" (i.e., expressions specifying the structure of answers) is desirable. With a rule-based language, constructions are rule heads, and queries are rule bodies. In order to relate a rule's construction to a rule's query (logic programming), variables can be employed.

As discussed in Section 2.13, the construction of complex results often requires considerable computation. The separation of querying and construction presented here allows for the separate optimization of both aspects, allowing easier adoption of efficient evaluation techniques.

Reasoning Capabilities

Versatility (Section 2.1) allows access to data in different representation formats, thereby addressing format heterogeneity. However, in a Web context, data often will be heterogeneous not only in the chosen representation format, but also in terms, structure, and so forth. Reasoning capabilities offer a means for the query author to deal with heterogeneous data and to infer new data.

Specific Reasoning as Theories

Many practical applications require special forms of reasoning; for instance, efficient equality reasoning is often performed using the so-called paramodulation rule instead of the equality axioms (transitivity, substitution, and symmetry). Also, temporal data might require conversions between different time zones and/or calendar systems that are expressed in a simpler format and more efficiently performed using arithmetic instead of logical axioms. Finally, reasoning with intervals of possible values instead of exact values (e.g., for appointment scheduling) is conveniently expressed and efficiently performed with constraint programming.

For this reason, it is desirable that a query language for the (conventional and Semantic) Web can be extended with so-called "theories" implementing specific forms of reasoning.

Such "theory extensions" can be realized in two manners:

- First, a theory can be implemented as an extension of the runtime system of the query language with additional language constructs for using the extension.
- Second, a theory can be implemented using the query language itself and made available to users of this query language through program libraries. In this case, theories are implemented by rules and queries. Based upon the XML syntax of the query language (Section 2.12), for example, such rule bases can then be queried using the query language itself and maintained and updated by a reactive language such as XChange (Bry & Ptrânjan, 2005).

Querying Ontologies and Ontology-Aware Querying

In a Semantic Web context, ontologies can be used in several alternative ways. First, they can be dealt with by a specialized ontology reasoner (the main disadvantage being the impossibility of adding new domain-specific constructs). Second, they can be regarded as descriptions to be used by a set of rules implementing the Semantics of the constructs employed by the ontology. (This is similar to a meta-interpreter and may be slow.) Alternatively, the ontology may be "compiled" to a set of rules.

As discussed in the previous point, the query language should allow for both approaches: extending the query language by specific theory reasoners for a certain ontology language (e.g., OWL-DL) as well as the ability to use rules written in the query language as means for implementing (at least certain aspects) of an ontology language. Examples for such aspects are the transitivity of the subsumption hierarchy represented in many ontologies or the type inference based on domain and range restrictions of properties.

The latter approach is based upon the ability to query the ontology together with the data classified by the ontology. This is possible due to the first design principle. Stated in terms of ontologies, we believe that a query language should be designed in such a way that it can query standard Web data (e.g., an article published on a Web site) in some XML document format metadata describing such Web data (e.g., resource descriptions in RDF stating author, usage restrictions, relations to other resources, reviews, etc.), and the ontology that provides the concepts and their relations for the resource description in RDF.

Querying and Evolution

When considering the vision of the Semantic Web, the ability to cope with both quickly evolving and rather static data is crucial. The design principles for a Web query language discussed in the remainder of this section are mostly agnostic of changes in the data; only a snapshot of the current data is considered for querying; synchronization and distribution issues are transparent to the query programmer.

In many cases, such an approach is very appropriate and allows the query programmer to concentrate on the correct specification of the query intent. However, there are also a large number of cases where information about changes in the data and the propagation of such and similar events is called for (e.g., event notification, change detection, and publish-subscribe systems).

For programming the reactive behavior of such systems, one often employs "event-condition-action" (or ECA) rules. We believe that the specification of both queries on occurring events (the "event" part of ECA-rules) and on the condition of the data, which should hold for a specific action to be performed, should be closely related to or even embed the general purpose query language whose principles are discussed in this chapter (e.g., the reactive language XChange [Bry & Ptrânjan, 2005] integrating the query language Xcerpt [Schaffert & Bry, 2004]).

Related Work

Although there have been numerous approaches for accessing Web data, few approaches consider the kind of versatility asked for by the design principles presented in this chapter. This section briefly discusses how the design principles previously introduced relate to selected query languages for XML and RDF data, but does not aim at a full survey over current Web query languages as presented (Furche et al., 2004).

Versatility

Most previous approaches to Web query languages beyond format-agnostic information retrieval systems such as search engines have focused on access to one particular kind of data only (e.g., XML or RDF data). Therefore, such languages fall short of realizing the design principles on versatility described in Section 2.1. Connected to the realization that the vision of a "Semantic Web" requires joint access to XML and RDF data, versatility (at least when restricted to these two W3C representation standards) has been increasingly recognized as a desirable if not necessary characteristic of a Web query language (Patel-Schneider & Simeon, 2002). The charter of the W3C working group on RDF Data Access even asks "for RDF data to be accessible within an XML Query context [and] a way to take a piece of RDF Query abstract syntax and map it into a piece of XML Query" (Prud'hommeaux, 2004).

This recognition, however, has led mostly to approaches where access to RDF data is added to already established XML query languages. Robie et al. (2001) proposes a library of XQuery accessor functions for normalizing RDF/XML and querying the resulting RDF triples. Notably, the functions for normalizing and querying actually are implemented in XQuery. In contrast, TreeHugger (Steer, 2003) provides a set of (external) extension functions for XSLT (1.0) (Clark, 1999). Both approaches suffer from the lack of expressiveness of the XQuery and XSLT data model when considering RDF data; XQuery and XSLT consider XML data as tree data where references (expressed using ID/IDREF or XLink) have to be resolved explicitly (e.g., by an explicit join or a specialized function). Therefore, Robie et al., (2001) maps RDF graphs to a flat, triple-like XML structure requiring explicit, value-based joins for graph traversal. TreeHugger maps the RDF graph to an XML tree, thus using the more efficient structural access, where possible, requiring special treatment, however, of RDF graphs that are not tree shaped. None of these approaches fulfills entirely the design principles proposed in Section 2.1, but they represent important steps in the direction of a versatile Web query language.

Data Selection

For the remainder of the design principles, Web query languages specialized for a certain representation format such as XML or RDF are worth considering. One of the most enlightening views on the state-of-the-art in both XML and RDF query languages is a view considering how data selection is specified in these languages. Both data formats allow structured information, and data selection facilities emphasize the selection of data based on its own structure and its position in some context (e.g., an XML document or an RDF graph). For specifying such structural relations, three approaches can be observed:

1. **Purely relational:** Where the structural relations are represented simply as relations, e.g., child(CONTEXT, X)Ủdescendant(X, Y) for selecting the descendants of a child of some node CONTEXT. This style is used in several RDF query languages (e.g., the widely used RDQL [Seaborne, 2004]) and current drafts of the upcoming W3C RDF query language SPARQL (Prud'hommeaux & Seaborne, 2004). For XML querying, this style has proven convenient for formal considerations of expressiveness and complexity of query languages, for example. In actual Web query languages, it can be observed only sparsely (e.g., in the Web extraction language Elog [Baumgartner et al., 2001]).

2. **Path-based:** Where the query language allows several structural relations along a path in the tree of graph structure to be expressed without explicit joins, e.g., child::*/descendant::* for selecting the descendants of childs of the context. This style, originating in object-oriented query languages, is used in the most popular XML query languages such as XPath (Clark & DeRose, 1999), XSLT ([Clark, 1999), and XQuery (Boag et al., 2004), but also in a number of other XML query languages (XpathLog, 2004) that shows that this style of data selection also can be used for data updates. Several ideas to extend this style to RDF query languages have been discussed (Palmer, 2003), but only RQL (Karvounarakis et al., 2004) proposes a full RDF query language using path expressions for data selection.

3. **Pattern-based:** As discussed in Section 2.2.1. This style is used (e.g., in XML-QL [Deutsch et al., 1998] and Xcerpt [Schaffert & Bry, 2004]) but is also well established for relational databases in the form "query-by-example" and Datalog.

Most Web query languages consider to some extent incomplete query specifications, as Web data is inherently inconsistent, and few assumptions about the schema of the data can be guaranteed. However, only few query languages take into account the two flavors of incomplete data selection discussed in Section 2.2.3 (e.g., Xcerpt [Schaffert & Bry, 2004] and SPARQL [Prud'hommeaux & Seaborne, 2004]).

Polynomial cores have been investigated most notably for XPath (and, therefore, by extension XQuery [Boag et al., 2004] and XSLT [Clark, 1999]); the results are presented, for example, in Gottlob et al. (2003) and Segoufin (2003).

Answers

Naturally, most XML query languages can construct answers in arbitrary XML. This, however, is not true of RDF query languages, many of which, such as RDQL

(Seaborne, 2004) do not even allow the construction of arbitrary RDF, but rather outputs only (n-ary) tuples of variable bindings.

Answer ranking and top-k answers historically have rarely been provided by the core of Web query languages, but rather have been added as an extension (Amer-Yahia et al., 2004), a W3C initiative on adding full-text search and answer ranking to XPath and XQuery (Boag et al., 2004). In relational databases, on the other hand, top-k answers are a very common language feature.

Query Programs

Declarativity and referential transparency have long been acknowledged as important design principles for any query language, as a declaratively specified query is more amenable to optimization while also easing query authoring in many cases.

Most of the Web query languages claim to be declarative languages and, oftentimes claim to offer a referentially transparent syntax. In the case of XQuery (Boag et al., 2004), the referential transparency of the language is doubtful due to side effects during element construction. For instance, the XQuery let $x = <a/> return $x is $x, where is the XQuery node comparator (i.e., tests whether two nodes are identical, evaluates to true, whereas the query <a/> is <a/> evaluates to false, although it is obtained from the first query by replacing all occurrences of $x with its value.[1] The reason for this behavior lies in the way elements are constructed in XQuery: In the first query, a single (empty) a is created, which is, of course, identical to itself. However, in the second case, two a elements are constructed, which are not identical, and, therefore, the node identity comparison using is fails. Interestingly, this behavior is related to XQuery's violation of design principle 2.4.4, that stipulates that querying and construction should be separated in a query language.

In contrast to referential transparency, answer-closedness cannot be observed in many Web query languages. With the exception of Xcerpt (Schaffert & Bry, 2004), Web query languages provide, if at all, only a limited form of answer-closedness, where only certain answers also can be used as queries.

Related to answer-closedness is the desire to be able to easily recognize the result of a query. This can be achieved by a strict separation of querying and construction, where the construction specifies a kind of form filled with data selected by the query. Such a strict separation is not used in most XML query languages but can be observed in many RDF query languages (e.g., RDF and SPARQL) due to the restricted form of construction considered in these languages (following a similar syntax as SQL, but restricting the SELECT clause to lists of variables, for example).

Section 2.4.3 proposes the use of (possibly recursive) rules for separation of concern, view specification. This has been a popular choice for Web query languages (e.g., XSLT [Clark, 1999], Algae [Prud'hommeaux, 2004]), in particular when combined with reasoning capabilities (e.g., in TRIPLE [Sintek, 2002], XPathLog [May, 2004]).

Reasoning Capabilities

Reasoning capabilities, as discussed in Section 2.5, are very convenient means to handle and enrich heterogeneous Web data. Nevertheless, the number of XML query languages featuring built-in reasoning capabilities is rather limited, examples being XPathLog (May, 2004) and Xcerpt (Schaffert & Bry, 2004). In contrast, several RDF query languages provide at least limited forms of reasoning for computing the transitive closure of arbitrary relations (e.g., TRIPLE [Sintek, 2002], Algae [Prud'hommeaux, 2004]. Some RDF query languages also consider ontology-aware querying with RDFS (Brickley et al., 2004) as ontology language. For XML query languages, this has not been considered at length.

Conclusion and Outlook

In this chapter, design principles for (Semantic) Web query languages have been derived from the experience with previous conventional Web query language proposals from academia and industry as well as recent Semantic Web query activities.

In contrast to most previous proposals, these design principles are focused on versatile query languages (i.e., query languages) able to query data in any of the heterogeneous representation formats used in both the standard and the Semantic Web.

As argued in Section 3, most previous approaches to Web query languages fail to address the design principles discussed in this chapter; most notably, very few consider access to heterogeneous representation formats.

Currently, the Web query language Xcerpt (Schaffert & Bry, 2004), which already reflects many of these design principles, is being further refined to a true versatile query language along the principles outlined in this chapter.

We believe that versatile query languages will be essential for providing efficient and effective access to data on the Web of the future, effective as the use of data from different representation formats allows to serve better answers (e.g., by enriching, filtering, or ranking data with metadata available in other representation formats). Efficient as previous approaches suffer from the separation of data access by representation formats requiring either multiple query languages or hard to comprehend and expensive data transformations.

Acknowledgments

We would like to thank Claude Kirchner (LORIA, Nancy, France) and Wolfgang May (Göttingen University, Göttingen, Germany) for providing numerous valuable comments on how to improve both presentation and content of an early draft of this chapter. We would also like to thank the anonymous reviewers for insightful comments on how to strengthen the arguments presented in this chapter.

This research has been funded by the European Commission and by the Swiss Federal Office for Education and Science within the 6th Framework Programme project REWERSE number 506779 (see http://rewerse.net).

References

Abiteboul, S., Hull, R., & Vianu, V. (1995). *Foundations of databases.* Addison-Wesley.

Amer-Yahia, S., et al. (2004). *XQuery and XPath full-text* [working draft]. W3C.

Alferes, J. J., May, W., & Bry, F. (2004). Towards generic query, update, and event languages for the Semantic Web. In *Proceedings of the Workshop on Principles and Practice of Semantic Web Reasoning.*

Baumgartner, R., Flesca, S., & Gottlob, G. (2001). The elog Web extraction language. In *Proceedings of the International Conference on Logic Programming, Artifical Intelligence, and Reasoning (LPAR).*

Bechhofer, S., et al. (2004). *OWL Web ontology language — reference.* W3C.

Berger, S., Bry, F., & Schaffert, S. (2003). A visual language for Web querying and reasoning. In *Proceedings of the Workshop on Principles and Practice of Semantic Web Reasoning.*

Berners-Lee, T. (1998). *Semantic Web road map.* W3C.

Berners-Lee, T., Hendler, J., & Lassila, O. (2001). The Semantic Web — a new form of Web content that is meaningful to computers will unleash a revolution of new possibilities. *Scientific American.*

Boag, S., et al. (Eds.) (2004). *XQuery 1.0: An XML query language* (W3C Working draft). Retrieved from http://www.w3.org/TR/xquery/

Boley, H., et al. (2002). *RuleML design. RuleML Initiative.* Retrieved from http://www.ruleml.org/indesign.html

Brickley, D., Guha, R., & McBride, B. (Eds.). (2004). *RDF vocabulary description language 1.0: RDF Schema* (W3C Recommendation).

Bry, F., Drabent, W., & Maluszynski, J. (2004). On subtyping of treestructured data — a polynomial approach. In *Proceedings of the Workshop on Principles and Practice of Semantic Web Reasoning.*

Bry, F., Furche, T., Ptrânjan, P.-L., & Schaffert, S. (2004). Data retrieval and evolution on the (Semantic) Web: A deductive approach. In *Proceedings of the Workshop on Principles and Practice of Semantic Web Reasoning.*

Bry, F. & Ptrânjan, P.-L. (2005). Reactivity on the Web: Paradigms and applications of the language XChange. In *Proceedings of the ACM Symposium on Applied Computing (SAC).*

Bry, F., Schaffert, S., & Schröder, A. (2004). A contribution to the semantics of Xcerpt, a Web query and transformation language. In *Proceedings of the Workshop Logische Programmierung.*

Chamberlin, D., Fankhauser, P., Florescu, D., Marchiori, M., & Robie, J. (Eds.). (2003). *XML query use cases* (W3C Recommendation).

Chandra, A. K., & Merlin, P.M. (1977). Optimal implementation of conjunctive queries in relational data bases. In *Proceedings of the ACM Symposium on Theory of Computing (STOC).*

Clark, J. (1999). *XSL transformation (XSLT) version 1.0* (W3C Recommendation).

Clark, J., & DeRose, S. (1999). *XML path language (XPath) version 1.0* (W3C Recommendation).

Courcelle, B. (1990). Graph rewriting: An algebraic and logic approach. In J. Leeuwen (Ed.), *Handbook of theoretical computer science* (pp. 193-242). Elsevier Science Publishers.

Cowan, J., & Tobin, R. (2004). *XML information set (second edition)* (W3C Recommendation).

DeRose, S., Maier, E., & Orchard, D. (Eds.). (2001). *XML linking language (XLink) version 1.0* (W3C Recommendation).

Deutsch, A., Fernandez, M., Florescu, D., Levy, A., & Suciu, D. (1998). *XML-QL: A query language for XML.* W3C.

Fernandez, M., Malhotra, A., Marsh, J., Nagy, M., & Walsh, N. (2004). *XQuery 1.0 and XPath 2.0 data model* (W3C Working draft).

Flum, J., Frick, M., & Grohe, M. (2002). Query evaluation via tree-decompositions. *Journal of the ACM, 49*(6).

Furche, T., et al. (2004). *Survey over existing query and transformation languages.* Deliverable I4-D1, REWERSE. http://rewerse.net/I4/deliverables#D1

Grohe, M., & Schweikardt, N. (2003). Comparing the succinctness of monadic query languages over finite trees. In *Proceedings of the Workshop on Computer Science Logic (CSL).*

Gottlob, G., Leone, N., & Scarcello, F. (2002). Hypertree decompositions and tractable queries. *Journal of Computer and System Sciences, 64*(3).

Gottlob, G., Koch, C., & Pichler, R. (2003). The complexity of XPath query evaluation. In *Proceedings of the ACM Symposium on Principles of Database Systems.*

Horrocks, I., et al. (2004). *SWRL: A Semantic Web rule language — combining OWL and ruleML* (W3C Member submission).

ISO/IEC 13250 Topic Maps. (1999). International organization for standardization, international standard.

Karvounarakis, G., et al. (2004). RQL: A functional query language for RDF. In P. Gray, P. King, & A. Poulovassilis (Eds.), *The functional approach to data management* (pp. 435-465). SpringerVerlag.

Klyne, G., Carroll, J. J., & McBride, B. (2004). *Resource description framework (RDF): Concepts and abstract syntax* (W3C Recommendation).

May, W. (2004). XPath-logic and XPathLog: A logic-programming style XML data manipulation language. *Theory and Practice of Logic Programming, 3*(4),499-526.

Olken, F., & McCarthy, J. (1998). Requirements and desiderata for an XML query language. In *Proceedings of Query Languages 1998 (W3C QL'98).*

Palmer, S.B. (2003). *Pondering RDF path.* Retrieved from http://infomesh.net/2003/rdfpath/

Patel-Schneider, P., & Simeon, J. (2002). The Yin/Yang Web: XML syntax and RDF semantics. In *Proceedings of the International World Wide Web Conference.*

Pepper, S., & Moore, G. (Eds.). (2001). *XML topic maps (XTM) 1.0.* TopicMaps. org, Specification.

Prud'hommeaux, E. (Ed.) (2004a). *RDF data access working group charter.* W3C. Retrieved from http://www.w3.org/2003/12/swa/dawg-charter

Prud'hommeaux, E. (2004b). *Algae RDF query language.* W3C. Retrieved from http://www.w3.org/2004/05/06Algae/

Prud'hommeaux, E., & Seaborne, A. (2004). *SPARQL query language for RDF* (W3C Working draft). Retrieved from http://www.w3.org/TR/rdf-sparql-query/

Robie, J., et al. (2001). The syntactic Web: Syntax and semantics on the Web. *Markup Languages: Theory and Practice, 3*(4), 411-440.

Schaffert, S., & Bry, F. (2004). Querying the Web reconsidered: A practical introduction to Xcerpt. In *Proceedings of the Extreme Markup Languages*.

Seaborne, A. (2004). *RDQL — a query language for RDF.* (W3C Member submission). Retrieved from http://www.w3.org/Submission/2004/SUBM-RDQ-20040109/

Segoufin, L. (2003). Typing and querying XML documents: Some complexity bounds. In *Proceedings of the ACM Symposium on Principles of Database Systems*.

Sintek, M. (2002). TRIPLE — a query, inference, and transformation language for the semantic Web. In *Proceedings of the International Semantic Web Conference*.

Steer, D. (2003). *TreeHugger 1.0 introduction.* Retrieved from http://www.semanticplanet.com/2003/08/rdft/spec

Vardi, M. Y. (1982). The complexity of relational query languages. In *Proceedings of the ACM Symposium on Theory of Computing (STOC)*.

Wilk, A., & Drabent, W. (2003). On types for XML query language Xcerpt. In *Proceedings of the Workshop on Principles and Practice of Semantic Web Reasoning*.

Zloof, M. (1975). Query by example. In *Proceedings of the AFIPS National Computer Conference*.

Endnote

[1]   This has been pointed out, in a slight variation, by Dana Florescu on the XML-DEV mailing list: http://lists.xml.org/archives/xml-dev/200412/msg00228.html

The chapter was previously published in the International Journal on Semantic Web & Information Systems, 1(2), 1-21, April-June 2005.

Section IV

Applications

Chapter IX

Semantic E-Business

Rahul Singh, The University of North Carolina at Greensboro, USA

Lakshmi Iyer, The University of North Carolina at Greensboro, USA

A. F. Salam, The University of North Carolina at Greensboro, USA

Abstract

We define semantic e-business as "an approach to managing knowledge for coordination of e-business processes through the systematic application of Semantic Web technologies." Advances in Semantic Web-based technologies offer the means to integrate heterogeneous systems across organizations in a meaningful way by incorporating ontology — a common, standard, and shareable vocabulary used to represent the meaning of system entities; knowledge representation, with structured collections of information and sets of inference rules that can be used to conduct automated reasoning; and intelligent agents that collect content from diverse sources and exchange semantically enriched information. These primary components of the Semantic Web vision form the foundation technology for semantic e-business. The challenge for research in information systems and e-business is to provide insight into the design of business models and technical architecture that demonstrate the potential of technical advancements in the computer and engineering sciences to be beneficial to business and consumers. Semantic e-business seeks to apply fundamental work done in Semantic Web technologies to support the transparent flow of semantically enriched information and knowledge — including content and know-how — to enable, enhance, and coordinate collaborative e-business processes within and across organizational boundaries. Semantic e-business processes are characterized by the seamless and transparent flow of semantically enriched information and knowledge. We present a holistic view of semantic e-business that integrates emergent and well-grounded Semantic Web technologies to improve the current state of the art in the transparency of e-business processes.

Introduction

The Semantic Web vision (Berners-Lee, Hendler, & Lassila, 2001) provides the foundation for semantic architecture to support the transparent exchange of information and knowledge among collaborating e-business organizations. Recent advances in Semantic Web-based technologies offer means for organizations to exchange knowledge in a meaningful way. This requires ontologies, to provide a standardized and shareable vocabulary to represent the meaning of system entities; knowledge representation, with structured collections of information and sets of inference rules that can be used to conduct automated reasoning; and intelligent agents that can exchange semantically enriched information and knowledge, and interpret the knowledge on behalf of the user (Hendler, 2001). It is increasingly clear that semantic technologies have the potential to enhance e-business processes. The challenge for research in information systems and e-business is to provide insight into the design of business models and technical architecture that demonstrate the potential of technical advancements in the computer and engineering sciences to be beneficial to business and consumers.

E-business is "an approach to achieving business goals in which technology for information exchange enables or facilitates execution of activities in and across value chains, as well as supporting decision making that underlies those activities" (Holsapple & Singh, 2000). Inter-organizational collaborations are effective means for organizations to improve the efficacy of their e-business processes and enhance their value propositions. Inter-organizational collaborative business processes require transparent information and knowledge exchange across partner firms. Businesses increasingly operate in a dynamic, knowledge-driven economy and function as knowledge-based organizations. Knowledge is defined as the highest order in the continuum of data and information, as having utility and specificity in its context domain. Functionally and in systems, the lines between useful information and knowledge are blurred (Grover & Davenport, 2001). For this research, we define knowledge as "information, in the context of a specific problem domain, upon which action can be advised or taken." Knowledge management includes facilities for the creation, exchange, storage, and retrieval of knowledge in an exchangeable and usable format, in addition to the critical facilities to use of knowledge to support business activity (O'Leary, 1998). It is important for e-business to explicitly recognize knowledge along with the processes and technologies for knowledge management.

We define semantic e-business as "an approach to managing knowledge for coordination of e-business processes through the systematic application of Semantic Web technologies." Semantic e-business applies fundamental work done in Semantic Web technologies, including ontologies, knowledge representation, multi-agent systems, and Web-services, to support the transparent flow of semantically enriched information and knowledge, including content and know-how, and enable collaborative e-business processes within and across organizational boundaries. In this article, we present an overview of the semantic e-business vision, with emphasis on the conceptual foundations and research directions in semantic e-business. In our view, semantic e-business is founded upon three primary streams of research literature: Semantic Web technologies, including ontologies, knowledge representation and intelligent software agents; knowledge management, including the creation, storage and retrieval, and the exchange of machine interpretable and useful information upon which action can be taken or advised; and e-business processes, including process automation, enterprise systems integration, and the coordination of workflows and activities within and across organizations. We provide a conceptual schematic of this grounding in Figure 1.

Figure 1. Semantic e-business vision founded upon existing work in Semantic Web technologies, knowledge management, and in the e-business processes literature

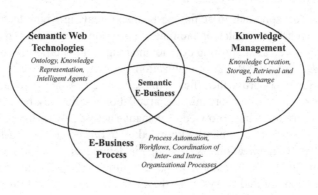

The following sections provide a detailed discussion of these foundations upon which Semantic e-business is envisioned. We provide some directions, from our own research initiatives and that of others, leading towards making the semantic e-business vision a reality. Interest in semantic e-business in the information systems community is beginning to gather momentum through the formation of special interest groups in the research and practitioner communities. We provide a description of some of the organizations that are playing an important role in this. This chapter concludes with a summary and directions for future research in semantic e-business.

Foundations

Semantic Web Technologies

The Semantic Web is an extension of the current Web in which information is given "well-defined meaning" to allow machines to "process and understand" the information presented to them (Berners-Lee et al., 2001).

According to Berners-Lee et al. (2001), the "Semantic Web" comprises and requires the following components in order to function:

- **Knowledge representation:** Structured collections of information and sets of inference rules that can be used to conduct automated reasoning. Knowledge representations must be linked into a single system.

- **Ontologies:** Systems must have a way to discover common meanings for entity representations. In philosophy, ontology is a theory about the nature of existence; in systems, ontology is a document that formally describes classes of objects and defines the relationship among them. In addition, we need ways to interpret ontology.

- **Agents:** Programs that collect content from diverse sources and exchange the result with other programs. Agents exchange "data enriched with semantics."

Intelligent software agents can reach a shared understanding by exchanging ontologies that provide the vocabulary needed for discussion. Agents can even bootstrap new reasoning capabilities when they discover new ontologies. Semantics makes it easier to take advantage of a service that only partially matches a request.

Figure 2. Semantic Web architecture (Source: www.w3.org/DesignIssues/diagrams/ sw-stack-2002.png; Berners Lee et al., 2001)

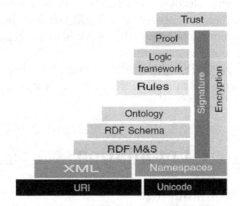

A typical process will involve the creation of a 'value chain' in which subassemblies of information are passed from one agent to another, each one 'adding value,' to construct the final product requested by the end user. Make no mistake: to create complicated value chains automatically on demand, some agents will exploit artificial-intelligence technologies in addition to the Semantic Web. (Berners-Lee et al., 2001)

XML-Based Technologies for Knowledge Representation and Exchange

Technologies for developing meaningful semantic representations of information and knowledge exist through XML (eXtensible Markup Language — www.xml. org, www.w3.org/XML/), RDF (Resource Description Framework — www.w3.org/ RDF/), and OWL (Web Ontology language — www.w3.org/TR/owl-features/). XML and its related standards make it feasible to store knowledge in a meaningful way while supporting unambiguous content representation and flexible exchange over heterogeneous platforms (Chiu, 2000). XML allows the creation of customized tags and languages using XML schema, which describe specific elements, the data types in each element, and their relationships. With the appropriate schema, XML documents can be parsed, validated, and processed by application software using XML parsers. Built upon accepted W3C standards, this provides the foundation for semantic technology for the capture, representation, exchange, and storage of knowledge that can be potentially used and shared by software agents. XML provides standardized representations of data structures for processing on heterogeneous systems without case-by-case programming. The use of XML-based technology, including ebXML (www.ebxml.org) and RossettaNet (www.RossettaNet.org), allows for the creation of common vocabularies for e-business to help automate business processes, allowing better collaboration and knowledge transfer between partners in semantically integrated systems.

Initiatives to develop technologies for the Semantic Web make the content of the Web unambiguously computer-interpretable to make it amenable to agent interoperability and automated reasoning techniques (McIlraith, Son, & Zeng, 2001). RDF was developed by the W3C as a metadata standard to provide a data model and syntactical conventions to represent data semantics in a standardized interoperable manner (McIlraith et al., 2001). The RDF working group also developed RDF Schema (RDFS), an object-oriented type system that provides an ontology modeling language. Recently, there have been several efforts to build on RDF and RDFS with AI-inspired knowledge representation languages such as SHOE, DAML-ONT, OIL, and DAML+OIL (Fensel, 2000). The Web Ontology Language (OWL) has been standardized by the W3C as a knowledge representation language for the Semantic Web. OWL documents represent domain ontologies and rules, and allow knowledge sharing among agents through the standard Web services architecture. Web services technology provides the envelope and transport mechanism for information exchange between software entities. Knowledge exchange architectures use Simple Object Access Protocol (SOAP—www.w3.org/TR/soap/) messages to carry relevant semantic information in the form of OWL documents between agents. The Web services framework consists of the Web Services Definition Language (WSDL — www.wsdl.org), which describes Web services in XML format and provides the basis for tools to create appropriate SOAP messages. These technologies provide the knowledge representation and exchange mechanism to allow collaborating organizations to seamlessly share information and knowledge to coordinate e-business processes.

Ontologies

Description logics (DLs) form a basis for developing ontology to further the sharing and use of a common understanding of a specific problem. Description logics model the domain of interest using constructs that describe domain-specific objects and the relationships between them (Baader et al., 2002). Domain-specific objects are represented using the concept construct, which is a unary predicate. Relationships between constructs are represented using the relations construct, which may be an n-ary predicate. Description logics, at the least, can be used to develop a model of the domain comprising:

- Specifications for the creation of complex concept and relation expressions built upon a set of atomic concepts and relations
- The cumulative set of description logics that forms the basis for a knowledge base containing the properties of domain-dependent concepts and relations specified through a set of assertions on the domain
- A set of reasoning procedures that allows suitable inferences from the concepts and the relationships between them

Ontologies provide a shared and common understanding of specific domains that can be communicated between disparate application systems, and therein provide a means to integrate the knowledge used by online processes employed by e-business organizations (Klein et al., 2001). Ontology describes the semantics of the constructs that are common to the online processes, including descriptions of the data semantics that are common descriptors of the domain context. Staab et al. (2001) describe an approach for ontology-based knowledge management through the concept of knowledge metadata, which contains two distinct forms of ontologies that describe the structure of the data itself and issues related to the content of data. We refer the reader to Kishore et al. (2004) for more comprehensive discussion of ontologies and information systems. Ontology documents can be created using FIPA-compliant content languages like BPEL, RDF, OWL, and DAML to generate standardized representations of the process knowledge. The structure of ontology documents will be based on description logics. The recent adoption of the OWL standards by the World Wide Web Consortium (www.w3c.org) includes OWL-DL, which specifies the representation of DL-based models into OWL documents.

In the semantic e-business vision, knowledge exchange and delivery can be facilitated by the availability and exchange of knowledge represented in OWL documents among intelligent software agents. Domain knowledge objects provide an abstraction to create, exchange, and use modular knowledge represented using OWL documents. This allows for a common vocabulary used for exchange of information and knowledge across all system participants. There are many benefits to storing this knowledge in XML format, including standardization of semantics, validation ability and 'well-formedness', ease of use, re-use, and storage. In addition, the ability to exchange complete XML documents in W3C standards affords integration on heterogeneous platforms. All exchanges between agents take place using the standard Web services architecture to allow for platform independence, and facilitate exchange of information and knowledge in OWL documents. Capturing and representing modular knowledge in XML format facilitates their storage in a knowledge repository — a repository that enables storage and retrieval of XML documents of multiple knowledge modules depending upon the problem domain. The benefits of such knowledge repositories are the historical capture of knowledge modules that are available to all agents in the agent community. This ensures that a newly instantiated agent has access to knowledge available to the entire system.

Intelligent Agents

Intelligent agents are action-oriented abstractions in electronic systems, entrusted to carry out various generic and specific goal-oriented actions on behalf of users (Papazoglou, 2001). The agent paradigm can support a range of decision-making activity, including information retrieval, generation of alternatives, preference order ranking of options and alternatives, and supporting analysis of the alternative-goal relationships. An intelligent agent is "a computer system situated in some environment and that is capable of flexible autonomous action in this environment in order to meet its design objectives" (Jennings & Wooldridge, 1998). The specific autonomous behavior expected of intelligent agents depends on the concrete application domain and the expected role and impact of intelligent agents on the potential solution for a particular problem for which the agents are designed to provide cognitive support. Criteria for application of agent technology require that the application domain should show natural distributivity with autonomous entities that are geographically distributed and work with distributed data; require flexible interaction without a priori assignment of tasks to actors; and be embedded in a dynamic environment (Muller, 1997).

Intelligent agents are able to organize, store, retrieve, search, and match information and knowledge for effective collaboration among Semantic e-business participants. A fundamental implication is that knowledge must be available in formats that allow for processing by software agents. Intelligent agents can be used for knowledge management to support Semantic e-business activities. The agent abstraction is created by extending an object with additional features for encapsulation and exchange of knowledge between agents to allow agents to deliver knowledge to users and support decision-making activity (Shoham, 1993). Agents work on a distributed platform and enable the transfer of knowledge by exposing their public methods as Web services using SOAP and XML. In this respect, the interactions among the agents are modeled as collaborative interactions, where the agents in the multi-agent community work together to provide decision support and knowledge-based explanations of the decision problem domain to the user.

Knowledge Management

Emerging business models are causing fundamental changes in organizational and inter-organizational business processes by replacing conflict with cooperation as a means to be economically efficient (Beam, 1998). Operationally, knowledge management (KM) is "a process that helps organizations find, select, organize, disseminate, and transfer important information and expertise necessary for activities such as problem solving, dynamic learning, strategic planning, and decision making" (Gupta, Iyer, & Aronson, 2000). From an organizational perspective, it is the management of corporate knowledge that can improve a range of organizational performance characteristics by enabling an enterprise to be more intelligent acting (Wiig, 1993). A system managing available knowledge must comprise facilities for the creation, exchange, storage, and retrieval of knowledge in an exchangeable and usable format, in addition to facilities to use the knowledge in a business activity (O'Leary, 1998). Many organizations are developing KM systems designed specifically to facilitate the exchange and integration of knowledge in business processes for increasing collaboration to gain a competitive advantage.

The semantic e-business vision is built upon transparent information and knowledge exchange across seamlessly integrated systems over globally available Internet technologies to enable information partnerships among participants across the entire value chain. Such transparency enhances the utility and extensibility of knowledge management initiatives of an organization by adding the ability to exchange specific and transparent knowledge, utilizing unambiguously interpretable, standards-based representation formats (Singh, Iyer, & Salam, 2003). Implementing and managing such high levels of integration over distributed and heterogeneous information platforms such as the Internet is a challenging task with significant potential benefits for organizations embracing such collaboration. Organizations can gain significant benefits from these initiatives including optimized inventory levels, higher revenues, improved customer satisfaction, increased productivity, and real-time resolution of problems and discrepancies throughout the supply chain. The vision is to achieve dynamic collaboration among business partners and customers throughout a trading community through transparent exchange of semantically enriched information and knowledge.

E-Business, E-Business Processes, and E-Marketplaces

Electronic data interchange (EDI) established the preliminary basis for automating business-to-business (B2B) e-commerce (EC) transactions through facilities for organizations to share process information electronically using standardized formats and semantics. Strategies such as supply chain management (SCM) and enterprise resource planning (ERP) go beyond process automation by streamlining and integrating internal and inter-organizational process for improved information availability across value-chain partners. While popular strategies such as SCM and ERP have improved transactional efficiencies, the lack of systems and process integration and the resultant lack of end-to-end value chain visibility continue to hinder collaborative and mutually beneficial partnerships. E-business processes require transparent information and knowledge transparency among business partners. The vision is to achieve dynamic collaboration among internal personnel, business partners, and customers throughout a trading community, electronic market, or other form of exchange characterized by the seamless and transparent exchange of meaningful information and knowledge. The resultant view is similar to the notions of real-time supply chains and infomediary-based e-marketplaces, where the virtual supply chain is viewed as an inter-organizational information system with seamless and transparent flows of information enabled through highly integrated systems (Rabin, 2003).

The timely sharing of accurate information among collaborating firms and transparency in the supply chain is critical for efficient workflows that support the business processes (Davenport & Brooks, 2004). Information technologies can help streamline business processes across organizations and improve the performance of the value chain by enabling better coordination of inter-firm processes through B2B e-marketplaces (Dai & Kauffman, 2002). The lack of integration of information and knowledge in systems that manage business processes is a stumbling block in enterprise innovation (Badii & Sharif, 2003). The consequent lack of transparencies in information flow across the value chain continue to hinder productive and collaborative partnerships among firms in B2B e-marketplaces. Current e-chains suffer from paucity in information transparency spanning all participant e-marketplaces in the e-supply chain. Integrative systems that support the transparent exchange of information and knowledge can enhance collaboration across organizational value chains by extending support for a range of e-business processes and provide aggregate or product-specific cumulative demand or supply conditions in a single e-marketplace and across multiple upstream or downstream links in the e-chain (Singh, Salam, & Iyer, forthcoming). Such systems must provide collaborating value chain partners with intelligent knowledge services capabilities for the seamless and transparent exchange of volatile and dynamic market information, both synchronously and asynchronously.

Reductions in transaction coordination costs gained through the effective application of information technologies partly explain the increasing use of markets over hierarchies by organizations to coordinate economic activities (Malone, Yates, & Benjamin, 1987). E-marketplaces offer value-added services by leveraging industry-specific expertise through deciphering complex information and contribute to transaction cost reductions. A survey by Davenport, Brooks, and Cantrell (2001) on B2B e-marketplaces identified lack of trust as a primary barrier for e-marketplace growth. Much of the risk associated with lack of trust can be reduced "as information becomes more codified, standardized, aggregated, integrated, distributed, and shaped for ready use" (Davenport et al., 2001). They also state that "currently achieved e-marketplace integration levels fall far below what is necessary." Investments in the IT infrastructure of the e-marketplace can further the effective use of process coordination and communication between participants. While asset-specific technology investments serve to reduce the transaction cost, this leads to significant increases in cost of switching partners. However, when such investments are made by the e-marketplace, the transaction cost reductions can benefit e-marketplace participants, while the increase in switching costs applies to switching from an e-marketplace participant to a non-participant firm.

Integrative technologies that support the transparent exchange of information and knowledge make it easier for the development of inter-organizational relationships through enhanced adaptability and standardization of content representation. This is increasingly prevalent through efforts such as ebXML (www.ebXML.org), Web services, and systems architecture standards, which allow standardization of content representation, with implications for technology adaptation and enterprise applications integration (Davenport & Brooks, 2004). By defining the standards for adaptability and standardization, e-marketplaces can help define the information technology standards that are in use by all participant organizations, allowing for easy interoperability and integration of key systems of participant organizations. In this regard, e-marketplaces are viewed as inter-organizational information systems that allow participant firms to integrate their information technologies in a Semantic e-business architecture that facilitates transparent information exchange (Choudhury, 1997).

Semantic E-Business Vision and Applications

Semantic e-business applies fundamental work done in semantic Web technologies, knowledge management, intelligent agent systems, and Web services to support the transparent flow of knowledge, content, and know-how, and enable semantically enriched collaborative e-business processes. Institutional trust among the collaborative partners engaged in semantic e-business processes, as well as information assurance of all flows between integrated systems in the semantic e-business network, is essential to the adoption of the vision. Semantic e-business requires a trusted and secure environment. Organizations develop descriptions of their business processes and business rules using semantic knowledge representation languages, such as OWL, in a format that allows for reasoning by intelligent software agents. Business processes consist of workflow descriptions that describe individual tasks at an atomic transactional level. At this transactional level, the individual services offered by organizations can be described using semantic languages. In addition, product ontologies and meta-ontologies describe the relationships between the various resources utilized, required, or created by an organization in the semantic e-business network. The semantic e-business framework (Figure 3) utilizes (existing) information technology infrastructure, including Web services architecture to provide the transport infrastructure for messages containing semantic content.

Figure 3. Semantic e-business utilizes Semantic Web technologies and existing information technology infrastructure for transparent information and knowledge flows in a secure and trusted environment

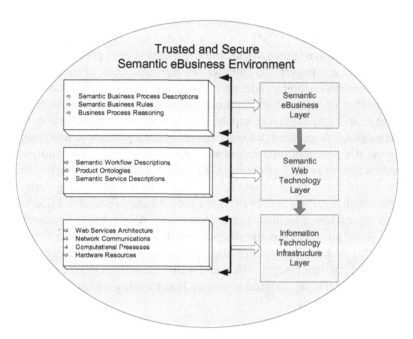

The application of Semantic Web technologies to enable semantic e-business provides the organizations the means to design collaborative and integrative, inter- and intra-organizational business processes and systems founded upon the seamless exchange of knowledge. Semantic e-business architectures can enable transparent information and knowledge exchange, and intelligent decision support to enhance online e-business processes. It can also help organizations fill the chasm that exists in the adaptation of emerging technologies to enable and enhance business processes through the use of distributed heterogeneous knowledge resources. The concept of semantic e-business is potentially applicable to industries with an online presence. Candidates for applications in business include supply chain management and e-marketplaces. In addition, multiple not-for-profit and government processes are also potential application areas, including the healthcare industry for improving the management of medical records and e-government applications for improving services offered online to citizens. The following scenarios present some areas where we believe semantic e-business can enhance information and knowledge exchange and improve the efficacy of e-business processes.

Potential Semantic E-Business Applications

Supply Chain Management

Supply chain management (SCM) is a common strategy employed by businesses to improve organizational processes to optimize the transfer of goods, information, and services between buyers and suppliers in the value chain (Poirier & Bauer, 2000). A fundamental ongoing endeavor of SCM is to foster information transparency (availability of information in an unambiguously interpretable format) that allows organizations to coordinate supply chain interactions efficiently in dynamic market conditions. A standard ontology for all trading partners is necessary for seamless transformation of information and knowledge essential for supply chain collaboration (Singh et al., forthcoming). Increasing complexity in supply chains make the timely sharing of accurate information among collaborating partners a critical element in the efficiency of workflows and e-business processes. Information and knowledge exchange facilitated through semantic Web technologies enable the creation of global information partnerships across the entire supply chain. Organizations embracing such paradigms can sustain their competitive advantages by having an effective and efficient e-supply chain and realize benefits such as reduced cycle times, lower product costs, reduced inventory, better quality decision making, and improved customer service.

E-Marketplaces

Infomediaries perform a critical role in bringing together buyers and suppliers in the e-marketplace and facilitating transactions between them. A detailed description of the value-added activities provided by infomediaries in e-marketplaces can be found in Grover and Teng (2001). The infomediary adds value through its role as an enterprise system hub responsible for the critical integration of the information flows across participant firms (Davenport & Brooks, 2004). Infomediaries become vital repositories of knowledge about buyers, suppliers, and the nature of exchanges among them including the past experiences of other buyers' reliability and trustworthiness of the supplier. They provide independent and observed post-transaction assessment of the commitments of the individual buyers and sellers to facilitate the development of coordination structures, leading to collaborative relationships in e-supply chains. The integration of intelligence and knowledge within and across e-marketplaces can enhance the coordination of activities among collaborating firms across e-marketplaces (Singh et al., 2003). Collaborations create information partnerships between organizations to enable the delivery of products and services to the customer in an efficient manner. Such information partnerships are founded upon the transparent exchange of information and knowledge between collaborating organizations in a dynamic manner across participants in the value chain.

Healthcare

Healthcare delivery is very complex and knowledge dependent. Information systems employed for healthcare store information in very disparate and heterogeneous clinical information system data repositories. Pollard (2004) states that knowledge management activities in healthcare center on acquiring and storage of information, and lacks the ability to share and transfer knowledge across systems and organizations to support individual user productivity. In addition the data acquired and stored in islands clinical information systems are in multiple formats. Common vocabulary to represent data and information is needed for efficient knowledge management (Desouza, 2002). The focus has been on building independent applications to make these systems talk to each other. The need is for models to integrate the data and knowledge in these disparate systems for effective knowledge sharing and use (Sittig et al., 2002). To serve the needs, relevant patient-centered knowledge must be accessible to the person supplying care in a timely manner in the workflow. Interoperability standards of emerging Semantic Web technologies can enable health information integration, providing the transparency for healthcare-related processes involving all entities within and between hospitals, as well as stakeholders such as pharmacies, insurance providers, healthcare providers, and clinical laboratories. Further research on using Semantic Web technologies is needed to deliver knowledge services proactively for improved decision making. Such innovations can lead to enhanced caregiver effectiveness, work satisfaction, patient satisfaction, and overall care quality in healthcare (Eysenbach, 2003).

E-Government

E-government refers to the use of Internet technologies for the delivery of government services to citizens and businesses (www.Webster-dictionary.org/definition/EGovernment). The aim of e-government is to streamline processes and improve interactions with business and industry, empower citizens with the right information, and improve the efficiency of government management. Given that e-government services extend across different organizational boundaries and infrastructures, there is a critical need to manage the knowledge and information resources stored in these disparate systems (Teswanich, Anutariya, & Wuwongse, 2002). Emerging Semantic Web technologies have the ability to enable transparent information and knowledge exchange to enhance e-government processes. Klischewski and Jeenicke (2004) examine the use of ontology-driven e-government applications based on Semantic Web technologies to support knowledge management related to e-government services. Further research to investigate requirements, design and develop systems, and examine success factors for systems development employing Semantic Web technologies for effective knowledge management within e-government services is needed.

Organizations and Research Groups Fostering a Semantic E-Business Vision

As research in the foundation technologies for the Semantic Web develops, the application of these technologies to enable semantic e-business is of increasing importance to the professional and academic communities. In this section we would like to inform the readers of several organizations that are involved in furthering research related to semantic e-business.

Association for Information Systems (AIS) (www.aisnet.org)

A professional organization, the Association for Information Systems (AIS) was founded in 1994 to serve as the premier global organization for academics specializing in information systems. This organization has formed several special interest groups (SIGs) to provide substantial benefits to IS students, academics, and practitioners by helping members exchange ideas and keep up to date on common research interests. The following SIGs contribute significantly to advacing Semantic e-business research:

- **Special interest group on Semantic Web and information systems, SIG-SEMIS (www.sigsemis.org):** SIG-SEMIS' goal is to cultivate the Semantic Web vision in IS. The main areas of emphasis in this SIG are: Semantic Web, knowledge management, information systems, e-learning, business intelligence, organizational learning, and emerging technologies. The SIG aims to "create knowledge capable of supporting high-quality knowledge and learning experience concerning the integration" of the above main areas. This integration will provide the participants of the SIG an opportunity to create and diffuse knowledge concerning the issues of Semantic Web in the IS research community.

- **Special interest group on agent-based information systems, SIG-ABIS (www.agentbasedis.org):** SIG-ABIS aims to advance knowledge "in the use of agent-based information systems, which includes complex adaptive systems and simulation experiments, to improve organizational performance. SIG-ABIS promises to fill an existing gap in the field, and therefore is more focused on the strategic and business issues with agent technology and less on the artifact itself, such as computational algorithms, which are well investigated by computer science related research groups."

- **Special interest group on ontology driven information system, SIG-ODIS (aps.cabit.wpcarey.asu.edu/sigodis/):** The objective of SIG-ODIS is to provide "a unifying international forum for the exchange of ideas about the field of ontology as it relates to design, evaluation, implementation, and study of ontology driven information systems." In helping develop awareness and foster research about the role and impact of computational ontologies on the design, development, and management of business information systems, SIG-ODIS also strives to build bridges between the IS discipline and other related disciplines, such as computer science, information science, philosophy, linguistics, and so forth, that pursue research in the broad area of computational ontologies.

- **Special interest group on process automation and management, SIG-PAM (www.sigpam.org):** SIG-PAM's objective is to address the "need of IS researchers and practitioners for information and knowledge sharing in the areas of process design, automation, and management in both organizational and inter-organizational contexts." The SIG collaborates with other not-for-profit organizations that have related focus on process theories and applications, such as the Workflow Management Coalition (WfMC), the Workflow and Reengineering International Association (WARIA), and the Computer Supported Collaborative Work (CSCW) Conference.

Hewlett-Packard (HP) Labs Semantic Web Research (www.hpl.hp.com/semWeb/)

The HP Labs Semantic Web research group recognizes that Semantic Web technologies can enable new and more flexible approaches to data integration, Web services, and knowledge discovery. The HP Labs' investment in the Semantic Web consists of the development of Semantic Web tools (such as Jena, a Java framework for writing Semantic Web applications) and associated technology, complemented by basic research and application-driven research. HP is also part of several collaborative ventures, including involvement in W3C initiatives (RDF and Web ontologies working groups) and European projects (Semantic Web Advanced Development Europe — SWAD-E, and Semantic Web-enabled Web Services — SWWS).

World Wide Web Consortium's Semantic Web Initiative (www.w3.org/2001/sw/)

The main goal of the W3C Semantic Web initiative is to create a universal medium for the exchange of data. "It is envisaged to smoothly interconnect personal information management, enterprise application integration, and the global sharing of commercial, scientific, and cultural data. The W3C Semantic Web activity has been established to serve a leadership role in both the design of specifications and the open, collaborative development of enabling technology."

In addition to these organizations, the formation of this new journal, *International Journal on Semantic Web and Information Systems*, provides an opportunity for the publication and exchange of research discussions of the Semantic Web in the context of information systems.

Summary and Research Directions

The realization of representing knowledge-rich processes is possible through the broad developments in the Semantic Web initiative of the World Wide Web Consortium. We defined semantic e-business as "an approach to managing knowledge for coordination of e-business processes through the systematic application of Semantic Web technologies." Advances in Semantic Web technologies — including ontologies, knowledge representation, multi-agent systems, and the Web services architecture — provide a strong theoretical foundation to develop system architecture that enables semantically enriched collaborative e-business process. Semantic e-business architecture enables transparent information and knowledge exchange and intelligent decision support to enhance online e-business processes.

Developments in the availability of content and business logic on-demand, through technologies such as Web services, offer the potential to allow organizations to create content-based and logic-driven information value chains, enabling the needed information transparencies for semantic e-business processes. Research is needed to understand how conceptualizations that comprise business processes can be captured, represented, shared, and processed by both human and intelligent agent-based information systems to create transparency in e-business processes. Further work on these dimensions is critical to the design of knowledge-based and intelligence-driven e-business processes in the digital economy.

Research is also needed in the development of business models that can take advantage of emergent technologies to support collaborative, knowledge-rich processes characteristic of semantic e-business. Equally important is the adaptation and assimilation of emergent technologies to enable semantic e-business processes, and the contribution to organizations' value propositions. Topics of research directions include the development of innovative, knowledge-rich business models that enhance collaborations in e-business processes, and innovative technical models that enable the vision of semantic e-business.

One of our current research initiatives involves developing models for the representation of knowledge, using ontologies and intelligent agents for semantic processing of cross-enterprise business processes over heterogeneous systems. For the Semantic Web to be a vibrant and humane environment for sharing knowledge and collaborating on a wide range of intellectual enterprises, the W3C must include in its Semantic Web initiatives research agenda the creation of policy-aware infrastructure, along with a trust language for the Semantic Web that can represent complex and evolving relationships.

References

Baader, F., Calvanese, D., McGuinness, D., Nardi, D., & Patel-Schneider, P. F. (2002). *The description logic handbook: Theory, implementation, and applications*. Cambridge University Press.

Badii, A., & Sharif, A. (2003). Information management and knowledge integration for enterprise innovation. *Logistics Information Management, 16*(2), 145-155.

Beam, H. H. (1998). The infinite resource: Creating and leading the knowledge enterprise. *The Academy of Management Executive, 12*(3).

Berners-Lee, T., Hendler, J., & Lassila, O. (2001, May). The Semantic Web. *Scientific American*, 34-43.

Chiu, C. (2000). Re-engineering information systems with XML. *Information Systems Management, 17*(4).

Choudhury, V. (1997). Strategic choices in the development of interorganizational information systems. *Information Systems Research, 8*(1), 1-24.

Dai, Q., & Kauffman, R. J. (2002). Business models for Internet-based B2B electronic markets. *International Journal of Electronic Commerce, 6*(4), 41-72.

Davenport, T. H., Brooks, J. D., & Cantrell, S. (2001, January). *B2B e-market survey: Summary of findings*. White Paper, Accenture Institute of Strategic Change.

Davenport, T. H., & Brooks, J. D. (2004). Enterprise systems and the supply chain. *Journal of Enterprise Information Management, 17*(1), 8-19.

Desouza, K. C. (2002). Knowledge management in hospitals: A process oriented view and staged look at managerial issues. *International Journal of Healthcare Technology & Management, 4*(6), 478-497.

Eysenbach, G. (2003). The Semantic Web and healthcare consumers: A new challenge and opportunity on the horizon? *International Journal of Healthcare Technology & Management, 5*(3/4/5), 194-212.

Fensel, D. (2000, November/December). *IEEE Intelligent Systems*, 67.

Grover, V., & Davenport, T. H. (2001). General perspectives on knowledge management: Fostering a research agenda. *Journal of Management Information Systems, 18*(1).

Grover, V., & Teng, J. T. C. (2001, April). E-commerce and the information market. *Communications of the ACM, 44*(4), 79-86.

Gupta, B., Iyer, L., & Aronson, J. E. (2000). Knowledge management: A taxonomy, practices and challenges. *Industrial Management and Data Systems, 100*(1), 17-21.

Hendler, J. (2001, March/April). Agents and the Semantic Web. *IEEE Intelligent Systems*, 30-37.

Holsapple, C., & Singh, M. (2000). Toward a unified view of electronic commerce, electronic business, and collaborative commerce: A knowledge management approach. *Knowledge and Process Management, 7*(3), 159.

Jennings, N. R., & Wooldridge, M. (1998). *Agent technology: Foundations, applications, and markets*. London: Springer-Verlag.

Kishore, R., Sharman, R., & Ramesh, R. (2004). Computational ontologies and information systems: I. foundations. *Communications of the Association for Information Systems, 14*, 158-183.

Klein, M., Fensel, D., van Harmelen, F., & Horrocks, I. (2001). The relation between ontologies and XML schemas. *Electronic Transactions on Artificial Intelligence (ETAI), Linköping Electronic Articles in Computer and Information Science, 6*(4).

Klischewski, R., & Jeenicke, M. (2004). Semantic Web technologies for information management within e-government services. In *Proceedings of the 37th Hawaii International Conference on System Sciences*.

Malone, T. W., Yates, J., & Benjamin, R. I. (1987). Electronic markets and electronic hierarchies. *Communications of the ACM, 30*(6), 484-497.

McIlraith, S., Son, T. C., & Zeng, H. (2001, March/April). Semantic Web services. *IEEE Intelligent Systems*, 46-53.

Muller, H. J. (1997). Towards agent systems engineering. *Data and Knowledge Engineering, 23*, 217-245.

O'Leary, D. (1998). Knowledge management systems: Converting and connecting. *IEEE Intelligent Systems and Their Applications, 13*(1).

Papazoglou, M. P. (2001). Agent oriented technology in support of e-business: Enabling the development of intelligent business agents for adaptive, reusable software. *Communications of the ACM, 44*(4), 71-77.

Poirier, C. C., & Bauer, M. (2000). *E-supply chain: Using the Internet to revolutionize your business*. Berrett-Koehler.

Pollard, D. (2004, June 15). Knowledge integration leading to personal knowledge management: Enabling better life science and medical product management and health delivery. *Knowledge Management Blog — The Ferryman*. Retrieved September 2004 from barryhardy.blogs.com/theferryman/2004/06/knowledge_integ.html.

Rabin, S. (2003). The real-time enterprise, the real-time supply chain. *Information Systems Management, 20*(2), 58-62.

Singh, R., Salam, A. F., & Iyer, L. (n.d.). Intelligent infomediary-based e-marketplaces: Agents in e-supply chains. *Communications of the ACM*, (forthcoming).

Singh, R., Iyer, L. S., & Salam A. F. (2003). Web service for knowledge management in e-marketplaces. *eService Journal, 3*(1).

Shoham, Y. (1993). Agent oriented programming. *Journal of Artificial Intelligence, 60*(1), 51-92.

Sittig, D. F., Hazlehurst, B. L., Palen, T., Hsu, J., Jimison, H., & Hornbrook, M. C. (2002). A clinical information system research agenda for Kaiser Permanente. *The Permanente Journal, 6*(3), 41-44.

Staab, S., Studer, R., Schnurr, H. P., & Sure, Y. (2001). Knowledge processes and ontologies. *IEEE Intelligent Systems*, (February).

Teswanich, W., Anutariya, C., & Wuwongse, V. (2002). Unified representation for e-government knowledge management. In *Proceedings of the 3rd International Workshop on Knowledge Management in E-Government*, University of Linz and University of Roskilde (pp. 199-209).

Wiig, K. M. (1993). *Knowledge management foundations*. Schema Press.

The chapter was previously published in the International Journal on Semantic Web & Information Systems, 1(1), 19-35, January-March 2005.

Chapter X

A Distributed Patient Identification Protocol Based on Control Numbers with Semantic Annotation

Marco Eichelberg, OFFIS, Germany

Thomas Aden, OFFIS, Germany

Wilfried Thoben, OFFIS, Germany

Abstract

One important problem of information systems in health care is the localisation and access to electronic patient records across health care institute boundaries, especially in an international setting. The complexity of the problem is increased by the absence of a globally accepted standard for electronic health care records, the absence of unique patient identifiers in most countries, and the strict data protection requirements that apply to clinical documents. This article describes a protocol that allows the identification of locations of patient records for a given patient and provides access to these records, if granted, under consideration of the legal and technical requirements. The protocol combines cryptographic techniques with semantic annotation and mediation and presents a simple Web-service-based access to clinical documents.

Introduction

Information technology used in the health care sector is most often characterised by heterogeneity of systems, longevity of data and devices, and high availability requirements. While the heterogeneity and longevity of systems is a consequence of the fact that expensive special-purpose devices such as MRI (magnetic resonance imaging) scanners are produced by only a few vendors and need to be integrated with the existing IT infrastructure, the longevity and availability requirements of medical data such as images and diagnostic reports are related directly to the care process. Since patient treatment needs to continue, even if some part of the IT infrastructure is off-line, a distributed data storage with loose message-based coupling between devices is used most often. This implies that data inconsistencies between systems are not unusual and need to be accounted for. These properties of IT systems in health care explain the pressing need for interface standardisation and interoperability in this field, reflected by comprehensive interface standards like DICOM (NEMA, 2004) and HL7 (2003). According to the CEN/ISSS eHealth Standardization Focus Group (2004), a study currently being performed at the request of the European Commission, the key strategic aims for applications of information and communication technology to health services include improving access to clinical records and enabling patient mobility and cross-border access to health care. While much work has been devoted to developing standard system interfaces for applications within a single health care enterprise (i.e., hospital or private practice), the digital cross-enterprise exchange of clinical records is certainly the exception rather than the norm today, particularly in the case of cross-border communication. A key issue in this field is the absence of a unique identifier that could be used to unambiguously identify records pertaining to a particular patient. In this article, we discuss requirements for locating and accessing clinical records across enterprise and country borders under consideration of data protection and propose a protocol based on control numbers and semantic annotation that addresses these requirements. This protocol is being developed within the framework of the ARTEMIS project, which is introduced in the following section.

The ARTEMIS Project

The ARTEMIS project (ARTEMIS Consortium, 2004; Dogac et al., in press), funded by the European Union, aims to improve the interoperability of clinical information systems among different organisations, based on Semantic Web Services and suitable domain ontologies. A health care organisation can join the ARTEMIS peer-to-peer (P2P) network and advertise electronic services, such as the provision of access to a patient's electronic health care record (given suitable authorisation) and access to different subsystems (e.g., patient admission or laboratory information systems). Within the ARTEMIS network, further services might be invoked dynamically, for example, in order to translate and map among different representations of health care information. In ARTEMIS, all participating health care organisations (peers) are coupled loosely via the ARTEMIS P2P network. Groups of participating organisations are coupled via so-called Super Peers, which are connected among each other. The project is carried out with partners from Turkey, Germany, Greece, and the United Kingdom.

The Patient Identification Protocol

While a number of projects currently are attempting to establish central electronic health record (EHR) archives for certain regions or countries, most clinical records are still kept and maintained at the place of their creation. This means that, given a patient with a disease requiring long-term treatment (such as diabetes), related clinical records may be located at one or more family doctors' practices, several specialists, labs, and a number of hospitals. In particular, the patient may not even be aware of all the locations where records relevant to a particular medical problem may be kept. Any protocol that attempts to make relevant clinical documents available in digital form needs to take this distributed nature of document storage into account. The advent of wide area networks such as the Internet, along with various VPN (virtual private network) technologies provides a solution to the underlying problem of a digital transport connection between document requestor and document provider, but it does not solve the problem of how to locate the relevant records.

The task of locating relevant medical records is complicated by the fact that there is no unique patient identifier that could be broadcast as a query in order to locate information pertaining to one patient. While countries such as Turkey, Norway, and Sweden maintain a national person identifier that commonly is used as the index key for medical records, no such unique identifier is available in most other countries either for historic reasons or due to data protection regulations. This means that a query applicable to cross-border health care delivery only can be based on the patient demographics that are commonly available, including the patient's name, date and place of birth, sex, nationality, and postal address.

It should be noted that the set of demographics available may depend on the location (i.e., a national patient identifier certainly would be included in any query within a country in which it is valid) and on the patient's health condition (i.e., whether the patient is able to provide the doctor with additional information not contained in the passport or driver's license, which may be the only source of information available for an emergency patient). It also should be noted that spelling errors in medical record archives are not uncommon and may need to be accounted for, using, for example, phonetic encoding techniques. An additional challenge for cross-border application is the different character sets used in different European countries. For example, names of patients of Turkish origin are certainly common in German hospital information systems, since this group accounts for more than 2% of the population. However, Turkish names may contain characters not present in the Latin-1 alphabet (ISO, 1999b) commonly used by information systems in Germany, since the Turkish language requires the Latin-9 alphabet (ISO, 1999a), which means that the spelling of one name may differ, depending on the character set supported by the information system.

Since medical records generally are considered to be sensitive personal information, it would neither be appropriate (or legal) for a health care enterprise to allow third parties to browse through the demographics of the local record archive, nor would it be appropriate if a request of the form Hospital X is looking for prior psychiatry records for patient Hans Friedrich Müller, born 12-24-1960 in Hamburg were made available widely (i.e., broadcast) to all health care institutes in the network that might possibly have such records available. Clearly, the query already communicates information to the recipient that needs to be protected under the applicable data protection rules; namely, the facts that Mr.Müller currently receives treatment at Hospital X and may have had a prior psychiatric treatment. We propose the use of control numbers along with semantic annotation and a probabilistic record linkage as a way of addressing the possible fuzziness of demographic data and at the same time preventing an inappropriate (i.e., premature and unlimited) communication of personal data.

Control Numbers and Record Linkage

Control numbers is a concept that is used in the epidemiological cancer registries in Germany to allow record linkage of anonymised records that describe cancer cases and are collected independently of multiple sources, as described by Thoben, Appelrath, and Sauer (1994). The patient identification protocol makes use of this concept in a modified form. The generation of a set of control numbers from a set of demographic values is performed through the following series of five processing steps, as shown in Figure 1:

- **Splitting:** This first step initialises the process. The available demographics are split into fields that later are converted into different control numbers. For example, the date of birth typically would be split into different components for year, month, and day.

Figure 1. Creation of control numbers

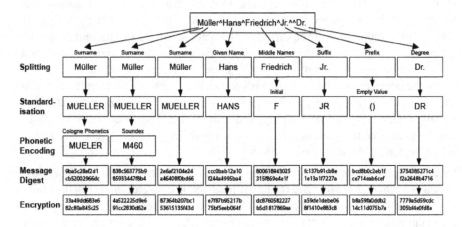

- **Standardisation:** This step addresses character set issues. Each component is standardised according to a set of rules that needs to be known to all parties participating in the protocol. Standardisation typically would involve conversion of names to upper-case ASCII characters, zero-padding of numbers such as day and month of birth, and the initialisation of unknown and empty fields with well known constants representing the concept of an unknown or empty value. The standardisation process certainly could be extended to Unicode to also cover multi-byte character sets such as Chinese or Japanese Kanji, for which a conversion of names to ASCII may not be appropriate, but this topic is not discussed further within the scope of this article.

- **Phonetic encoding:** Optionally, name components may be encoded with a phonetic encoding, such as the Soundex coding system used by the United States Census Bureau, the Metaphone algorithm or the Cologne phonetics for the German language (Postel, 1969). It should be noted that phonetic encoding is highly language-specific, and therefore, different encodings are likely to be used in different countries. For this reason, a name component always would be converted to at least two different control numbers, one with and one without phonetic encoding.

- **Message digest:** Each standardised and possibly phonetically encoded field in the set of demographics is subjected to a cryptographic message digest algorithm such as MD5, SHA-1, or RIPEMD-160 in this step. Due to the cryptographic properties of this class of algorithms, it is not possible to efficiently construct a matching input string to a given message digest; that is, the digest function is not reversible. It should be noted, however, that the set of possible input values for a patient's sex, year, month and day of birth, and so forth is rather limited. A dictionary-based attack, therefore, would quickly re-identify the plain-text source for these fields, along with most of the given names and family names that also could be determined by means of a dictionary attack.

- **Encryption:** In the final step, each message digest is encrypted with a secret encryption key that needs to be known by all parties in the protocol that generate control numbers to be compared with each other. Each encrypted message digest is called a control number, and the complete set of control numbers describes the patient demographics in a form that does not allow for the reproduction of any plain-text field by any party that does not have access to the encryption key, but it allows for a comparison of two different sets of control numbers without the need for access to the encryption key.

Given a set of control numbers describing a query and a larger number of sets of control numbers describing all patients in a record repository, matches in the repository can be identified using record linkage, defined by Winkler (1999) as "the methodology of bringing together corresponding records from two or more files or finding duplicates within files." We propose the use of a probabilistic rather than a deterministic record linkage algorithm, as described by Jaro (1989) as well as Blakely and Salmond (2002). This class of algorithms not only compares each pair of control numbers for equality, but it also considers the significance of each control number, based on an estimation of the true positive rate and the false positive rate; that is, the probabilities of a pair of identical control numbers of representing the same or different patients. The probabilistic record linkage also allows one to compensate to a certain degree for missing data (control numbers that are not available at the record repository), typing errors, and so forth. Basically, the algorithm allows a person to identify the most promising matches from a larger set. The final choice of records that would be treated as definitive matches depends on a threshold and possibly on human choice. Further issues in record linkage, such as array comparison, are discussed in Aden, Eichelberg, and Thoben (2004).

Blocking Variables

The protocol as previously described would require every record repository to create a set of control numbers for each patient in the repository and to repeat this for each incoming query because of the encryption key, which would change with each request. This, of course, is not practical for a large number of patients. Therefore, the protocol uses the concept of so-called blocking variables to reduce the number of possible candidate records for which control numbers have to be computed and evaluated. Blocking variables are simply plain-text demographics that are transmitted in unencrypted form (a transport level encryption can be used, of course, but the blocking variables are available to the record repository in plain-text form). Blocking variables must be chosen carefully to make sure that a patient cannot be identified from the blocking variables alone. As an example, the day of birth (not including month and year) certainly would not be sufficient to identify any specific patient but would reduce the number of candidates for which control numbers would have to be computed by a factor of up to 30. Similarly, a postal code of the place of residence or the place of birth would not be sufficient to identify a patient, even when combined with the day of birth, but would reduce significantly the number of candidates in most record repositories (except for hospitals actually located at the given place, where a large number of patients may have the same place of birth or residence). The set of blocking variables needs to be chosen carefully in order to reduce the number of candidate records as much as possible while avoiding the risk of exposing the patient's identity.

Semantic Annotation

As previously described, we can expect different countries to use different, though certainly overlapping, sets of control numbers accounting for country- or region-specific aspects such as phonetic encoding or national unique patient identifiers. Since control numbers only can be compared for binary equality but not evaluated in any other way, it is of prime importance for all parties participating in the protocol to understand exactly what each control number (and each blocking variable) means and which control number is supported by which party. The use of ontology-based semantic annotation allows one to introduce the amount of flexibility into the protocol that is needed to make it work in an international setting, where different sets of control numbers might be supported by different actors. Each request or response dataset consisting of a list of control numbers and blocking variables is encoded as a Web ontology language (OWL) (Dean & Schreiber, 2004) instance that describes the demographics from which each entry was generated, as well as the processing steps that were applied to the entry. Figure 2 shows the core demographics ontology defined for this purpose. A DemographicsOntology used by a health care enterprise to describe the supported set of control numbers and blocking variables consists of a set of DemographicsValue entities that are either control numbers or blocking variables (the asterisk in the hasValues relationship type denotes a one-to-many relationship). For control numbers, the processing steps are described through properties; for blocking variables, the BlockVariable Encoding describes the standardisation process or value range. Since different countries typically will use different sets of control numbers, more than one DemographicsOntology might exist. The country-, region-, or hospital-specific demographics ontologies (called local ontologies) are defined as extensions to the core ontology. Figure 3 shows a subset of such a local ontology, describing a single blocking variable (the patient's

Figure 2. Demographics ontology describing control numbers and blocking variables

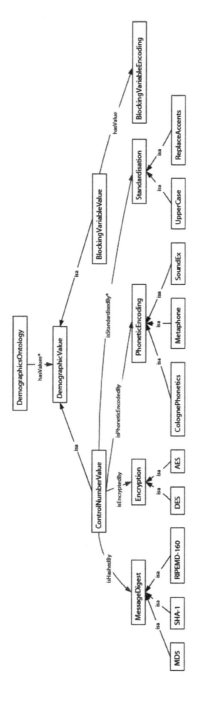

Figure 3. Local ontology describing control numbers and blocking variables for one country or institute

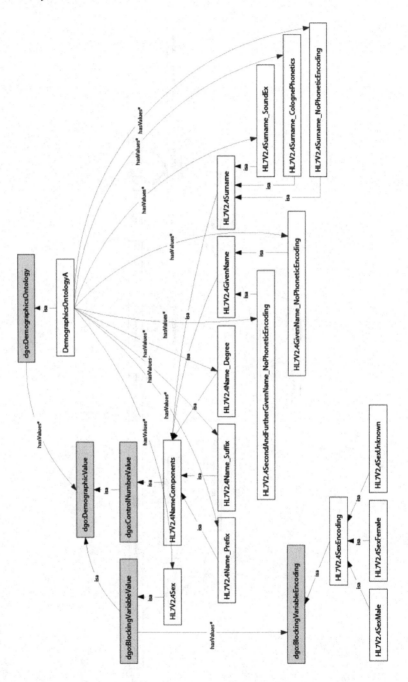

sex) and a set of control numbers for the name components as defined in HL7. All ontology classes shown in grey with the prefix dgo: in their name refer to the core ontology. OWL restrictions on properties that are not shown in this figure define the algorithms used in the local ontology for standardisation, phonetic encoding, message digest, and encryption. Also not shown is a binary property isUnique defined for each subclass of DemographicValue that denotes control numbers that guarantee a unique identification of the patient for a match. These properties are used to initialise the weights of the record linkage process accordingly. If the requestor and a record repository in the protocol use different local ontologies, then a direct or indirect mapping between these ontologies is used, which is available both to the record repository (for the purpose of interpreting the blocking variables) and the record linkage server, which is introduced next. A mapping would be defined as an ontology describing owl:equivalentClass relationships between ontology classes in the different ontologies, allowing for a reconciliation between the ontology instances using rather simple inference rules. Instance nodes (i.e., individual control numbers or blocking variables) for which no equivalence in the other local ontology can be found simply are omitted from the record linkage process.

Knowledge Distribution

As described, the security of the control numbers is based on the combination of a message digest algorithm followed by an encryption with a session key. The session key, which is randomly generated for each query, guarantees that responses from different queries cannot be compared in order to derive information from the evaluation of a large set of queries. However, the problem of dictionary attacks still remains: Any entity that has access to both a set of control numbers and the session key could attempt to decrypt the control numbers and use a dictionary of names, dates, and so forth to re-identify the patient described by the control numbers. In order to prevent this, the following simple policy needs to be established:

Any entity in the network that has access to the session key must not be granted access to any set of control numbers except the control numbers generated by this entity itself.

This means that the initiator of a query for a specific patient (called the requestor) cannot receive the control numbers generated by the record repositories responding to the query. The record repositories, on the other hand, cannot be given access to the control numbers in the query, because they need to access the session key in order to generate their own sets of control numbers for all patients matching the blocking variables. Fortunately, the record linkage process does not require access to the session key—only to the control numbers in the query and the responses that were pre-filtered by the record repositories using the blocking variables. Therefore, the protocol needs to introduce additional actors between requestor and record repositories in order to guarantee that no patient-related information is leaked through the protocol before explicit authorisation has been granted. The actors and their transactions in a slightly simplified form are shown in Figure 4. The complete protocol is detailed in Eichelberg, Aden, and Riesmeier (2004). Figure 4 shows the actors involved in the protocols as ovals and the transactions (i.e., message exchange between them) as boxes with an arrow indicating the direction of the information flow. Only a single record repository is shown in the diagram; however, the protocol is designed to work with a potentially large number of record repositories and possibly with more than one instance of the other actors involved. The two additional actors involved are as follows:

- **Record linkage server (RLS):** An entity in the network that receives a set of control numbers from the requestor describing the patient to be identified and a possibly large number of sets of control numbers generated by the record repositories, based on the blocking variables and the session key. The RLS performs the probabilistic record linkage and identifies a number of candidates; that is, patient records in the record repositories that have a high probability of referring to the same patient described by the query control numbers. Once the RLS has completed its work and authorisation has been given by the record repositories (see discussion that follows), the set of best matches (based on a threshold value) is reported back to the requestor completing the patient identification process. Since the RLS does not have access to the session key, it cannot re-identify the patient demographics from the control numbers it receives. The RLS must be a trusted component in the network in the sense that both requestor and record repositories have to rely on the RLS to never give away any control numbers it receives and never trying to obtain a session key in order to perform a re-identification of patient demographics.

- **Trusted third party (TTP):** An entity in the network that enables distribution of the query containing the session key and blocking variables among the record repositories in the network, preventing any direct communication between requestor and record repositories at this stage. The TTP also can act as a gatekeeper to the network in the sense that only requestors accepted by the TTP are able to initiate patient identification queries, and only repositories accepted by the TTP are able to provide information to the RLS. Each match retrieved by the requestor from the RLS consists of a resource identifier (e.g., URL), under which the record repository that has provided this matching record can be contacted, a set of flags indicating for each of the control numbers in the query whether or not they matched or were missing in the response, and a candidate identifier, a simple numeric identifier generated by the record

Figure 4. Actors and transactions in the patient identification protocol (simplified)

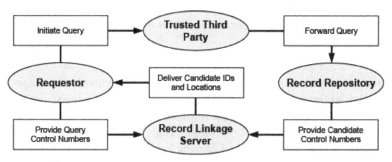

repository as an alias to the local patient ID that identifies a specific patient in the context of the current query transaction and can be used to request medical records for this specific patient.

Medical Record Access

Once a requestor has identified one or more record repositories that have clinical documents pertaining to the current patient available, the appropriate documents have to be selected, requested, retrieved and displayed. This comprises the second phase of the protocol described in this article. Since no global standard for electronic health care records exists at this time that could be used to provide record access in the cross-border scenario previously described, we suggest using the retrieve information for display (RID) (IHE, 2004) protocol defined by the integrating the healthcare enterprise (IHE) initiative (Eichelberg, Poiseau, Wein, & Riesmeier, 2003) for this purpose. IHE is a non-profit initiative addressing the issue of system integration in health care with strong participation from industry, science, and medical professional societies in North America, Europe and Japan. While IHE does not develop standards as such, it selects and recommends appropriate standards for specific use cases and develops restrictions (application profiles) for these standards that allow for a simplified system integration. The result of this technical work is published as the IHE Technical Framework and revised annually. The IHE Technical Framework for IT Infrastructure (IHE, 2004) gives the following short overview about the purpose of the RID integration profile:

The retrieve information for display integration profile (RID) provides simple and rapid read-only access to patient-centric clinical information that is located outside the user's current application but is important for better patient care (for example, access to lab reports from radiology department). It supports access to existing persistent documents in well-known presentation formats such as HL7 CDA (Level 1), PDF, JPEG, etc. It also supports access to specific key patient-centric information such as allergies, current medications, summary of reports, etc. for presentation to a clinician.

IHE interface definitions are based on actors (the IT systems involved in the protocol) and transactions (interfaces between actors). In the case of RID, the actors are called information source and display. The information source, which corresponds to the record repository in the previous discussion, is a system that maintains a database of persistent clinical documents and specific key patient-centric information such as allergies, current medications, summary of reports, and so forth. The display, which corresponds to the requestor, is a system that accesses the information source, retrieves patient-centric information or persistent documents, and displays them to a human observer. The focus of the integration is visual presentation, not a complete integration of the structured databases on which the actors might be based. Documents are exchanged in well-known presentation formats. Communication between display and information source is always initiated by the display and implemented as a Web Service using the Web Services description language (WSDL) with a binding to HTTP GET.

The RID protocol is ideal for integration with the patient identification process described before, because the only a priori information that the display needs when accessing a record repository is the patient identifier. This identifier is provided by the patient identification protocol in the form of the candidate identifier, which describes a single patient and is only valid in the context of a single query transaction. Figure 5 shows how an existing RID information source at the record repository

Figure 5. Access to medical records based on IHE retrieve information for display

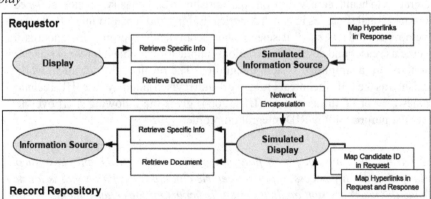

Figure 6. Sequence of transactions for patient identification and medical record access

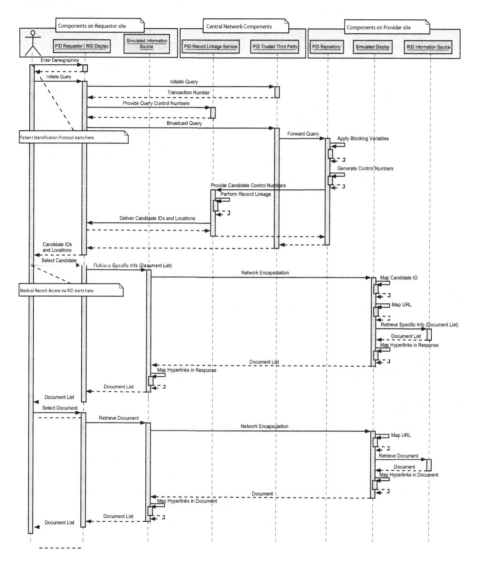

site and an existing RID display system at the requestor site can be combined with an additional layer of middleware to provide medical record access in combination with the patient identification protocol.

On the repository site, a simulated display receives the incoming requests from the requestor, replaces the candidate ID generated during the patient identification process by the real patient ID locally used in the hospital, and forwards the request to the existing information source, to which this actor looks like any local display actor. Before forwarding the response to the requestor, all hyperlinks in the response have to be replaced with links pointing to the simulated display, because these hyperlinks typically will refer to resources that cannot be reached directly from the outside world (due to firewall protection and network address translation). Subsequent requests for these mapped hyperlinks simply would be redirected from the simulated display to the original resource. In a similar manner, a hyperlink lookup scheme can be implemented on the requestor site inside the simulated information source to address firewall and network address translation issues. As a side effect, the two simulated actors can provide a secure tunneling of the request and response message, which is usually transmitted in clear text form within a hospital, using any available transport level security protocol. Figure 6 shows the combined sequence of transactions for the patient identification protocol and the following medical record access. In this figure, the PID requestor from Figure 4 and the RID display from Figure 5 have been grouped into a single system providing the user interface to the end user. This is the typical use case and also reflects the ARTEMIS implementation. The scalability aspect of the protocol (i.e., involvement of multiple TTPs and repositories) is not shown for reasons of clarity. The grouped requestor/display actor and the simulated information source are part of the IT infrastructure of the user's site. The TTP and the RLS are central components provided by the network, and all other actors are located at the repository site.

Data Protection and Patient Consent

The EU data protection directive (Council of the European Communities, 1995) and the recommendation of the Council of Europe on the protection of medical data (Council of Europe, 1997) determine that neither person identifying data nor medical records are allowed to be exchanged between different organisations unless either the patient agrees on the exchange of the identifying data and medical records for a specific purpose or the vital interests of the patient are touched. Therefore, in most cases, an explicit patient consent will be a prerequisite to an exchange of medical records.

Since the patient is most likely to be at the health care institute searching for and requesting to access clinical records (i.e., the requestor), the question arises how the patient consent can be demonstrated to the record repository; in particular, if the exact location of the repository is unknown. It should be noted that no information that would allow one to identify a patient or derive any information about a patient is exchanged in the patient identification protocol, until the RLS provides a list of matches to the requestor that is in the last step of the first phase of the protocol depicted in Figure 4. This list of matches enables the requestor to identify resources (i.e., health care institutes) that have clinical documents for the given patient available with a certain probability. The second more significant exchange of information takes place during the second phase of the protocol when the requestor uses the modified Retrieve Information for Display protocol to request and access clinical documents for a specific patient. Correspondingly, there are two places at which additional barriers can be installed in the protocol, barriers that will be opened automatically or manually once the patient consent has been demonstrated to the record repository:

- The requestor may deposit a proof of the patient consent at the RLS when initiating the query. The RLS would make this document available only to those record repositories that have been identified as matches in the record linkage and request permission to report them back to the requestor. Only repositories granting this permission would ever be reported to the requestor.

- The RID access to clinical documents for a specific candidate may require additional authorisation at the repository site requiring a prior communication of the proof of patient consent. It also would be possible to restrict access within the RID protocol to specific documents or document types (e.g., radiology reports).

Two different approaches for demonstrating patient consent are conceivable — the use of a public key infrastructure (PKI) for patients or a conventional out-of-band communication using possibly digitised letters, telephone, mail, or fax conversation. A PKI for patients would allow for a solution of the issue of patient consent in a fully digital manner by providing a digital signature of the patient authorising the request. This, however, would require that certificates and security tokens for the private key, such as smartcards, be issued for all patients. While a few countries, including Belgium, Taiwan, and Germany, have plans for a PKI for the health care sector (Dietzel & Riepe, 2004), there are no such plans in many other countries, and there is no sign of a global or at least a European-wide harmonisation of these PKIs (the European health insurance card does not include PKI functionality).

Since a PKI-based solution will not be available in the foreseeable future for cross-border communication, a conventional approach needs to be supported. As an example, the patient may be asked to sign a letter of consent at the requesting health care institute, and a digitised copy of this letter could be deposited with the RLS and made available to the record repositories for which matches were found during the record linkage process. The data protection officer at each health care institute operating a record repository would check the letter of consent and, if appropriate, give permission to the RLS to report the location of the record repository back to the requestor and grant access to certain clinical documents. In cases where an original handwritten signature is legally required, the digitised document could be accompanied by a contact address at the requesting health care institute where a delivery of an original document (e.g., by express service) could be requested. While it is not realistic to assume a working PKI for patients as a prerequisite to a digital cross-border exchange of clinical records, a working PKI for the health care institutes connected to the network could be implemented rather easily, again utilising the gatekeeper role of the TTP entity in the network. This would assure that only authenticated entities could participate in the protocol either as a requestor or as a record repository and, therefore, would provide a minimum level of quality control of the data communicated within the network.

Results

The patient identification protocol establishes a concept that, to our knowledge, has not been available in the health care sector before — an undirected search for patient records (i.e., a search that does not require a priori information about the location of the records) that does not violate data protection requirements. The concept matches well with the peer-to-peer network structure established in the context of the ARTEMIS project, where many health care institutes may form a network of services in a very dynamic manner. The use of semantic annotation allows one to cope with the fact that different institutes identify patients with different demographics and that no globally unique identifier for patients will be available for the foreseeable future. The possibility of including national extensions allows one to maximise the specificity of the search algorithm in environments that can make use of such extensions, while the inclusion of phonetic encoding allows one to improve sensitivity by gracefully handling spelling errors. The integration of the Retrieve Information for Display protocol for the second phase (i.e., the request and transmission of clinical documents once their location has been identified) provides a simple read-only access to clinical documents that easily can be integrated with the existing legacy systems.

An implementation of the patient identification protocol is currently under development in the context of the ARTEMIS project. The implementation is based on the ARTEMIS middleware, which provides for the peer-to-peer infrastructure required by the protocol; that is, message transmission and broadcast facilities based on the JXTA peer-to-peer communication platform (Gong, 2002), a policy-based security architecture for a secure communication over unsecured networks and a pre-selection of record repositories that participate in a query based on geographical location (e.g., "we are looking for records located in Germany only"). Pilot applications that will evaluate the protocol in a clinical setting are planned in the UK and in Turkey. From these prototypes, we expect practical experience about use patterns, performance, and scalability of the protocol. Krieg, Hense, Lehnert, and Mattauch (2001) report about an evaluation of the probabilistic record linkage based on control numbers, which is used in the Münster Cancer Registry in Germany. They use a set of 19 control numbers computed from the patient's name (including name of birth, prior name, and phonetic encoding of the name components) and the day of birth. The clear-text blocking variables comprise the month and year of birth, the patient's sex, and place of residence. They evaluated 27,262 record linkage processes performed in the year 1998 for a database of 101,880 patients. In this case, the record linkage provided a false positive rate (i.e., patients that were incorrectly selected as a match) of 0.36% and a false negative rate (i.e., matches in the database that were not found) of 1.81%. Krieg et al. (2001) emphasise that these figures depend significantly on the size of the database. Nevertheless, the figures indicate that the patient identification protocol provides good results even with a rather limited set of demographics available. It should be noted that in countries that have a national patient identifier available, the record linkage process would be able to provide 0% false positive and false negative rate in repositories that support the national patient ID while still providing results in the order of magnitude shown above for other repositories (i.e., other countries). Additional work will be needed to improve the internationalisation of the splitting and standardisation algorithms for control number generation, which currently are based mainly on German experiences with epidemiological cancer registries. Fine-tuning may be needed for the parameters of the record linkage process in order to maximise specificity and sensitivity of the record linkage process.

Conclusion

The patient identification protocol described in this article provides a solution for a common problem in the health care sector that is likely to become very important with the increasing mobility of the workforce in Europe — locating and accessing prior clinical records for the continuity of care. The solution combines techniques from different domains — control numbers, blocking variables, and record linkage procedures as used in epidemiological registries, knowledge distribution, and TTP services from cryptographic communication protocols, semantic annotation, and ontology-based mediation, core technologies of the Semantic Web. The protocol reflects the way clinical records typically are stored, indexed, and accessed in today's health care information systems. While the advent of a universally accepted standard for electronic health care records possibly could render the patient identification protocol obsolete in the future, there is no indication at the moment that such a standard is going to be established in the foreseeable future, and even then, the issue of historical records would remain for a number of years. Therefore, the authors believe that the patient identification protocol can be a significant help in improving access to clinical information while safeguarding data protection rules and protecting the patient's right of self-determination regarding his or her clinical records.

Acknowledgment

This work is supported by the European Commission through the IST-1-002103-STP ARTEMIS R&D project.

References

Aden, T., Eichelberg, M., & Thoben, W. (2004). A fault-tolerant cryptographic protocol for patient record requests. In *Proceedings of EuroPACS-MIR 2004 in the Enlarged Europe* (pp. 103-106). Trieste, Italy: E.U.T. Edizioni Università di Trieste.

ARTEMIS Consortium. (2004). *The ARTEMIS Project*. Retrieved from http://www. srdc.metu.edu.tr/webpage/projects/artemis/

Blakely, T., & Salmond, C. (2002). Probabilistic record linkage and a method to calculate the positive predictive value. *International Journal of Epidemiology, 31*, 1246-1252.

CEN/ISSS eHealth Standardization Focus Group. (2004). *Current and future standardization issues in the e-health domain: Achieving interoperability* (Draft 4.1). Geneva, Switzerland: European Committee for Standardization/Information Society Standardization System.

Council of Europe. (1997). *Recommendation No. R(97)5 of the Committee of Ministers to Member States on the Protection of Medical Data* (Technical report). Strasbourg, France: Council of Europe Publishing.

Council of the European Communities. (1995). Directive 95/46/EC of the European Parliament and of the Council of 24 October 1995 on the protection of individuals with regard to the processing of personal data and on the free movement of such data. *Official Journal of the European Communities, L281*, 31-39.

Dean, M., & Schreiber, G. (2004). *OWL Web ontology language reference (W3C Recommendation)*. Cambridge, MA: World Wide Web Consortium.

Dietzel, G., & Riepe, C. (2004). Modernizing health care in Germany by introducing the eHealthcard. *Swiss Medical Informatics, 52*, 18-22.

Dogac, A., et al. (in press a). Exploiting ebXML registry semantic constructs for handling archetype metadata in healthcare informatics. *International Journal of Metadata, Semantics and Ontologies.*

Dogac, A., et al. (in press b). Artemis: Deploying semantically enriched Web Services in the healthcare domain. *Information Systems Journal*.

Eichelberg, M., Aden, T., & Riesmeier, J. (2004). *Relevant electronic healthcare record standards and protocols for accessing medical information* (ARTEMIS deliverable D5.1.1). Oldenburg, Germany: ARTEMIS Consortium.

Eichelberg, M., Poiseau, E., Wein, B. B., & Riesmeier, J. (2003). IHE Europe: Extending the IHE initiative to the European health care market. In H. K. Huang, & O. M. Ratib (Eds.), *Medical imaging 2003: PACS and integrated medical information systems: Design and evaluation* (Vol. 5033, pp. 1-10).

Gong, L. (2002). *Project JXTA: A technology overview* (Technical report). Palo Alto, CA: Sun Microsystems, Inc.

HL7. (2003). *Application protocol for electronic data exchange in health care environments (Version 2.5) (ANSI Standard)*. Ann Arbor, MI: Health Level Seven.

IHE. (2004). *IT infrastructure technical framework revision 1.1* (Technical Report). Oak Brook, IL: Integrating the Healthcare Enterprise.

ISO. (1999a). *Information processing: 8-bit single-byte coded graphic character sets. Part 13: Latin alphabet No. 9 (International Standard No. 8859-13)*. Geneva, Switzerland: International Organization for Standardization.

ISO. (1999b). *Information processing: 8-bit single-byte coded graphic character sets. Part 1: Latin alphabet No. 1 (International Standard No. 8859-1)*. Geneva, Switzerland: International Organization for Standardization.

Jaro, M. A. (1989). Advances in record linkage methodology as applied to matching the 1985 census of Tampa, Florida. *Journal of the American Statistical Association, 84*(406), 414-420.

Krieg, V., Hense, H.-W., Lehnert, M., & Mattauch, V. (2001). Record linage mit kryptographierten Identitätsdaten in einem bevölkerungsbezogenen Krebsregister. *Gesundheitswesen, 63*, 376-382.

NEMA. (2004). *Digital imaging and communications in medicine (DICOM) (NEMA Standards Publication No. PS 3.x–2004)*. Rosslyn, VA: National Electrical Manufacturers Association.

Postel, H.-J. (1969). Die Kölner Phonetik — Ein Verfahren zur Identifizierung von Personennamen auf der Grundlage der Gestaltanalyse. *IBM-Nachrichten, 19*, 925-931.

The chapter was previously published in the International Journal on Semantic Web & Information Systems, 1(4), 24-43, October-December 2005.

Chapter XI

Family History Information Exchange Services Using HL7 Clinical Genomics Standard Specifications

Amnon Shabo (Shvo), IBM Research Lab, Haifa

Kevin S. Hughes, Massachusetts General Hospital,
Partners Health Care, USA

Abstract

A number of family history applications are in use by health care professionals (e.g., CAGENE, Progeny, Partners Health care Family History Program) as well as by patients (e.g., the U.S. Surgeon General's Family History Program). Each has its own proprietary data format for pedigree drawing and for the maintenance of family history health information. Interoperability between applications is essentially non-existent. To date, disparate family history applications cannot easily exchange patient information. The receiving application should be able to understand the semantics of the incoming family history and enable the user to view and/or to edit it using the receiving applications interface. We envision that any family history application will be able to send and receive an individual's family history informa-

tion using the newly created HL7 Clinical Genomics Specifications through the Semantic Web, using services that will transform one format to the other through the HL7 canonical representation.

Introduction

The need to represent a patient's family history information associated with clinical and genomic data was introduced as a storyboard to the Clinical Genomics Special Interest Group (SIG) in HL7 (CG, 2005). The SIG develops HL7 standards (HL7, 2005) to enable the exchange of interrelated clinical and personalized genomic data between disparate organizations (e.g., health care providers, genetic labs, research facilities, pharmaceutical companies). Agreed-upon standards to allow this exchange are crucial, as it is envisioned that the use of genomic data in health care practice will become ubiquitous in the near future. A few emerging cases for this include tissue typing, genetic testing (e.g., cystic fibrosis, BRCA1, BRCA2), and pharmacogenomics clinical trials. These cases are represented in the SIG storyboards, which have led to the development of the genotype model as the basic unit of genomic data representation, focusing on a specific chromosomal locus.

It was determined that there was a set of basic information required to record a family history and to create a pedigree for the purpose of breast cancer risk assessment (Thull & Vogel, 2004). For each family member, this set included the information about his or her relationships to other members of the family and the information regarding his or her health. Relationship information included the type of relative, a personal identifier, and the identifier of the person's mother and father. Health information data included disease type, age at diagnosis, current age or age of death, genetic syndrome suspected, genetic test done, genetic test result as raw data, and interpretation of genetic test.

The explosion in our knowledge of genetics has increased our understanding of the hereditary basis of many diseases. While we present here the example of exchanging family history and risk information relative to breast cancer, we believe this model can be used for the exchange of any hereditary risk information.

An outline of the patient's family history is presented in Appendix A. Populating this data set with patient data results is the example shown in Table 1.

Storyboard Presentation

The following fictitious scenario demonstrates the potential use of the Semantic Web (Berners-Lee, Hendler & Lassila, 2001) in offering services of exchanging family history information. Note that this is an abridged version of the full presentation contained in the HL7 specifications (CG, 2005).

1. Martha Francis is 39 years old. Her mother had ovarian cancer and was found to have a deleterious BRCA1 mutation. She has two sisters, a husband, and a daughter. She is not of Ashkenazi Jewish descent.

2. She makes an appointment at a risk clinic. The clinic instructs her to use the Surgeon General's Family History (Yoon, 2002) Web-based tool to prepare for the visit. She brings up the Surgeon General's Family History tool and enters her family history.

3. She then sends the data to the risk clinic prior to her appointment with that clinic, where a CAGENE application receives the data.

4. The counselor at the risk clinic (nurse geneticist, nurse practitioner, genetic counselor, doctor, etc.) uses the CAGENE application (a pedigree drawing program that runs risk models), where the patient's family history already has been received. The counselor edits the data after confirming and clarifying various issues with the patient and adds additional information that was not entered at home.

Table 1. Example of a cancer patient's family history instance

ID	Father ID	Mother ID	Relationship	Vital Status	Current age or age of death	Disease	Age of diagnosis	Genetic test	Result	Interpretation
1	3	2	Client-F	ALIVE	47	NONE	0	N/A	N/A	N/A
2	5	4	Mother	DEAD	72	Ovarian	40	N/A	N/A	N/A
3	7	6	Father	ALIVE	75	NONE	0	N/A	N/A	N/A
4	0	0	Maternal Grandmother	ALIVE	98	NONE	0	N/A	N/A	N/A
5	0	0	Maternal Grandfather	ALIVE	67	NONE	0	N/A	N/A	N/A
6	0	0	Paternal Grandmother	ALIVE	78	NONE	0	N/A	N/A	N/A
7	0	0	Paternal Grandfather	ALIVE	87	NONE	0	N/A	N/A	N/A
8	3	2	Sister	DEAD	67	Ovarian	60	N/A	N/A	N/A
9	3	2	Sister	DEAD	55	Ovarian	80	N/A	N/A	N/A
1	0	0	Husband	ALIVE	57	NO	0	N/A	N/A	N/A
11	1	1	Daughter	DEAD	33	Breast	30	BRCA1	185delAG	DELETERIOUS MUTATION

5. The patient is considered to be at high risk, and she is told that she is a candidate for genetic testing. This includes a thorough discussion of the pros and cons of testing. The patient decides not to have testing and leaves.

6. The counselor at the risk clinic sends back the updated family history to the Surgeon General History tool, so that the patient can use it in future encounters, if needed.

In this fictitious scenario, both the Surgeon General and CAGENE programs use publicly available Web Services that transform the data to the format needed by the receiving application, if it is not yet complying with the HL7 specs. The various aspects by which this kind of storyboard relates to the current processes are described in Table 2, where the left column shows the current practice, and the right column shows the proposed improvements. The scenario described in Table 2 is more complex than the previous, as it includes the use of three more family history programs with their own data formats as well as results from a genetic testing facility.

The Family History Exchange Model

Following the previous analysis of a patient's family history outline as well as the contextual storyboard presentation, we have developed an HL7 model to allow the representation of a pedigree with an unlimited depth of generations. The model addresses the storyboard requirements while making use of the Genotype model for embedding genomic data at any level of granularity available and needed.

The modeling effort is based on the new HL7 reference information model (RIM) from which all HL7 V3 specs are derived (e.g., labs, pharmacy, clinical documents, clinical trials, etc.). The HL7 RIM (RIM, 2005) has four core classes that basically allow the representation of an entity playing a role that has a participation in an act. For example, a person is playing a role of a relative that has a participation in an observation act of clinical and genomic data. By using the dedicated HL7 tools, we created UML-like models, where we refined the core RIM classes and associated them in a way that represents a pedigree. We then were able to generate automatically an XML schema from these models and to experiment with family history information exchange.

Figure 1 shows a bird's eye view of the family history model utilizing the genotype model to represent optional genomic data for the patient and each of his or her relatives.

Table 2. How semantic interoperability of family history information can improve current practices

CURRENT MEDICAL APPROACH	ENVISIONED APPROACH
Martha Francis is a 39-year-old woman with ovarian cancer. She has a family history of breast and ovarian cancer and believes she may be carrying a BRCA1 or BRCA2 mutation (which predisposes to breast and ovarian cancer).	Martha Francis is a 39-year-old woman with ovarian cancer. She has a family history of breast and ovarian cancer and believes she may be carrying a BRCA1 or BRCA2 mutation (which predisposes to breast and ovarian cancer).
She downloads the Surgeon General's Family History tool onto her computer at home and enters her family history.	She uses the Surgeon General's Family History Web-based tool from her home and enters her family history.
She then prints out her information onto paper and brings the paper to her clinician.	She then sends the data to her clinician (the Surgeon General's tool uses Web Services to export its data to the HL7 format and then to transform it to the clinician's system format).
Her clinician types the information from the paper into the homegrown electronic medical record (EHR).	Her clinician is able to see her family history as part of the homegrown electronic health record (EHR) system used in the clinician's office.
The clinician reviews the family history with the patient and makes corrections and additions in the EHR.	The clinician reviews the family history with the patient and makes corrections and additions in family history information of the patient's EHR.
The patient is considered to be at high risk of having a mutation, and this information is given to her.	The patient is considered to be at high risk of having a mutation, and this information is given to her.
She is referred to a risk clinic.	She is referred to a risk clinic.
Francis' family history details are printed on paper and sent to the risk clinic.	Francis' family history details are sent to the risk clinic (the clinician's system uses Web Services to export its data to the HL7 format and then to transform it to the risk clinic's required format).
The counselor at the risk clinic (nurse geneticist, nurse practitioner, genetic counselor, doctor, etc.) types the data into a number of programs: (1) Progeny (Progeny, 2005) to draw a pedigree; (2) CAGENE (CaGene, 2005) to run risk models; and (3) a homegrown Microsoft Access database to hold various and sundry other data. The counselor then reviews the family history information collected by the primary clinician, edits it, reviews results of the risk model algorithms, decides what genetic syndrome her family might have, and categorizes the patient as to degree of risk.	The counselor at the risk clinic (nurse geneticist, nurse practitioner, genetic counselor, doctor, etc.) imports the patient's family history information into a number of programs: (1) Progeny (Progeny, 2005) to draw a pedigree; (2) CAGENE (CaGene, 2005) to run risk models; and (3) a homegrown Microsoft Access database to hold various and sundry other data. The counselor then reviews the family history information collected by the primary clinician, edits it, reviews results of the risk model algorithms, decides what genetic syndrome her family might have, and categorizes the patient as to degree of risk.
The counselor speaks with the patient and adds additional information to the databases.	The counselor speaks with the patient and adds additional information to the databases.
If there have been any changes or additions to the family history, the counselor runs the computer models again.	If there have been any changes or additions to the family history, the counselor runs the computer models again.

Table 2. continued

CURRENT MEDICAL APPROACH	ENVISIONED APPROACH
The patient is considered to be at high risk, and she is told she is a candidate for genetic testing. This includes a thorough discussion of the pros and cons of testing.	The patient is considered to be at high risk, and she is told she is a candidate for genetic testing. This includes a thorough discussion of the pros and cons of testing.
The order for testing is issued, and the family history information is included with the lab requisition (required by the testing laboratory). The family history information is transcribed by hand onto a paper lab requisition, which is sent to the testing facility along with a blood sample.	The order for testing is issued, and the family history information is included with the lab requisition (required by the testing laboratory). The data is sent to the testing facility through the aforementioned family history Web Services, along with a delivery of a blood sample.
At the central testing facility, the family history data is typed into the database (homegrown).	At the central testing facility, the HL7 message received from the family history Web Services is imported into the database (homegrown).
Testing of the BRCA1 and BRCA 2 genes for mutations is undertaken.	Testing of the BRCA1 and BRCA 2 genes for mutations is undertaken.
The results are entered into the database.	The results are entered into the database.
Identified mutations are assessed for functional significance by determining if they are truncating (deleterious), or if they are irrelevant (no change in amino acid coded by that codon). All other mutations are compared to known mutations to determine if information is available on their functional significance. In this case, a mutation is identified in BRCA1 and the mutation is deleterious.	Identified mutations are assessed for functional significance by determining if they are truncating (deleterious) or if they are irrelevant (no change in amino acid coded by that codon). All other mutations are compared to known mutations to determine if information is available on their functional significance. In this case, a mutation is identified in BRCA1 and the mutation is deleterious.
The actual mutations and the assessment of functional significance are printed on paper, which is sent to the counselor.	The actual mutations and possibly the entire gene sequences as well as the assessment of functional significance are exported using the HL7 Genotype model, which is part of the family history standard specification. The Genotype model is known to clinical genomics Web Services that annotate the genomic data by the most updated knowledge and to associate it with the patient clinical history. The annotated results are sent to the counselor.
The counselor types the results into his or her databases, makes comments, and then prints a final report, which is sent to the primary provider and to the patient.	The counselor receives the results through his or her family history program and further annotates it. The counselor then sends the information to the primary provider and to the patient so both can update their records. As in all information exchanges thus far, this is seamlessly accomplished through publicly available Web Services that can transform all known family history formats through HL7 standards specifications.

Figure 1. A bird's eye view of the HL7 family history model

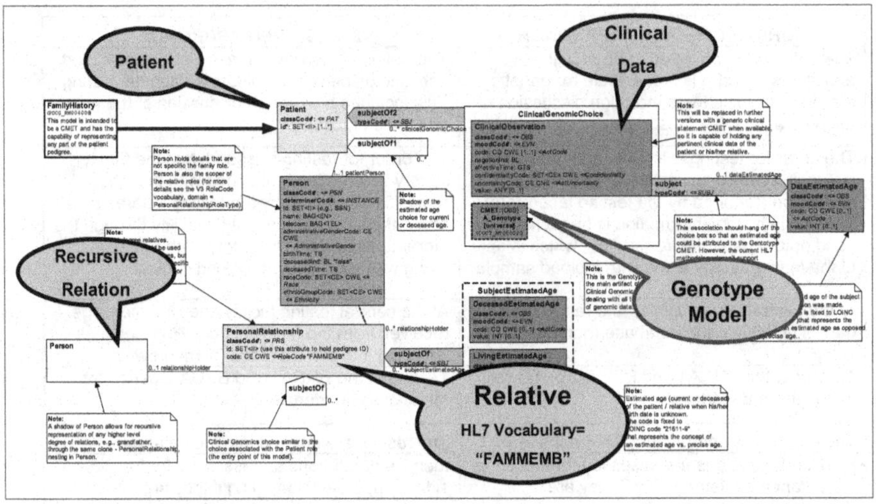

Underlying Standards and Technologies

The following sections describe standards and technologies that underlie the family history model and enable its potential use in the Semantic Web.

HL7 Standards as a Foundation for Semantic Interoperability

The HL7 standard specifications focus on the seventh layer of the ISO open systems interconnection model (i.e., the semantic level that defines the contents of the messages exchanged between disparate systems within and across enterprises). An outstanding example of such use of HL7 is the principle design of the UK NHS NPfIT (National Health Service — National Program for IT) (Williams et al., 2004). It is a radical approach to change the entire strategy for information service provision in England and Wales. The plan is to have a foundation layer of nationwide applications running over a new broadband infrastructure and exchanging information using HL7 version 3 messages extended and localized by the requirements of this program. Three main applications are built on these new infrastructures: (1) a national e-booking system that enables the patient to participate in where and when an appointment is made; (2) an electronic transmission of prescriptions that will enable prescriptions to be sent electronically between GPs and retail pharmacies; and (3) a national integrated patient care service. The national patient record system, comprising a medical snapshot of every patient, will be fed into a national spine on top of the IT infrastructure. The spine will link the full range of the IT services specified locally. As a result, electronic patient records will be held centrally and will be available from all parts of the NHS with improved debugging, duplication, and management facilities, compared to today's dispersed and fragmented systems. The UK multi-billion-dollar NPfIT implementation (started in 2004) is a quantum leap compared to the current health care situation in the UK, and it is all built around HL7 standard specifications — a crucial enabler of semantic interoperability on a large national scale. A similar initiative for National Health Information Infrastructure is evolving in the US, although with different architecture — less centralized than the UK (ONCHIT, 2005). As in the UK, it also is built around health care standards as main enablers of semantic interoperability. More national health IT initiatives are going on these days around the globe, some of which are based on HL7 standards; for example, in Finland (Porrasmaa, 2004), The Netherlands (NICTIZ, 2005), Canada (InfoWay, 2005), and Australia (HealthConnect, 2005).

Development Methodologies and Technologies

The development of HL7 specifications follows the HL7 development framework (HDF, 2005), a methodology that dictates the use of pure UML models to represent the domain analysis and activity in the storyboards of interest to each working group (e.g., laboratory, pharmacy, medical records, clinical genomics). After the completion of these domain-specific UML models to the satisfaction of the domain experts, the working group represents these models through the HL7 RIM building blocks, resulting in an HL7 domain information model (a UML-like model with HL7-specific constraints). The latter then serves as a basis of creating several HL7 message information models that can be serialized to hierarchical message descriptions and organized into interaction sets. The aforementioned artifacts are being balloted and sent to ANSI. For implementation purposes, the HL7 specifications could be translated to some implementable technology like XML. The resulting XML schemas are not considered part of the balloted content but rather one option of implementation, taking into account that at a later time, there might be new implementation technologies for the same standard specifications. Note that only HL7 Message Information Models can be translated to XML schemas, as they are serializable models as opposed to Domain Information Models that can be more complex, encompassing all relevant data and associations in the domain.

The process of creating HL7 specifications is facilitated by a suite of tools developed specifically for HL7; a drawing tool allows the designer to draw an HL7 model from a pallet of RIM core classes. It also allows the validation of the model and its storage in a design repository. Another tool serializes a Message Information Model into a hierarchical message description (HMD) exported into an XML format. Finally, a schema generator, which is part of the HL7 XML ITS (implementable technology specification), generates an XML schema out of the HMD representation.

The Genotype Model

As aforementioned, the family history model utilizes the HL7 genotype model to carry genomic data relevant to the patient's family history. The genotype model is intended to be used as a shared component in any HL7 specification that conveys genomic data. It embeds various types of genomic data relating to a chromosomal locus, including sequence variations, gene expression, and proteomics. Within the Genotype model, we have utilized existing bioinformatics markups that are commonly used by the bioinformatics community (e.g., MAGE-ML for gene expression data or BSML for DNA sequences). Those bioinformatics markups represent the raw genomic data and are encapsulated in HL7 objects. On the other hand, only portions of the raw and mass genomic data are relevant to clinical practice. To that end, we have constrained the full-blown bioinformatics markup schemas and excluded areas that describe pure research data. More importantly, the genotype model also includes specialized HL7 objects (e.g., sequence variation of SNP type) that hold those portions of the raw genomic data that seem to be significant to clinical practice. Those specialized objects have attributes that represent the essential genomic data along with optional annotation. They are populated through a bubbling-up process that dedicated applications carry out. The bubbling-up process should take into account the goals of clinical care, the patient-specific history, and the most current knowledge about relevant clinical-genomic correlations. Once populated, those specialized objects can be associated with clinical phenotypes, represented either internally within the genotype model or elsewhere; for example, as diagnoses and allergies residing in the patient medical records.

Figure 2 shows a bird's eye view of the genotype model, distinguishing between the encapsulating objects vs. bubble-up objects.

Figure 3 illustrates a possible use of the encapsulate and bubble-up paradigm in the case of family history data. The genetic testing lab sends raw genomic data encapsulated in the genotype encapsulating objects (e.g., full sequencing of the BRCA1 gene, expressed with BSML and encapsulated in the sequence object of the genotype model). When this portion of the HL7 message arrives at the EHR system, it gets appended to the patient's family history. We then envision that specialized decision support services will parse the family history and bubble up those SNPs in the raw data that are most clinically significant to the goal of assessing patient risk, resulting in annotation and enrichment of the data to be more useful to clinical practice. Thus, we envision that services will not only enable the exchange of information from one proprietary format to the other but also leverage it to be more effective to the receiving user.

Figure 2. A bird's eye view of the Genotype model (blue callouts point to encapsulating objects while yellow callouts point to bubbled-up objects)

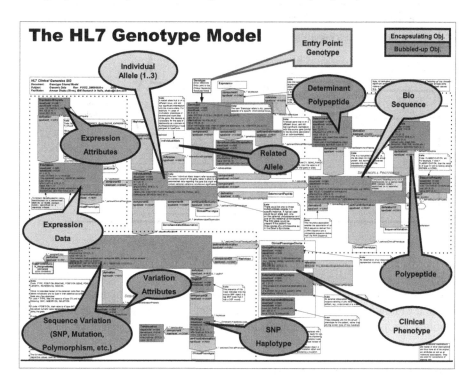

Note that several bubbling-up processes could be performed at the same time (e.g., different algorithms, ontologies, etc.) and in different times (e.g., when new discoveries become available and the same raw data can be interpreted differently). Therefore, it is important not to abstract away the raw genomic data of a specific patient but rather encapsulate it and make it available to any processes that attempt to associate it with clinical data and facilitate a clinical decision at the point of care.

The Clinical Statement Model

The clinical data in the family history model might be represented using a shared model of a clinical statement, which is under development in HL7 by various working groups (e.g., the Structured Documents Committee, the Orders and Observations

Figure 3. Encapsulate and bubble up family history clinical genomics data

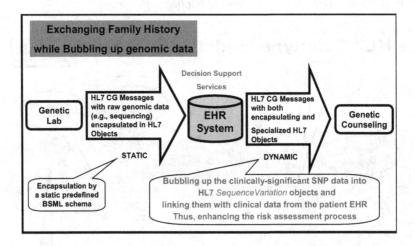

Committee, the Patient Care Committee). The clinical statement model provides the grammar of how various discrete acts (observations, procedures, substance administrations, etc.) are associated to generate a meaningful clinical statement.

The EHR Functional Model

The HL7 EHR functional model (recently approved as a DSTU – Draft Standard for Trial Use) has a family history function stating the information found in Table 3.

It is expected that this draft standard will be mandatory in the near future and that every EHR system will comply with certain profiles derived from this standard. The U.S. government is developing an incentives program (through the CMS, for example) to encourage providers to adopt EHR systems that comply with this standard (conformance metrics are being developed) as well as to encourage EHR vendors to offer their systems in accordance with the standards functions (Dickinson, Fischetti, & Heard, 2003).

The HL7 Health Care Services Standardization Effort

Further to the aforementioned EHR functional model, there is a new effort to define standard services for EHR systems, undertaken jointly by HL7 and OMG. This will

Table 3. Family history function statements in the HL7 EHR functional model

Function Name	Subject-to-Subject Relationship
Function Statement	Capture relationships among patients and others to facilitate appropriate access to their health record on this basis (e.g., parent of a child), if appropriate.
Functional Description	A user may assign the relationship of parent to a person who is their offspring. This relationship may facilitate access to their health record as parent of a young child.
Rationale	Support delivery of effective healthcare; facilitate management of chronic conditions.

lead to the realization of a Semantic Web for health care, as functions defined in the functional model will be available as Web services, either by the enterprise EHR system or by trusted third parties, who will provide Web services for interoperability of EHR systems as well as for decision support and annotation.

In order to move forward in this direction, it is necessary for health care enterprises to implement a service-oriented architecture while establishing service offerings within such architecture. Realization of service-oriented health care interoperability is based on identifying the business functions and behavior being performed by a set of agreed-upon services as well as defining conformance metrics. This work is predicated on the availability of a robust semantic model describing precisely the information payload across organizations (Rubin, 2005).

OWL and the HL7 Templates

The specifications developed thus far in HL7 are general-purpose specs and are not customized or constrained to specific requirements from the various clinical domains and their subspecialties. For example, there is a generic specification of a clinical document, but there is not a standard way of representing a discharge summary. The HL7 Templates SIG's mission is to address this issue of specialization and customization by offering mechanisms for constraining the generic specifications (Elkin & Kernberg, 2005). Template specifications eventually will constitute the majority of the HL7 standards, including specialized domains such as clinical genomics. One candidate formalism for expressing templates is OWL (Heflin, 2004), and once approved as a standard template mechanism (currently under ballot), the HL7 clinical genomics SIG will attempt to represent its specifications using OWL. Using OWL representations will allow designers to better constrain the generic specifications and to elaborate them in order to create a rich set of specialized data constructs in their clinical domain. The current HL7 methodology and tooling do not permit the structured representation of constraints over generic HL7 models. The current practice is to use a constraint box pointing to a class or attribute in the model and to specify the constraint in free text. This is a limited mechanism that will be improved once these balloted models can be constrained using languages such as OWL. In addition, OWL representations will make the HL7 specs a better fit for the Semantic Web.

Implementation

We have implemented the family history model by automatically generating the XML schema from the model and crafting XML samples with actual patients' family history data that validate against that schema. We also added patient-specific BRCA sequences to illustrate the benefits of encapsulating raw genomic data in the context of BRCA risk assessment. We are now working with various stakeholders (owners of family history programs and diagnostic facilities, such as myriad genetics) to make their programs interoperable with the HL7 specification.

As an example, we show here fragments of a family history sample XML instance that represents clinical and genomics data of a patient who has a mother and a father (each has two parents), two sisters, a husband, and a daughter. The full sample is presented in Appendix B.

The XML instance starts with the patient as the root element (see Table 4).

Note that the patient as well as each of her relatives has optional nested ID elements that identify their ID and role; for example, NMTH is an HL7 code that means natural mother.

The fragment in Table 5 describes the daughter of the patient who died of breast cancer. The genomic data appear first, identifying a specific allele of the BRCA2 gene.

The fragment in Table 6 shows an elaboration of that BRCA2 allele by encapsulating sequences from that allele that might consist of personal SNPs beyond those variations that identified this allele. Note that the DNA sequences below are presented for illustration purposes only and are not necessarily accurate.

Finally, the fragment in Table 7 shows a few of the SNPs from the BRCA2 allele, represented with BSML within the encapsulated object (using the isoform element). In contrast, the element derived sequence variation represents an object of the geno-type model that holds the results of the bubbling-up processing, picking on a specific

Table 4. Family history XML sample: The root element fragment

```
<Patient xmlns="urn:hl7-org:v3" xmlns:xsi="http://www.w3.org/2001/XMLSchema-instance"
    xsi:schemaLocation="urn:hl7-org:v3POCG_MT004008.xsd">
    <id extension="555.001-SUBJ"/>
    <id extension="555.002-NMTH"/>
    <id extension="555.003-NFTH"/>
    <!-- PATIENT-->
    <patientPerson>
        <administrativeGenderCode code="F"/>
        <birthTime value="1957"/>
        ...
```

Table 5. Family history XML sample: The daughter fragment

```
<!-- DAUGHTER-->
        <relationshipHolder>
            <id extension="555.011-SUBJ"/>
            <id extension="555.001-NMTH"/>
            <id extension="555.01-NFTH"/>
            <code code="DAU"/>
            <relationshipHolder>
                <deceasedInd value="true"/>
            </relationshipHolder>
        <!-- GENOMIC DATA-->
        <subjectOf>
            <Genotype>
                <component2>
                    <individualAllele>
                        <text>breast cancer 2, early onset</text>
                        <value code="U43746" displayName="BRCA2" codeSystemName
                                                        ="HUGO"/>
            ...
```

Table 6. Family history XML sample: The sequencing fragment

```
<sequence>
    <code code="BSMLcon3"/>
        <value>
            <Definitions>
                <Sequences>
                    <Sequence id="seq1" molecule="dna"
                        ic-acckey="U14680 REGION: 101..199"
                    db-source="GenBank" title="BRCA1, exon 2" representation="raw"
                    local-acckey="this could be used by the genetic lab">
                        <Seq-data>
                            GCTCCCA CTCCATGAGG TATTTCTTCA
                            CATCCGTGTC CCGGCCCGGC CGCGGGGAGC CCCGCTTCAT
                            CGCCGTGGGC TACGTGGACG ACACGCAGTT CGTGCGGTTC
                            GACAGCGACG CCGCGAGCCA GAGGATGGAG CCGCGGGCGC
                            CGTGGATAGA GCAGGAGGGG CCGGAGTATT GGGACCAGGA
                            GACACGGAAT GTGAAGGCCC AGTCACAGAC TGACCGAGTG
                            GACCTGGGGA CCCTGCGCGG CTACTACAAC CAGAGCGAGG
                            CCG
                        </Seq-data>
                    </Sequence>
                    ...
```

Table 7. Family history XML sample: The bubbling-up fragment

```
            <Isoforms>
                <Isoform-set>
                    <Isoform id="SNP123" seqref="seq1" location="9" change="T"/>
                        <Isoform id="SNP456" seqref="seq1" location="32" change="C"/>
                        <Isoform id="SNP789" seqref="seq2" location="124" change="G"/>
                    </Isoform-set>
            </Isoforms>
        </Definitions>
    </value>
    <methodCode code="SBT"/>
    <derivation4>
        <derivedSequenceVariation>
            <code code="DNA"/>
            <text>
                <reference value="#SNP456"/>
            </text>
            <!--MUTATION-->
            <value xsi:type="CE" code="185delAG"/>
            <interpretationCode code="DELETERIOUS"/>
            <pertinentInformation>
                <pertinentClinicalPhenotype>
                    <reference typeCode="SUBJ">
                        <referredToExternalClinicalPhenotype>
                            <id root="2.16.840.1.113883" extension="diagnosis1"/>
                        </referredToExternalClinicalPhenotype>
                    </reference>
                </pertinentClinicalPhenotype>
            </pertinentInformation>
        ...
```

SNP and representing it as a deleterious mutation. The mutation is then associated with clinical phenotypes (clinical observation from the patient medical records).

Note that only the observation id appears in this XML instance, because it is represented by the ISO OID (object identifier) standard, which ensures uniqueness of object identifiers across systems and organizations and thus enables services to resolve the location of an object such as this patient's diagnosis and to get it from where it is being stored.

The value element is the end of the encapsulation portion, because the raw genomic data is encapsulated in the value attribute of the HL7 sequence object. The reference tag allows referencing back to the BSML Isoform element. This referencing mechanism enables the association of bubbled-up objects like the 185delAG mutation with encapsulated data as evidence. On the other hand, the mutation object is associated with clinical information to enable its usability within EHR systems.

Conclusion

The vision of the Semantic Web could play a major role in the current efforts to achieve interoperability of disparate health information systems. In this article, we have focused on the use case of exchanging family history data, which is crucial for breast cancer patients. In particular, elaborated family history with raw genomic data is becoming more important as clinical genomics correlations are now a standard part of modern health care.

While we have focused on breast cancer family history, this model has the generalizability to be utilized to exchange family history information for any hereditary condition. Hereditary conditions (benign or malignant) tend to be defined by the number of relatives with a condition or conditions, the age at which those conditions occur, and the closeness of that relative to the patient (degree of relative). In addition, if genetic testing is undertaken, the genetic mutation is discovered. Our model collects this information in a uniform format.

For example, let us consider a family suspected of having hemochromatosis (Toland, 2000), a benign condition that causes the cells of the body to retain more iron than they need, which can lead to diabetes, heart disease, liver disease, and arthritis. The important information would be the presence of liver disease, diabetes, and so forth in various relatives, the age of onset of these conditions in each relative, the bloodline and the ability to show the relative in a pedigree, and whether genetic testing was done, which test was done, what the actual result was, and what the interpretation is. All these data items have placeholders in the HL7 model described in this article.

As a more abstract conception, in thinking about other indicators of hereditary conditions, we can conceive of a condition where the genetic test is not available or was not performed, but a laboratory test might give useful information. In our model, laboratory test results can be transmitted for each individual and can be displayed on a pedigree or run through a model. Some conditions may require the interaction of multiple genes, and our model allows the representation of multiple genetic test results for each relative.

Whatever condition is suspected or whatever data is collected, our model allows the transmission of this data from clinician to clinician as a message and, in addition, allows this information to be used to draw pedigrees and to run computer models of risk.

The importance of drawing a pedigree should not be underestimated. A pedigree is a graphical display of the family history information that allows the clinician to visualize the diseases and the relationships, and thus to be able to interpret the data better. In addition, the data is in a format that can be imported easily into computer models of risk in order to provide quantitative analyses of the likelihood of the condition for various family members.

Our HL7 model allows the transmission of all pertinent information for any hereditary condition of which we currently can conceive and has the flexibility to be extended to future, more complex genetic conditions.

We envision the use of services based on health standards over the Web that various family history specialized applications will be able to use to seamlessly exchange family history data. These services will be part of the entire set of health services being defined by major standardization bodies such as HL7 and OMG. In the development of the family history model, we used the HL7 development methodology and the HL7 dedicated tooling. We thus defined the semantics of the payload of family history services, and as the aforementioned health services technical framework becomes available, our family history model could be utilized by those services as the domain-specific ontology.

Acknowledgment

The work described in this article has been carried out partly within the HL7 Clinical Genomics Special Interest Group, and the authors wish to thank its members for their contributions and reviews of the family history specification.

References

Berners-Lee, T., Hendler, J., & Lassila, O. (2001, May). The Semantic Web. *Scientific American.*

Bray, T., Paoli, J., Sperberg-McQueen, C., Maler, E., & Yergeau, F. (2004, February). *Extensible markup language (XML) 1.0* (3rd ed., W3C Recommendation).

CAGENE (CancerGene). (2005). Retrieved April 1, 2005, from The University of Texas Southwestern Medical Center at Dallas at http://www3.utsouthwestern.edu/cancergene/cancergene.htm

CG. (2005). Clinical genomics domain. V3 ballot package. Retrieved April 1, 2005, from http://www.hl7.org

Dickinson, G., Fischetti, L., & Heard, S. (2003). *Functional model and standard, draft standard for trial use, Release 1.0.* Retrieved April 1, 2005, from http://www.hl7.org

Elkin, P. L., & Kernberg, M. (2005). *HL7 standard V3 template architecture 3.3.* Retrieved April 1, 2005, from http://www.hl7.org

HDF. (2005). *HL7 development framework.* Retrieved April 1, 2005, from http://www.hl7.org

HealthConnect: A Health Information Network for all Australians. (n.d.). Retrieved July 2, 2005, from http://www.healthconnect.gov.au/index.htm

Heflin, J. (2004). *OWL Web ontology language use cases and requirements* (W3C Recommendation). Retrieved April 1, 2005, from http://www.w3.org/TR/webont-req/

HL7. (2005). *What is HL7?* Retrieved April 1, 2005, from http://www.hl7.org

InfoWay: Canada interoperable electronic health record (EHR) solutions and related telehealth development. (n.d.). Retrieved July 2, 2005, from http://www.infoway-inforoute.ca/home.php?lang=en

NICTIZ: National IT Institute for Health Care in the Netherlands. (n.d.). Retrieved July 2, 2005, from http://www.nictiz.nl

ONCHIT. (2004, July 21). *The decade of health information technology: Delivering consumer-centric and information-rich health care.* Framework for strategic action. Washington, DC: Department of Health & Human Services. Retrieved July 2, 2005, from http://www.hhs.gov/

Porrasmaa, J. (2004, October). *HL7 and common services in health information systems: Finnish experiences.* Paper presented at the 5th HL7 International Affiliates Meeting and 2nd International Conference on the Clinical Document Architecture, Acapulco, Mexico.

Progeny: A unique pedigree software (genogram) program. (2005). Retrieved April 1, 2005, from http://www.progeny2000.com/

Radhakrishnan, R., & Wookey, M. (2005). *Model driven architecture enabling service oriented architectures.* Retrieved April 1, 2005, from http://www.omg.org

RIM. (2005). *Reference information model. Foundations V3 ballot package.* Retrieved April 1, 2005, from http://www.hl7.org

Rubin, K. (2005). *Health care services specification (HSS) project: The impetus for collaboration between HL7 and OMG.* Retrieved April 1, 2005, from http://www.hl7.org

Thull, D. L., & Vogel, V. G. (2004). Recognition and management of hereditary breast cancer syndromes. *The Oncologist, 9*(1), 13-24.

Toland, E. A. (2000). *Hereditary hemochromatosis: Is genetic testing available?* Retrieved July 2, 2005, from http://www.genetichealth.com/HCROM_Genetic_Testing_for_ Hemochromatosis.shtml

Williams, R., Bunduchi, R., Gerst, M., Graham, I., Pollock, N., Procter, R, et al. (2004, August). *Understanding the evolution of standards: Alignment and reconfiguration in standards development and implementation arenas.* Paper presented at the 4SEASST Conference, Paris.

Yoon, P. W., et al. (2002). Can family history be used as a tool for public health and preventive medicine? *Genetics in Medicine 2002, 4*(4), 304-310. Retrieved April 1, 2005, from http://www.cdc.gov/genomics/info/reports/research/famhist_yoon.htm

Appendix A

Outlining Family History Data of a Breast Cancer Patient

Patient ID				
	Relative type (Self)			
	Cancer			
		Year diagnosed		
		Age diagnosed		
	Genetic syndrome suspected			
		Genetic test done		
			Genetic test result specific	
			Genetic test result interpretation	
	Mother ID number			
	Father ID number			
	Relative ID number			
		Relative type (Brother, sister…)		
		Cancer		
			Year diagnosed	
			Age diagnosed	
		Genetic syndrome suspected		
			Genetic test done	
				Genetic test result specific
				Genetic test result interpretation
		Mother ID number		
		Father ID number		
	Relative ID number			
		Relative type (Brother, sister…)		
		Cancer		
			Year diagnosed	
			Age diagnosed	
		Genetic syndrome suspected		
			Genetic test done	
				Genetic test result specific
				Genetic test result interpretation
		Mother ID number		
		Father ID number		

Appendix B

The Family History XML Sample

```
<?xml version="1.0" encoding="UTF-8"?>
<!--Sample of Family History model showing a flat version of a patient's pedigree as well as the ability to represent clinical and
genomic data of the patient and any of his or her relatives. The pedigree represented in this sample file is as follows:
Patient has a mother and a father (each has two parents), two sisters, a husband, and a daughter.

This file is valid against the schema that was generated using the HL7 Schema Generator with the input of the HMD resulting from
the Visio model with the Genotype model plugged in as a CMET, which, in turn, includes the BSML and MAGE-ML constrained
schemas for the raw genomic data.

For comments, please e-mail Amnon Shabo (Shvo) at shabo@il.ibm.com (IBM Research Lab in Haifa).
-->
<Patient xmlns="urn:hl7-org:v3" xmlns:xsi="http://www.w3.org/2001/XMLSchema-instance" xsi:schemaLocation="urn:hl7-org:v3
POCG_MT004008.xsd">
    <id extension="555.001-SUBJ"/>
    <id extension="555.002-NMTH"/>
    <id extension="555.003-NFTH"/>
    <!-- PATIENT-->
    <patientPerson>
        <administrativeGenderCode code="F"/>
        <birthTime value="1957"/>
        <!-- MOTHER-->
        <relationshipHolder>
            <id extension="555.002-SUBJ"/>
            <id extension="555.004-NMTH"/>
            <id extension="555.005-NFTH"/>
            <code code="NMTH"/>
            <relationshipHolder>
                <!-- The value 'true' means that this person is dead. Default value is 'false'-->
                <deceasedInd value="true"/>
            </relationshipHolder>
            <subjectOf>
                <clinicalGenomicChoiceClinicalObservation>
                    <!-- Ovarian Cancer observation of the patient's mother-->
                    <code code="V1043" codeSystemName="ICD" displayName="HX OF OVARIAN MALIGNANCY"/>
                    <!-- The following construct represents the estimated age at which the above diagnosis was made
                    (40)-->
                    <subject>
                        <estimatedAge>
                            <value value="40"/>
                        </estimatedAge>
                    </subject>
                </clinicalGenomicChoiceClinicalObservation>
            </subjectOf>
            <!-- The following construct represents the estimated deceased age (72)-->
            <subjectOf>
                <clinicalGenomicChoiceEstimatedDeceasedAge>
                    <value value="72"/>
                </clinicalGenomicChoiceEstimatedDeceasedAge>
            </subjectOf>
        </relationshipHolder>
        <!-- end of MOTHER data-->
        <!-- FATHER-->
        <relationshipHolder>
            <id extension="555.003-SUBJ"/>
            <id extension="555.006-NMTH"/>
            <id extension="555.007-NFTH"/>
            <code code="NFTH"/>
            <!-- The following construct represents the estimated age (75)
            Note that the code element will be fixed in the schema to the LOINC code below,
            so there is no need to send it in each instance, and it appears here for illustration purposes.-->
            <subjectOf>
                <clinicalGenomicChoiceEstimatedAge>
                    <code code="21611-9" displayName="ESTIMATED AGE" codeSystemName="LOINC"/>
                    <value value="75"/>
                </clinicalGenomicChoiceEstimatedAge>
            </subjectOf>
        </relationshipHolder>
        <!-- end of FATHER data-->
```

```
<relationshipHolder>
    <!-- MATERNAL GRANDFATHER -->
    <id extension="555.004-SUBJ"/>
    <code code="GRFTH"/>
    <subjectOf>
        <clinicalGenomicChoiceEstimatedAge>
            <value value="98"/>
        </clinicalGenomicChoiceEstimatedAge>
    </subjectOf>
</relationshipHolder>
<!-- end of maternal grandfather data-->
<relationshipHolder>
    <!-- MATERNAL GRANDMOTHER -->
    <id extension="555.005-SUBJ"/>
    <code code="GRMTH"/>
    <subjectOf>
        <clinicalGenomicChoiceEstimatedAge>
            <value value="67"/>
        </clinicalGenomicChoiceEstimatedAge>
    </subjectOf>
</relationshipHolder>
<!-- end of maternal grandmother data-->
<relationshipHolder>
    <!-- PATERNAL GRANDFATHER -->
    <id extension="555.006-SUBJ"/>
    <code code="GRFTH"/>
    <subjectOf>
        <clinicalGenomicChoiceEstimatedAge>
            <value value="78"/>
        </clinicalGenomicChoiceEstimatedAge>
    </subjectOf>
</relationshipHolder>
<!-- end of paternal grandfather data-->
<relationshipHolder>
    <!-- PATERNAL GRANDMOTHER -->
    <id extension="555.007-SUBJ"/>
    <code code="GRMTH"/>
    <subjectOf>
        <clinicalGenomicChoiceEstimatedAge>
            <value value="87"/>
        </clinicalGenomicChoiceEstimatedAge>
    </subjectOf>
</relationshipHolder>
<!-- end of paternal grandmother data-->
<!-- SISTER-->
<relationshipHolder>
    <id extension="555.008-SUBJ"/>
    <id extension="555.002-NMTH"/>
    <id extension="555.003-NFTH"/>
    <code code="SIS"/>
    <relationshipHolder>
        <deceasedInd value="true"/>
    </relationshipHolder>
    <subjectOf>
        <clinicalGenomicChoiceClinicalObservation>
            <!-- Ovarian Cancer observation of the patient's sister-->
            <code code="V1043" codeSystemName="ICD" displayName="HX OF OVARIAN MALIGNANCY"/>
            <subject>
                <estimatedAge>
                    <value value="60"/>
                </estimatedAge>
            </subject>
        </clinicalGenomicChoiceClinicalObservation>
    </subjectOf>
    <subjectOf>
        <clinicalGenomicChoiceEstimatedDeceasedAge>
            <value value="67"/>
        </clinicalGenomicChoiceEstimatedDeceasedAge>
    </subjectOf>
</relationshipHolder>
<!-- end of first SISTER data-->
```

```
<!-- SISTER-->
<relationshipHolder>
    <id extension="555.009-SUBJ"/>
    <id extension="555.002-NMTH"/>
    <id extension="555.003-NFTH"/>
    <code code="SIS"/>
    <relationshipHolder>
        <deceasedInd value="true"/>
    </relationshipHolder>
    <subjectOf>
        <clinicalGenomicChoiceClinicalObservation>
            <!-- Ovarian Cancer observation of the patient's sister-->
            <code code="V1043" codeSystemName="ICD" displayName="HX OF OVARIAN MALIGNANCY"/>
            <subject>
                <estimatedAge>
                    <value value="50"/>
                </estimatedAge>
            </subject>
        </clinicalGenomicChoiceClinicalObservation>
    </subjectOf>
    <subjectOf>
        <clinicalGenomicChoiceEstimatedDeceasedAge>
            <value value="55"/>
        </clinicalGenomicChoiceEstimatedDeceasedAge>
    </subjectOf>
</relationshipHolder>
<!-- end of second SISTER data-->
<!-- HUSBAND-->
<relationshipHolder>
    <id extension="555.01-SUBJ"/>
    <code code="HUSB"/>
    <subjectOf>
        <clinicalGenomicChoiceEstimatedAge>
            <value value="57"/>
        </clinicalGenomicChoiceEstimatedAge>
    </subjectOf>
</relationshipHolder>
<!-- end of HUSBAND data-->
<!-- DAUGHTER-->
<relationshipHolder>
    <id extension="555.011-SUBJ"/>
    <id extension="555.001-NMTH"/>
    <id extension="555.01-NFTH"/>
    <code code="DAU"/>
    <relationshipHolder>
        <deceasedInd value="true"/>
    </relationshipHolder>
    <!-- GENOMIC DATA-->
    <subjectOf>
        <Genotype>
            <component2>
                <individualAllele>
                    <text>breast cancer 2, early onset</text>
                    <value code="U43746" displayName="BRCA2" codeSystemName="HUGO"/>
                    <component1>
                        <sequence>
                            <!-- full sequence of the daughter's BRCA2 gene goes here so that applications
                            could look for more information such as SNPs that are not recognized as mutations.
                            (note that the actual sequences below are not accurate and are presented for
                            illustration purposes only) -->
                            <code code="BSMLcon3"/>
                            <value>
                                <Definitions>
                                    <Sequences>
                                        <Sequence id="seq1" molecule="dna" ic-acckey="U14680 REGION:
                                            101..199" db-source="GenBank" title="BRCA1, exon 2"
                                            representation="raw" local-acckey="this could be used by the
                                            genetic lab">
                                            <Seq-data>
```

```
                              GCTCCCA CTCCATGAGG TATTTCTTCA
                              CATCCGTGTC CCGGCCCGGC CGCGGGGAGC
                              CCCGCTTCAT CGCCGTGGGC
                              TACGTGGACG ACACGCAGTT CGTGCGGTTC
                              GACAGCGACG CCGCGAGCCA
                              GAGGATGGAG CCGCGGGCGC CGTGGATAGA
                              GCAGGAGGGG CCGGAGTATT
                              GGGACCAGGA GACACGGAAT GTGAAGGCCC
                              AGTCACAGAC TGACCGAGTG
                              GACCTGGGGA CCCTGCGCGG CTACTACAAC
                              CAGAGCGAGG CCG
                         </Seq-data>
                    </Sequence>
                    <Sequence id="seq2" molecule="dna" ic-acckey="U14680 REGION:
                         200..253" db-source="GenBank" title="BRCA1, exon 3"
                         representation="raw" local-acckey="this could be used by the
                         genetic lab">
                         <Seq-data>
                              GTTCTCA
                              CACCATCCAG ATAATGTATG GCTGCGACGT
                              GGGGTCGGAC GGGCGCTTCC
                              TCCGCGGGTA CCGGCAGGAC GCCTACGACG
                              GCAAGGATTA CATCGCCCTG
                              AACGAGGACC TGCGCTCTTG GACCGCGGCG
                              GACATGGCGG CTCAGATCAC
                              CAAGCGCAAG TGGGAGGCGG CCCATGTGGC
                              GGAGCAGCAG AGAGCCTACC
                              TGGATGGCAC GTGCGTGGAG TGGCTCCGCA
                              GATACCTGGA GAACGGGAAG
                              GAGACGCTGC AGCGCACGG
                         </Seq-data>
                    </Sequence>
               </Sequences>
               <Isoforms>
                    <Isoform-set>
                         <!--The isoform tag in BSML can be used to represent an SNP.
                         The 'seqref' attribute is used to refer to the sequence where the
                         SNP occurs.
                         (Note that the SNPs are not based on real data but rather were made
                         up for illustration purposes only)-->
                         <Isoform id="SNP123" seqref="seq1" location="9" change="T"/>
                         <Isoform id="SNP456" seqref="seq1" location="32" change="C"/>
                         <Isoform id="SNP789" seqref="seq2" location="124"
                                                            change="G"/>
                    </Isoform-set>
               </Isoforms>
          </Definitions>
     </value>
     <!-- The following attribute belongs to the HL7 Sequence class and represents the
          sequencing method.
          Its vocabulary has not been nailed down yet, and several options are suggested
          in the Genotype documentation.-->
     <methodCode code="SBT"/>
     <derivation4>
          <derivedSequenceVariation>
               <code code="DNA"/>
               <text>
                    <!-- The HL7 'text' attribute is of ED data type and this data type has a
                         reference tag that allows the
                         pointing to the BSML Isoform element.
                         This referencing enables the linking between the bubbled-up
                         object like this sequence variation one,
                         to the encapsulated data in the Sequence class.-->
                    <reference value="#SNP456"/>
               </text>
               <value xsi:type="CE" code="185delAG"/>
               <!-- The interpretationCode value should be drawn from the
                    ObservationInterpretation vocabulary that doesn't have the
                    DELETERIOUS value (abnormal is the closest)
               but has been proposed to RIM Harmonization in November 2004 and was
               accepted in principle.-->
               <interpretationCode code="DELETERIOUS"/>
```

```
<pertinentInformation>
    <pertinentClinicalPhenotype>
        <!-- The use of the ID attribute populated with an OID value could
        facilitate the access to the location where the actual instance of
        the referred diagnosis resides (e.g., in the patient medical
        records)-->
        <reference typeCode="SUBJ">
            <referredToExternalClinicalPhenotype>
                <id root="2.16.840.1.113883" extension="diagnosis1"/>
            </referredToExternalClinicalPhenotype>
        </reference>
    </pertinentClinicalPhenotype>
</pertinentInformation>
<derivation>
    <derivedSequenceVariationProperty>
        <code code="TYPE"/>
        <value xsi:type="CV" code="MUTATION"/>
    </derivedSequenceVariationProperty>
</derivation>
                            </derivedSequenceVariation>
                        </derivation4>
                    </sequence>
                </component1>
            </individualAllele>
        </component2>
    </Genotype>
</subjectOf>
<!-- CLINICAL DATA-->
<subjectOf>
    <clinicalGenomicChoiceClinicalObservation>
        <!-- Ovarian Cancer observation of the patient's daughter-->
        <code code="V1043" codeSystemName="ICD" displayName="HX OF OVARIAN MALIGNANCY"/>
        <subject>
            <estimatedAge>
                <value value="30"/>
            </estimatedAge>
        </subject>
    </clinicalGenomicChoiceClinicalObservation>
</subjectOf>
<subjectOf>
    <clinicalGenomicChoiceEstimatedDeceasedAge>
        <value value="33"/>
    </clinicalGenomicChoiceEstimatedDeceasedAge>
</subjectOf>
        </relationshipHolder>
        <!-- end of DAUGHTER data-->
    </patientPerson>
    <!-- end of PATIENT data-->
</Patient>
```

This chapter was previously published in the International Journal on Semantic Web & Information Systems, 1(4), 44-67, October-December, 2005.

Chapter XII

Archetype-Based Semantic Interoperability of Web Service Messages in the Health Care Domain

Veli Bicer, Middle East Technical University (METU), Turkey

Ozgur Kilic, Middle East Technical University (METU), Turkey

Asuman Dogac, Middle East Technical University (METU), Turkey

Gokce B. Laleci, Middle East Technical University (METU), Turkey

Abstract

In this chapter, we describe an infrastructure enabling archetype-based semantic interoperability of Web service messages exchanged in the health care domain. We annotate the Web service messages with the OWL representation of the archetypes. Then, by providing the ontology mapping between the archetypes, we show that the interoperability of the Web service message instances can be achieved automatically. An OWL mapping tool, called OWLmt, has been developed for this purpose. OWLmt uses OWL-QL engine, which enables the mapping tool to reason over the source archetype instances while generating the target archetype instances according to the mapping patterns defined through a GUI.

Introduction

Health care is one of the few domains where sharing information is the norm rather than the exception (Heard, Beale, Mori, & Pishec, 2003). On the other hand, today there is no universally accepted standard for the digital representation of clinical data. There is a multitude of medical information systems storing clinical information in all kinds of proprietary formats.

We address this interoperability problem within the scope of the ARTEMIS project by wrapping and exposing the existing health care applications as Web services. However, given the complexity of the clinical domain, the Web service messages exchanged have numerous segments of different types and optionality. To make any use of these messages at the receiving end, their semantics must be clearly defined.

In a previous effort described in Dogac et al. (in press), we annotated Web services through the reference information models of electronic healthcare record (EHR) standards. EHR standards define the interfaces for clinical content exchange. The prominent EHR standards include openEHR (openEHR Community, 2005), HL7 CDA (HL7 Clinical Document Architecture, 2004), and CEN TC/251 prEN 13606-1 (referred to as EHRcom) (CEN TC/251 prEN 13606-1, 2004). Although such an approach allowed us to achieve a certain degree of interoperability, there were further problems to be addressed as follows:

- The reference information models of EHRs contain generic classes rather than having a class for each specialized clinical concept. Therefore, given a class in source ontology, the corresponding class in the target ontology is not clear unless the context is known. For example, an instance of an ENTRY class in EHRcom corresponds to one of the instances of ACT or ORGANIZER or OBSERVATION or PROCEDURE classes in HL7 CDA.

- Another problem in mapping reference information models one into another is as follows: different reference information models structure their classes differently. As an example, both CEN EHRcom and HL7 CDA have a class name called SECTION, and sections can have nested sections. When the sections of a clinical document are organized differently, then generating the same hierarchy for the target domain as in the source domain would not be correct.

In this chapter, we address these problems by using archetypes to complement the work described in Dogac et al. (in press). An archetype is a reusable, formal expression of a distinct, domain-level concept such as blood pressure, physical examination, or laboratory result, expressed in the form of constraints on data whose instances conform to some reference information model (Beale & Heard, 2003). The reference information model can be CEN EHRcom (CEN TC/251 prEN 13606-1, 2004), openEHR (openEHR Architecture Specifications, 2005), or the HL7 CDA schema (HL7 Clinical Document Architecture, 2004).

We use the Web ontology language (OWL) (OWL, 2004) representation of the archetypes to semantically annotate the Web service messages. We then provide the mapping between the OWL representations of archetypes through an OWL ontology mapping tool called OWLmt (OWLmt, 2005). The mapping definition produced by OWLmt is used by OWLmt engine to automatically transform the Web service message instances one into other when two health care institutes conforming to different archetypes want to exchange messages.

Related Work

Semantic heterogeneity occurs when there is a disagreement about the meaning, interpretation, or intended use of the same or related data (Sheth & Larsen, 1990). Since medical information systems today store clinical information about patients in all kinds of proprietary formats, there is a need to address the interoperability problem. For this purpose, several EHR standards that allow the structure of clinical content for the purpose of exchange are currently under development. A very detailed survey and analysis of electronic health care records is presented in Eichelberg, Aden, Dogac, and Laleci (2005).

However, since there are more than one electronic health care record standards, the semantic heterogeneity problem is still unavoidable among health care systems. HL7 and openEHR offer different reference information models for the health care domain. For example, an instance of an ENTRY class in openEHR corresponds to one of the instances of ACT, ORGANIZER, OBSERVATION, or PROCEDURE classes in HL7 CDA.

Two approaches are described in Kashyap and Sheth (1996) for providing interoperability based on ontologies. One is to build a common ontology; the other is reusing existing ontologies and combining them. Instead of building a common ontology, we resolve the semantic heterogeneity among health care standards by reusing existing ontologies and combining them through ontology mapping, which allows the exchange of information among health care information systems conforming to different standards.

Archetypes and Representing
Archetypes in OWL

Archetypes are constraint-based models of domain entities, and each archetype describes configurations of data instances whose classes conform to a reference information model. Having a small but generic reference information model helps the EHR system to handle many different medical concepts. Yet, the small number of generic concepts in the reference information model is not enough to describe the semantics of the domain-specific concepts, which are described through archetypes.

An archetype is composed of three parts: header section, definition section, and ontology section. The header section contains a unique identifier for the archetype, a code identifying the clinical concept defined by the archetype. The header section also includes some descriptive information such as author, version, and status. The definition section contains the restrictions in a tree-like structure created from the reference information model. This structure constrains the cardinality and content of the information model instances complying with the archetype. Codes representing the meanings of nodes and constraints on text or terms, bindings to terminologies such as SNOMED (SNOMED Clinical Terms, 2005) or LOINC (LOINC, 2005), are stated in the ontology section of an archetype. A formal language for expressing archetypes (i.e., archetype definition language [ADL]) is described in ADL (2003).

As already mentioned, ADL specializes the classes of the generic information model by constraining their attributes. The applicable constraints are as follows (ADL, 2003):

- Constraints on the range of data-valued properties.

- Constraints on the range of object-valued properties.

- Constraints on the existence of a property, indicating whether the property is optional or mandatory.

- Constraints on the cardinality of a property, indicating whether the property refers to a container type, the number of member items it must have, and their optionality, and whether it has a list or a set structure.

- Constraints on a property with occurrences, indicating how many times in runtime data an instance of a given class conforming to a particular constraint can occur. It only has significance for objects, which are children of a container property.

It is also possible to reuse previously defined archetypes and archetype fragments. There are two constructs for this purpose: The first one is the use node construct, which is used to reference an archetype fragment by a path expression. The use node references an archetype fragment within the archetype. The second one is the allow archetype construct, which is used to reference other archetypes by defining criteria for allowable archetypes. As an example to an archetype definition in ADL, a part of Complete Blood Count archetype definition is presented in Figure 1. The complete ADL definition can be found in Complete Blood Count Archetype ADL Definition (2005). Here, the Observation class from the reference information model is restricted to create Complete Blood Count archetype by restricting its CODED TEXT value to ac0001 term (ac0001 term is defined as complete blood count in the constraint definitions part of the ADL and declared to be equivalent to Loinc::700-0 term in the term bindings part) and by defining its content to be a list of Haemoglobin, Haematocrit, and Platelet Count test result elements.

In ARTEMIS architecture, OWL representations of the archetypes are exploited. OWL describes the structure of a domain in terms of classes and properties. Classes can be names (URIs) or expressions. The following set of constructors is provided for building class expressions: owl:intersectionOf, owl:unionOf, owl:complementOf, owl:oneOf, owl:allValuesFrom, owl:someValuesFrom, owl:hasValue.

In OWL, properties can have multiple domains and multiple ranges. Multiple domain (range) expressions restrict the domain (range) of a property to the intersection of the class expressions.

Another aspect of the language is the axioms supported. These axioms make it possible to assert subsumption or equivalence with respect to classes or properties (Baader, Horrocks, & Sattler, 2004). The following are the set of OWL axioms: rdfs:subClassOf, owl:sameClassAs, rdfs:subPropertyOf, owl:samePropertyAs, owl:disjointWith, owl:sameIndividualAs, owl:differentIndividualFrom, owl:inverseOf, owl:transitiveProperty, owl:functional Property, owl:inverse FunctionalProperty.

In HL7 Template and Archetype Architecture Version 3.0. (2003) and openEHR Community (2005), the OWL representations of reference information models of archetypes are given. The first step in representing archetypes in OWL is to construct the reference information model of the domain in OWL. A simple algorithm for mapping object model to OWL is given in HL7 Template and Archetype Architecture Version 3.0. (2003). First, each class in the reference information model is represented as an OWL class. Second, each relationship is represented as an ObjectProperty, and each data-valued property is represented as DatatypeProperty in OWL. Finally, cardinalities of relationships and properties are represented by cardinality restrictions in OWL. The next step is representing archetypes in OWL, based on the reference information model as described in ADL (2003) and HL7 Template and Archetype Architecture Version 3.0. (2003). As stated in HL7 Template and Archetype Architecture Version 3.0. (2003), each ADL object node generates

Figure 1. The ADL definition of complete blood count archetype

```
OBSERVATION[at1000.1] matches {-- complete blood picture
  name matches {
        CODED_TEXT matches {
                code matches {[ac0001]} -- complete blood count}}
  data matches {
        LIST_S[at1001] matches {-- battery
                items cardinality matches {0..*} \epsilon {
                ELEMENT[at1002.1] matches {-- haemaglobin
                        name matches {
                                CODED_TEXT matches {
                                        code matches {[ac0003]} -- haemaglobin}}
                        value matches {
                                QUANTITY matches {
                                        value matches {0..1000}
                                        units matches {^g/l|g/dl|.+^}}}}
                ELEMENT[at1002.2] occurrences matches {0..1} matches
        {-- haematocrit
                name matches {
                        CODED_TEXT matches {
                                code matches {[ac0004]}-- haematocrit}}
                        value matches {
                        QUANTITY matches {
                                value matches {0..100}
                                units matches {"%"}}}}
                ELEMENT[at1002.3] occurrences matches {0..1} matches
        {-- platelet count
                name matches {
                        CODED_TEXT matches {
                                code matches {[ac0005]} -- platelet count}}
                                value matches {
                        QUANTITY matches {
                                value matches {0..100000}
                                units matches {"/cm^3"}
                        }}}}}}}
```

an OWL class declaration. Object-valued properties are restricted through these OWL classes.

ARTEMIS Semantic Infrastructure

The aim of the ARTEMIS project (ARTEMIS Consortium, 2004) is to allow health care organizations to keep their proprietary systems and yet expose the functionality of their applications through Web services. ARTEMIS has a peer-to-peer infrastructure to facilitate the semantic discovery of Web services and service registries (Dogac et al., in press).

The full sharability of data and information requires two levels of interoperability:

- The functional (syntactic) interoperability, which is the ability of two or more systems to exchange information. This involves agreeing on the common network protocols, such as Internet or value added networks; the transport binding such as HTTP, FTP, or SMTP and the message format like ASCII text, XML (extensible markup language) or EDI (electronic data interchange). Web services provide functional interoperability through well-accepted standards like SOAP (2003) and WSDL (2005). However, note that in order to access and consume Web services through programs, you must know their operational and message semantics in advance.
- Semantic interoperability is the ability for information shared by systems to be understood at the level of formally defined domain concepts so that the information is computer processable by the receiving system. In other words, semantic interoperability requires the semantics of data to be defined through formally defined domain-specific concepts in standard ontology languages (ISO TC/215, 2003).

To provide semantic interoperability in ARTEMIS, the Web services are annotated with the following semantics:

- **Operational semantics of Web services:** In order to facilitate the discovery of the Web services, there is a need for semantics to describe what the service does; in other words, what the service functionality semantics is in the domain. For example, in the health care domain, when a user is looking for a service to admit a patient to a hospital, the user should be able to locate such a service through its meaning, independent of what the service is called and in which language it is in. Note that WSDL (2005) does not provide this information.

In ARTEMIS, HL7 categorization of health care events are used to annotate Web service functionality, since HL7 exposes the business logic in the health care domain. If further ontologies are developed for this purpose, they easily can be accommodated in the ARTEMIS architecture through ontology mapping.

- **Message semantics of Web services:** When invoking a Web service, there is also a need to know the meaning associated with the messages or documents exchanged through the Web service. In other words, service functionality semantics may suffice only when all the Web services use the same message

Figure 2. Artemis semantic architecture

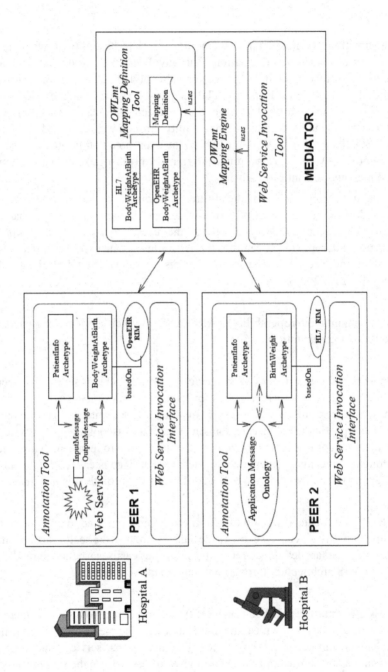

standards. For example, a GetClinicalInformation Web service may include the messages to pass information on diagnosis, allergies, encounters, and observation results about a patient. Unless both the sending and the receiving ends of the message conform to the same EHR standard, interoperability cannot be achieved.

ARTEMIS proposes to semantically enrich the Web service messages through archetypes. As depicted in Figure 2, through an annotation tool provided by the ARTEMIS infrastructure, the health care institutes can annotate the input and output messages of their Web services with archetypes. For example, Hospital A in Figure 2 declares that its Web service accepts a PatientInfo Archetype Instance based on OpenEHR RIM as an input and returns a BodyWeightAtBirth Archetype Instance based on OpenEHR RIM as an output. Note that the consumer application of the Web service may be compliant with another standard. ARTEMIS enables the service consumers to speak their own language. For this purpose, the annotation tool enables the health care institutes to define their application message schemas in terms of archetypes. For example, Hospital B in Figure 2 declares that its messaging structure will provide and accept PatientInfo and BirthWeight information as archetype instances based on HL7 RIM while invoking the Web services provided in the ARTEMIS network.

In the ARTEMIS architecture, the OWL representations of archetype definitions and instances are used. To interoperate the archetype instances based on different EHR standards, the ARTEMIS mediator provides an OWL mapping tool called OWLmt. Through a graphical interface, OWLmt tool enables the user to define the mappings between archetype definitions, and the resulting mapping definitions are stored at the mediator. When a health care institute wants to join the ARTEMIS network, they advertise their Web services to the mediator by semantically annotating them through archetypes. When one of the health care institutes wishes to invoke a Web service provided by another institute in the ARTEMIS Network, the Web service invocation request is delivered to the mediator. The health care institute provides the Web service input to the mediator in terms of the archetype instances it conforms. Then the mediator invocation tool consults the OWLmt Mapping Engine to transform the archetype instances from one EHR reference information model standard to another, using the mapping definitions that previously have been generated through the OWLmt Mapping Definition Tool. Finally, the Web service is invoked with the archetype instance to which the provider conforms. The output of the Web service is processed in the same manner and presented to the requester as an archetype instance based on the EHR standard to which the requester conforms. In the following sections, the details of this process are elaborated through examples.

Archetype-Based Interoperability
of Web Service Messages

Since there is more than one EHR standard such as openEHR (openEHR Community, 2005), HL7 CDA (HL7 Clinical Document Architecture, 2004), and CEN EN
13606 EHRcom (CEN TC/251 prEN 13606-1, 2004), each with different reference
information models and archetypes, annotating Web service messages with archetypes does not solve the interoperability problem.

Therefore, we need to transform archetypes of one standard into another through
ontology mapping. For this purpose, we use the OWL representation of both the
involved reference information models and the archetypes. Then, through an OWL
ontology mapping tool that we developed, called OWLmt, we map the reference
information models and the archetype schemas one into other. Once such a mapping
is achieved, OWLmt automatically transforms a Web service message annotated
with an archetype in one standard into another.

In this section, we explain this process through a running example. For this purpose,
we first generate the OWL descriptions of an archetype based on openEHR and
another one based on HL7. We then present the OWL mapping tool and depict its
functionality through the running example.

Example OpenEHR and HL7 Archetypes in OWL

Figure 3 depicts an archetype in ADL that represents the body weight at birth concept. This concept is described by restricting the OBSERVATION class in openEHR
Reference Model.

The OWL representation of the archetype in Figure 3 is presented in openEHR Body
Weight at Birth Archetype OWL Definition (2005). In brief, each restriction on an
object-valued property introduces a new class, which is a subclass of the class on
which the restriction is defined in the ADL document. For the example, in Figure 3,
the data property of the OBSERVATION class is defined as having a type HISTORY,
which is further restricted. In OWL, this restriction on history class is handled by
introducing a subclass of history called body weight at birth history. On the other
hand, each restriction on a data-valued property either introduces a user-derived
datatype for further restricting datatype of the property or produces owl:hasValue
or owl:oneOf restrictions on the property for restricting the value of the property
to one value or set of values, respectively. Note that user-derived datatypes can be
represented in XML schema and referenced from the OWL representation of the
archetype.

Figure 3. An example body weight at birth OpenEHR archetype in ADL

```
archetype
        openEHR-EHR-OBSERVATION.weight-birth.v1
specialize
        openEHR-EHR-OBSERVATION.weight.v1
concept
        [at0000.1] -- Body weight at birth
description
...
definition
  OBSERVATION[at0000.1] matches { -- Body weight at birth
    data matches {
      HISTORY[at0002] matches { -- history
        events cardinality matches {1..1; ordered} matches {
          EVENT[at0003] matches { -- Birth
            data matches {
              Simple[at0001] matches { -- Birth simple
                item matches {
                  ELEMENT[at0004.1] matches { -- Birth weight
                    value matches {
                      C_QUANTITY
                        property = <"mass">
                        units = <"kg">
                        magnitude = <|0.0..10.0|>
      } } } } } } } } }
      state matches {0..1} matches {
        List[at0008] matches { -- state structure
          items cardinality matches {1..1; ordered} matches {
            ELEMENT[at0009] occurrences matches {0..*} matches {
            -- Clothing
              value matches {
                CODED_TEXT matches {
                  code matches {[local::
                  at0010, -- Dressed
                  at0011] -- Naked
                  }
                  assumed_value matches {"at0011"}
      } } } } } }
      other_participations matches {0..1} matches{
        List [at0014] matches { -- participation structure
          items cardinality matches {1..1; ordered} matches {
            PARTIPICATION [at0012] matches{ --Baby
              function matches {
                CODED_TEXT matches {
                  code matches {
                  [local::at0013] -- Patient
                  }}}}}}}}    ...
```

Figure 4. An example body weight at birth HL7 archetype in ADL

```
archetype
        HL7-OBSERVATION.weight-birth.v1
specialize
        HL7-OBSERVATION.weight-birth.v1
concept
        [at0000.1] -- Body weight at birth
description
        author = <"Veli Bicer <veli@srdc.metu.edu.tr>">
        submission = <
                organisation = <"METU-SRDC">
                date = <2005-01-10>
        >
                version = <"version">
        status = <"draft">
        revision = <"1.0">
        description("en") = <
                purpose = <"Describe the observation for the body weight at birth">
                use = <"">
                misuse = <"">
        >
        adl_version = <"1.2">
        rights = <"">

definition
        Observation[at0000] matches { -- birth_weight
        classCode cardinality matches {1} matches {[hl7_ClassCode::OBS]}
        moodCode cardinality matches {1} matches {[hl7_ClassCode::EVN]}
        id matches {*}
                code cardinality matches {1} matches {[at0001],[at0002]}
        confidentialityCode cardinality matches {1..*} matches
        {[hl7_Confidentiality::N]}
        uncertaintyCode matches {[hl7_ActUncertainty::N]}
        value cardinality matches {1} matches {/.*kg[^ ]/}
        hasParticipation cardinality matches {1..*} matches{
          Participation matches{
            hasRole cardinality matches {1..*} matches{
              Patient{
                classCode cardinality matches {1} matches
                {[hl7_ClassCode::PAT]}
                player cardinality matches {1..*} matches{
                  Person matches{
                    classCode cardinality matches {1} matches
                    {[hl7_ClassCode::PSN]}
        }}}}}}
        }
        ...
```

Figure 4 depicts the body weight at birth ADL archetype based on the HL7 Version 3 Reference Information Model, whose OWL representation is presented in HL7 Body Weight at Birth Archetype OWL Definition (2005).

Ontology Mapping

In the Example OpenEHR and HL7 Archetypes in OWL subsection, we present ADL descriptions of two archetypes. As depicted in Figures 3 and 4, the archetypes differ in terms of structure and format of the data they represent. The main cause of this difference is that the archetypes refer to different reference models (i.e., openEHR RIM and HL7 RIM). Thus, the interoperability between these archetypes becomes a difficult task, although they represent the same concept — weight at birth.

ARTEMIS mediator provides an ontology mapping tool — OWLmt — that enables us to define the mapping between different OWL schemas. In this section, we describe an ontology mapping process in OWL to achieve the interoperability between the archetypes based on different reference models. Once such a mapping definition is stored at the mediator, the mediator will interoperate the Web service messages represented as archetypes between the health care institutes conforming to different EHR standards.

Ontology mapping is the process where two ontologies with an overlapping content are related at the conceptual level to produce a mapping definition. The source ontology instances then are automatically transformed into the target ontology instances according to the mapping definitions. The architecture of the OWLmt tool (see Figure 5) allows mapping patterns to be specified through a GUI. These patterns are stored in a document called Mapping Definition. The mapping engine uses the Mapping Definition to automatically transform source ontology instances into target ontology instances.

The OWLmt mapping tool has the following mapping capabilities:

- **Matching the source ontology classes to the target ontology classes:** We have developed the following four conceptual mapping patterns to represent the matching between the classes of the source and target ontology classes: EquivalentTo, SimilarTo, IntersectionOf, and UnionOf. The identical classes are mapped through EquivalentTo pattern. SimilarTo implies that the involved classes have overlapping content. As an example, the body weight at birth class which is a subclass of observation class in the openEHR archetype is similar to the birth weight, class which is inherited from the Observation class in the HL7 archetype, since they both represent the weight at birth concept. The SimilarTo patterns in OWLmt are represented in OWL (see Figure 6).

How similar classes are further related is described through property mapping patterns.

The IntersectionOf pattern creates the corresponding instances of the target class as the intersection of the declared source class instances. Similarly, the UnionOf pattern implies the union of the source classes' instances to create the corresponding instances of the target class.

In some cases, a class in a source ontology can be more general than a class in the target ontology. In this case, the instances of the source ontology that make up the instances of the target ontology are defined through knowledge interchange format (KIF) (2005) conditions to be executed by the mapping engine. As an example, assume that a SimilarTo pattern is defined between the body weight at birth class of the openEHR archetype and the birth weight class of HL7 archetype. The body weight at birth class in the openEHR archetype has a property state with the cardinality of zero or one (see Figure 3). On the other hand, the code property of the birth weight class of the HL7 archetype (see Figure 4) has either LOINC (2005) value of 8351-9 (weight at birth with clothes) or LOINC value of 8350-1 (weight at birth without clothes), depending on the value of the code value under the state property in the openEHR archetype. However, the code value is mandatory in the HL7 archetype, unlike the optionality of the state property in the openEHR. Therefore, we add a condition in KIF format to the SimilarTo pattern (see Figure 6) to ensure that there exists at least one state property of the body weight at birth instance in order to map it to an instance of birth weight class.

- **Matching the source ontology Object Properties to target ontology Object Properties:** ObjectPropertyTransform pattern is used to define the matching from one or more object properties in the source ontology to one or more object properties in the target ontology. As an example, consider the openEHR archetype in the Example OpenEHR and HL7 Archetypes in OWL subsection. According to the openEHR specifications (openEHR Architecture Specifications, 2005), the body weight at birth class has an other participations object property inherited from the Observation class, referring to a list of the Participation class in order to represent the parties that participate in the body weight at birth observation. With the help of this object property, we have defined a path from body weight at birth class to the PARTY REF in order to state the patient who is involved in this particular observation. Likewise, in the HL7 archetype, there is also a path from the birth weight class to the person with a set of object properties such as hasParticipation, hasRole, and player. Although these two paths have different structures and involve different properties (e.g., other participations and hasRole) and classes (e.g., List in openEHR and Patient in HL7), they represent the same content; that is, patient of an observation (see Figure 7). Therefore, in the mapping process, an ObjectPropertyTransform pattern is defined to match these paths to one another. These path expressions are stated as parameters in the ObjectPropertyTransform pattern in KIF format. For example, the path between the body weight at birth and PARTY REF can be represented in the source ontology through the following path: (rdf:type ?x Body weight at birth) (other participations ?x ?y) (rdf:type ?y List) (items ?y ?z) (rdf:type ?z PARTICIPATION) (performer ?z ?k) (rdf:type ?k PARTY REF).

This path corresponds to the following path in the target ontology: (rdf:type ?x birth weight) (hasParticipation ?x ?y) (rdf:type ?y Participation) (hasRole ?y ?z) (rdf:type ?z Patient) (player ?z ?k) (rdf:type ?k Person).

Through such patterns, the OWLmt constructs the specified paths among the instances of the target ontology in the execution step, based on the paths defined among the instances of the source ontology.

- **Matching source ontology Data Properties to target ontology Data Properties:** Through the DatatypePropertyTransform pattern, the data type properties of an instance in the source ontology are mapped to corresponding target ontology instance data type properties. OWLmt supports a set of basic XPath (XQuery 1.0 and XPath 2.0, 2004) functions and operators such as concat, split, and substring. In some cases, there is a further need for a programmatic approach in order to specify complex functions (e.g., need to use if-then-else, switch-case, or for-next). Therefore, we have introduced JavaScript support to OWLmt. By specifying the JavaScript to be used in the DatatypeProperty-Transform pattern, the complex functions (enriched by the Java SDK libraries) can be applied in the value transformations.

As an example, the OWL representations of the archetypes (see Figures 3 and 4) include data type properties that involve the same kind of data. For instance, units and magnitude data type properties in openEHR archetype correspond to the value data type property in the HL7 archetype. To map the values stored in units and magnitude data type properties to the value data type property, we state a Datatype PropertyTransform pattern. This pattern takes the paths of the data type properties units and magnitude in KIF format as input parameters and relates them to the value data type property. The basic concat operation is sufficient to concatenate the values stored in the units and magnitude and to assign the result to the value through the mapping engine.

There is also a relation between the code property, which states the clothing status of a patient in openEHR archetype, and the code property of the birth weight in the HL7 archetype. Based on the value of the code (e.g., naked or dressed) in openEHR archetype instance, the code data type property in HL7 archetype has either the LOINC value 8351-9 or the LOINC value 8350-1. To achieve such a mapping, the JavaScript code (see Figure 8) can be used in the DatatypePropertyTransform pattern.

Figure 5. Architecture of OWLmt

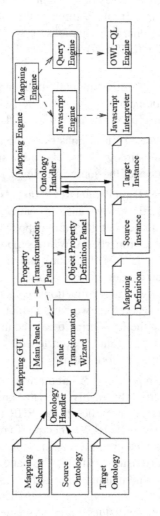

Once the mapping between two ontologies is specified by using the Mapping GUI, it can be serialized as a Mapping Definition in order to be used in the execution step as presented in the Transforming the Archetypes Instances subsection. The Mapping Definition itself is an OWL document whose structure is specified through Mapping Schema. In the mapping definition, the patterns are used to define the mappings

Figure 6. An example SimilarTo pattern

```
<SimilarTo rdf:about= "http://www.srdc.metu.edu.tr/Map#SimilarTo_1">
        <similarToInput rdf:resource= "http://www.sample.org/openEHRweight-
birth#Body_weight_at_birth"/>
        <similarToOutput rdf:resource= "http://www.sample.org/hl7weight-birth.owl#birth_weight"/>
        <operationName>SimilarTo_1</operationName>
        <Condition>(and (rdf:type ?x
                http://www.sample.org/openEHRweight-birth#Body_weight_at_birth)
                (state ?x ?y))
        </Condition>
...
</SimilarTo>
```

among the classes and properties of the source and target ontology. The patterns are also specified as OWL class instances in the Mapping Specification. As an example, SimilarTo pattern is shown in Figure 6.

However, the use of OWL as a mapping definition language has some shortcomings, as stated in Brujin and Polleres (2004). One of the shortcomings of using OWL as a mapping definition language is its tight coupling between the source and the target ontologies. A mapping definition needs to import other related (source and target) ontologies with owl:import. This results in a tight coupling between ontolo-

Figure 7. Mapping object properties

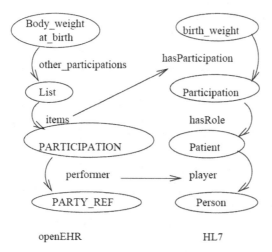

Figure 8. An example JavaScript

```
function copy_code(openEHR_code)
{
        if(openEHR_code.equals("Naked"))
        return "8351-9";
        else if(openEHR_code.equals(Dressed")
        return "8350-1";
}
```

gies, which is undesirable, because it makes one ontology dependent on another in the sense that axioms and definitions in one ontology use classes and properties from the other ontology. This can result in such things as the necessity to use the other externally specified ontology in order to perform certain local reasoning tasks (Brujin & Polleres, 2004).

Therefore, rather than using pure OWL, we specify queries in our mapping definition in OWL-QL KIF syntax which are then executed by the mapping engine. Furthermore, the value transformations also should be expressed in the Mapping Definition. We specify the value transformations as JavaScript strings of the DatatypePropertyTransform pattern.

Transforming the Archetype Instances

Consider the example presented in Figure 2. Hospital B, using the archetype instances based on HL7, wishes to invoke the Web service provided by Hospital A in order to receive the BirthWeight information for a patient. Through the Web service Invocation Interface provided by the ARTEMIS peer, Hospital B provides the Web service input as PatientInfo archetype instance based on HL7 RIM and wishes to receive the result as a BirthWeight archetype instance again based on HL7 RIM. Note that Hospital A has declared to the mediator that its Web service exchanges are based on OpenEHR archetypes. When the mediator invokes this Web service on behalf of Hospital B, the invocation tool in the mediator consults to the OWLmt Mapping Engine for transforming the archetype instances from source ontology to the target ontology. In this section, we detail how this instance transformation is achieved through the OWLmt mapping engine.

The OWLmt mapping engine creates the target archetype instances in OWL, using the mapping patterns in the Mapping Definition and the instances of the source archetype. It uses OWL Query Language (OWL-QL) (Fikes, Hayes, & Horrocks, 2003) to retrieve required data from the source ontology instances. While executing the

Figure 9. The state_structure class

```
<owl:Class rdf:ID="state_structure">
        <rdfs:subClassOf rdf:resource= "openEHR:List"/>
        <rdfs:subClassOf>
                <owl:Restriction rdf:ID="RestrictionOnitems">
                        <owl:allValuesFrom>
                                <owl:Class rdf:ID="Clothing">
                                        <rdfs:subClassOf rdf:resource= "openEHR:ELEMENT"/>
....
                                </owl:Class>
                        </owl:allValuesFrom>
                        <owl:onProperty>
                                <owl:ObjectProperty rdf:resource= "openEHR:items"/>
                        </owl:onProperty>
                </owl:Restriction>
        </rdfs:subClassOf>
        <rdfs:subClassOf>
                <owl:Restriction>``birth\_weight"
                        <owl:onProperty>
                                <owl:ObjectProperty rdf:resource="openEHR:items"/>
                        </owl:onProperty>
                        <owl:minCardinality rdf:datatype= http://www.w3.org/2001/XMLSchema#int">
                        0</owl:minCardinality>
                        <owl:maxCardinality rdf:datatype=http://www.w3.org/2001/XMLSchema#int">
                        1</owl:maxCardinality>
                </owl:Restriction>
        </rdfs:subClassOf>
</owl:Class>
```

class and property mapping patterns, the query strings defined through the mapping GUI are sent to the OWL-QL engine with the URL of the source ontology instances. The query engine executes the query strings and returns the query results.

During this process, OWL-QL uses the reasoning capabilities of Java theorem prover (JTP) (2005) to infer new facts from the source ontology and use them in order to construct the target ontology instance. To illustrate this, consider the archetypes introduced in the Example OpenEHR and HL7 Archetypes in OWL subsection. The range of the state object property of body weight at birth class in openEHR archetype is the state structure, which is a subclass of list and involves a restriction. State structure in OWL is depicted in Figure 9.

The items object property of state structure is involved in an owl:allValuesFrom restriction. Its range is stated to be the clothing class, as depicted in Figure 9.

The mapping engine uses the information in the source ontology to infer new knowledge at instance level. This new knowledge lets OWLmt obtain more accurate query results in the execution step. In the running example, the following rules are used to derive the fact that InferredInstance is an instance of the clothing: (rdf:type MyStateStructure state_structure) (rdfs:subClassOf state_structure RestrictionO-nitems) -> (rdf:type MyStateStructure RestrictionOnitems).

Figure 10. The openEHR archetype instance

```
<state_structure rdf:ID="MyStateStructure">
        <openEHR:items rdf:resource="#InferredInstance"/>
</state_structure>
```

Figure 11. Source instance

```
<Body_weight_at_birth rdf:ID="Instance1">
        <openEHR:state>
                <state_structure rdf:ID="Instance2">
                        <openEHR:items rdf:resource="#Instance3"/>
                </state_structure>
        </openEHR:state>
...
</Body_weight_at_birth>
<Clothing rdf:ID="Instance3">
        <openEHR:value>
                <openEHR:CODED_TEXT rdf:ID="Instance4">
                        <openEHR:code>Naked</openEHR:code>
                </openEHR:CODED_TEXT>
        </openEHR:value>
</Clothing>
```

This rule derives the fact that MyStateStructure has rdf:type of RestrictionOnitems. With the derivation of this fact, all the predicates of the following rule become true: (owl:onProperty RestrictionOnitems items) (owl:all ValuesFrom RestrictionOnitemsClothing) (rdf:type MyStateStructureRestriction Onitems) (items MyStateStructure MyClothingType) -> (rdf:type MyClothingType Clothing).

According to the data obtained by querying the source ontology instance, the OWLmt mapping engine executes the conceptual mapping patterns to create the corresponding instances in the target ontology. The conditions specified for each conceptual mapping pattern also are applied to ensure the accuracy in the mapping process. In this step, the instances that do not satisfy a particular condition in the pattern are discarded.

As an example, when the mapping engine executes the SimilarTo pattern (see Figure 6), the body weight at birth instance is obtained (see Figure 11) as a result of the query of the source instance. The mapping engine then creates the corresponding birth weight instance (see Figure 12) in the target ontology.

After the creation of the class instances in the target ontology, the property mapping patterns are applied to create the object and datatype properties for the instances in the target ontology. During the mapping of the datatype properties, the value

Figure 12. Target instance

```
<birth_weight rdf:ID="TInstance1">
        <HL7:code>8351-9</HL7:code>
...
</birth_weight>
```

transformations specified in the corresponding patterns are applied. OWLmt mapping engine uses JavaScript in order to transform the values from the source ontology to the target ontology programmatically. In order to achieve this, it sends the JavaScript specified in the corresponding property mapping pattern to the JavaScript Interpreter (RHINO, 2005) with the data obtained from the source ontology instance. The result from the execution of the JavaScript is set as the value of the datatype property in the target ontology. For example, as a result of executing the DatatypePropertyTransform pattern, which includes the JavaScript (see Figure 8), the code datatype property with LOINC code of 8351-9 (see Figure 12) is created in the target instance according to the naked value indicated in openEHR instance, as depicted in Figure 11.

As a result of these steps, the archetype instance based on the source RIM is transformed to the archetype instance, based on the target RIM, providing the interoperability of the Web services exchanging such messages.

Conclusion and Future Work

Web services have the capacity to bring many advantages to the health care domain, such as seamless integration of disparate health care applications conforming to different and, at times, competing standards. Also, Web services will extend the life of the existing health care software by exposing previously proprietary functions as Web services.

To the best of our knowledge, the ARTEMIS project is the first initiative to use semantically enriched Web services in the health care domain. In fact, only very recently did Web services start to appear in the medical domain. An important industry initiative to use Web services is integrating the health care enterprise (IHE) (IHE IT Infrastructure Integration Profiles, 2003). IHE has defined a few basic Web services, such as retrieve information for display integration profile (RID). Yet, since IHE does not address semantic issues, in order to use the IHE Web services, it is necessary to conform to their exact specification by calling the Web services with the names they have specified and by providing the messages as instructed in its specification.

However, given the complexity of the health care domain and the proliferation of standards and the terminologies to represent the same data, semantic annotation of the Web service messages is essential.

In this chapter, we describe how interoperability among different health care systems conforming to different EHR standards can be achieved by semantically annotating the Web service messages through archetypes. An archetype is a set of constraints on the generic EHR reference information model, which ensures that clinical concepts are correctly represented without actually storing them, since there are very many (more than 300,000) clinical concepts. The semantic differences among the archetypes are then handled through an OWL mapping tool that is developed.

As a future work, we plan to semantically annotate the IHE Web services that currently are being integrated into the ARTEMIS infrastructure. How IHE Web services are integrated to the ARTEMIS architecture is described in Aden and Eichelberg (2005).

Acknowledgment

This work is supported by the European Commission through IST-1-002103-STP ARTEMIS project and in part by the Scientific and Technical Research Council of Turkey (TÜB0TAK), Project No: EEEAG 104E013.

References

Aden, T., & Eichelberg, M. (2005). *Cross-enterprise search and access to clinical information based on IHE retrieve information for display.* Paper presented at EuroPACS-MIR 2005.

Archetype definition language 1.2 draft. (2003). Australia: Ocean Informatics, the OpenEHR Foundation.

ARTEMIS Consortium. (2004). The ARTEMIS Project. Retrieved from http://www.srdc.metu.edu.tr/webpage/projects/artemis

Baader, F., Horrocks, I., & Sattler, U. (2004). *Handbook on ontologies.* Description Logics.

Beale, T., & Heard, S. (2003). *Archetype definitions and principles* (Revision 0.5). Australia: Ocean Informatics, the OpenEHR Foundation.

Brujin, J., & Polleres, A. (2004). *Towards an ontology mapping specification language for the Semantic Web* (DERI Technical report).

Complete Blood Count Archetype ADL Definition. (2005). Retrieved from http://my.openehr.org/wsvn/knowledge/archetypes/dev/adl/openehr/ehr/entry/observation/openEHR-EHR-OBSERVATION.cbc.v1.adl?op=file&rev= 0&sc=0

CEN TC/251 prEN 13606-1, Health informatics electronic health record communication. Part 1: Reference model, draft for CEN enquiry. (2004). Brussels, Belgium: CEN/TC 251 Health Informatics, European Committee for Standardization.

Dogac, A., et al. (in press). ARTEMIS: Deploying semantically enriched Web services in the health care domain. *Information Systems Journal.*

Eichelberg, M., Aden, T., Dogac, A., & Laleci, G. B. (2005). *A survey and analysis of electronic health care record standards.* Unpublished manuscript.

Fikes, R., Hayes, P., & Horrocks, I. (2003). *OWL-QL: A language for deductive query answering on the Semantic Web* (Tech. Rep.). Stanford, CA: Stanford University, Knowledge Systems Laboratory.

Heard, S., Beale, T., Mori, A. R., & Pishec, O. (2003). *Templates and archetypes: How do we know what we are talking about* (Technical report).

HL7 Body Weight at Birth Archetype OWL Definition. (2005). Retrieved from http://www.srdc.metu.edu.tr/~veli/hl7_Weight_Birth_Archetype.owl

HL7 Clinical Document Architecture, Release 2.0 (HL7 v3 Standard). (2004). Ann Arbor, MI: Health Level Seven.

HL7 Template and Archetype Architecture Version 3.0 (Technical report). (2003). Health Level Seven Template Special Interest Group.

IHE IT Infrastructure Integration Profiles. (2003). *The key to integrated systems: integration profiles.* Oak Brook, IL: Integrating the Health Care Enterprise.

ISO TC/215. (2003). Health Informatics — requirements for an Electronic Health Record Architecture (ISO Technical Specification 18308). International Organization for Standardization, Health Informatics.

JTP. (2005). *Java Theorem Prover.* Retrieved from http://www.ksl.stanford.edu/software/JTP/

Kashyap, V., & Sheth, A. P. (1996). Semantic and schematic similarities between database objects: A context-based approach. *VLDB Journal, 5*(4), 276-304.

KIF. (2005). *Knowldge interchange format.* Retrieved from http://logic.stanford.edu/kif/kif.html

LOINC. (2005). *Logical observation identifiers names and codes* (Version 2.15). Indianapolis, IN: Regenstrief Institute.

openEHR Architecture Specifications. (2005). Retrieved from http://www.openehr. org/getting_started/t_openehr_primer.htm

openEHR Body Weight at Birth Archetype OWL Definition. (2005). Retrieved from http://www.srdc.metu.edu.tr/~veli/openEHRweight-birth.owl

openEHR Community. (2005). Retrieved from http://www.openehr.org/

OWL. (2004). Web ontology language. In *Proceedings of the World Wide Web Consortium.*

OWLmt. (2005). *OWL mapping tool.* Retrieved from http://www.srdc.metu.edu. tr/artemis/owlmt/

RHINO. (2005). *JavaScript for Java.* Retrieved from http://www.mozilla.org/ rhino/

Sheth, A. P., & Larsen, J. (1990). Federated database systems for managing distrib-uted, heterogeneous and autonomous databases. *ACM Computing Surveys: Special Issue on Heterogeneous Databases, 22*(3), 183-236.

SNOMED Clinical Terms. (2005). Retrieved from http://www.snomed.org/snomedct/ index.html

SOAP. (2003). Simple object access protocol (Version 1.2). In *Proceedings of the World Wide Web Consortium.*

WSDL. (2005). Web service description language (Version 2.0). Part 0: Primer (W3C Working Draft). In *Proceedings of the World Wide Web Consortium.*

XQuery 1.0 and XPath 2.0. (2004). *Functions and operators* (W3C Working Draft). Retrieved from http://www.w3.org/TR/xpath-functions/

The chapter was previously published in the International Journal on Semantic Web & Information Systems, 1(4), 1-23, October-December 2005.

About the Authors

Miltiadis Lytras holds a PhD from the Department of Management Science and Technology of the Athens University of Economics and Business (AUEB), Greece. His first degree was in informatics (AUEB, Greece) while his further studies include an MBA from AUEB as well as a postgraduate diploma in adult learning (Selete Patras). His research focuses on e-learning, knowledge management and the Semantic Web, with more than 35 publications in these areas. He is guest co-editing a special issue of the *International Journal of Distance Education Technologies* with the special theme "Knowledge Management Technologies for E-Learning" as well as one in the *IEEE Educational Technology and Society Journal* with the theme "Ontologies and the Semantic Web for E-Learning" (with Gerd Wagner, Paloma Diaz, Demetrios Sampson, Lisa Neal). In Greece, he has published the book *Knowledge Management and E-Learning*, while he co-edits with Professor Ambjorn Naeve the book *Intelligent Learning Infrastructures for Knowledge Intensive Organizations: A Semantic Web Perspective*. In early 2005, he published the authored book *Knowledge Management Strategies: Applied Technologies Handbook* with Idea Group Inc. He is the founder of the Semantic Web and Information Systems Special Interest Group in Association for Information Systems and serves on the SIG Board (www.sigsemis.org). He has been a program committee member in eight international conferences and serves on the editorial board of two international journals. His teaching experience, especially in adults seminars, exceeds 3,500 hours in themes including e-business, information systems, knowledge management, e-learning, IT skills and management. He has participated in 15 Greek and European funded projects.

Amit Sheth is an educator, researcher and entrepreneur. He joined the University of Georgia, USA, and started the LSDIS Lab in 1994. Earlier, he served in R&D groups at Bellcore (now Telcordia Technologies), Unisys, and Honeywell. In August 1999, Sheth founded Taalee, Inc., a VC funded enterprise software and Internet infrastructure startup based on the technology developed at the LSDIS lab. He managed Taalee as its CEO until June 2001. Following Taalee's acquisition/merger, he served as CTO and co-founder of Semagix, Inc. (formerly Voquette, Inc). His research has led to several commercial products and applications. He has published more than 175 papers and articles (in the areas of semantic interoperability, federated databases, workflow management, Semantic Web), given over 130 invited talks and colloquia including 19 keynotes, (co-)organized/chaired 12 conferences/workshops, and served on over 90 program committees. He is the co-editor-in-chief of the *International Journal on Semantic Web and Information Systems*, is on five journal editorial boards, is a member of the W3C Advisory Committee the Semantic Web Services Architecture committee. For more information, visit http://lsdis.cs.uga.edu/~amit and http://www.semagix.com/company_team.html.

* * *

Thomas Aden is a member of the Healthcare Information and Communication Systems R&D division at the OFFIS Research Institute in Oldenburg, Germany. He is a graduate of the Carl von Ossietzky University of Oldenburg where he received his MS in computer science (2001). His research topics in the field of medical informatics include data warehousing and data quality applications, in particular in the context of epidemiological cancer registration, as well as application of the Semantic Web in health care.

Anthony Aristar received his PhD in linguistics from the University of Texas (1984). He was a researcher at Microelectronics & Computer Technology Corporation, 1984-1989; an assistant professor, University of Australia, 1990-1991; an assistant professor, Texas A&M University, 1991-1995; and an associate professor, Texas A&M University, 1996-1998. He joined the Department of English at Wayne State University, USA, in 1998 where he is currently an associate professor. Dr. Aristar is chairman of the OLAC working group on language codes; moderator and founder of LINGUIST List; and organizer of several endangered languages related workshops.

Liviu Badea is a senior researcher and heads the artificial intelligence lab within the National Institute for Research and Development in Informatics, Romania. His main areas of research include: knowledge representation and reasoning, intelligent information integration, Semantic Web, bioinformatics, and machine learning.

Veli Bicer is an MS student at the Middle East Technical University (METU), Computer Engineering Department, Turkey, and a senior researcher at SRDC. His research interests include semantic interoperability, Web service technology, and health care informatics.

François Bry is currently investigating methods and applications emphasizing XML, semistructured data, document modelling, and query answering and reactivity on the Web. Formerly, he worked on knowledge representation, deductive databases, automated theorem proving, and logic programming. Since 1994, he has been full professor at the Institute for Informatics, University of Munich, Germany. From 1984-1993, he was with the European Computer-Industry Research Centre (ECRC), Munich. Before 1983, he worked in a few companies in Paris, among others on an early word processor. In 1981, he received a PhD from the University of Paris. He has been visiting at several universities and research centers. He has given invited talks at many major research centers, universities, and scientific conferences. He has contributed and contributes to scientific conferences as an author, program committee member or chairman. He has been or is involved in research projects founded by the European Commission (ESPRIT, FP6) and in doctoral schools founded by the German Foundation for Research (DFG). He is the scientific coordinator of the European Network of Excellence REWERSE (http://rewerse.net) launched by the European Commission in 2004.

Artem Chebotko is a PhD student in the Department of Computer Science at Wayne State University, USA. His research interests include databases and the Semantic Web. He is a student member of the IEEE.

Oscar Corcho has worked at iSOCO as a research manager since March 2004. Previously, he belonged to the Ontological Engineering Group of the AI Department of the Computer Science School, Universidad Politécnica de Madrid (UPM). He graduated in computer science from UPM in 2000 and received the third Spanish award in computer science from the Spanish Government. He obtained an MSc in software engineering from UPM (2001) and a PhD in artificial intelligence (2004). His research activities include ontology languages and tools, the ontology translation problem and the Semantic Web and grid. He has published the books *Ontological Engineering* and *A Layered Declarative Approach to Ontology Translation with Knowledge Preservation*. He has published more than 30 journal and conference/workshop papers on ontology languages and tools in important forums for the ontology community (ISWC, EKAW, KAW, KCAP, AI Magazine, IEEE Intelligent Systems), and reviews papers in many conferences, workshops and journals. He chaired the demo/industrial sessions at EKAW2002 and co-organised the ISWC2003 and ISWC2004 Workshops on Evaluation of Ontology Tools (EON2003, EON2004).

Matteo Cristani (PhD, computer science) is an assistant professor with the Department of Computer Science, Università di Verona, Italy. His main research interests are knowledge representation and ontology of physical systems. He published in outstanding international journals and recognized international conferences, such as *Artificial Intelligent*, *Journal of Artificial Intelligent Research*, *ECAI*, *KR*, and *IJCAI*.

Roberta Cuel (PhD, organizational studies) is a research fellow on knowledge management at the Università di Verona, Italy. Cuel's main interests include: the interdependencies between technologies and organizations — in particular, the impact (non impacts) of innovative technologies on teams, communities, and organizational models; the study of distributed tools and processes that allow organizational learning and knowledge management; knowledge representation systems and tools — such as ontologies, classifications, and taxonomies — as mechanisms for knowledge reification processes.

Yu Deng graduated from Wayne State University, USA, with an MS in computer science (2004). Her research interests include databases and the Semantic Web.

Asuman Dogac is a full professor with the Computer Engineering Department, Middle East Technical University (METU), Ankara, Turkey. She is founding director of the Software Research and Development Center (SRDC), METU. Her research interests include health care informatics, Web Services, and semantic interoperability.

Marco Eichelberg is a member of the Healthcare Information and Communication Systems R&D division at the OFFIS research institute in Oldenburg, Germany. He is a graduate of the Carl von Ossietzky University of Oldenburg. Dr. Eichelberg has been involved in research on telemedicine, applications of medical imaging and PACS, communication standards, conformance and interoperability as well as IT security for more than 10 years. He has actively contributed to standardisation in CEN/TC 251 and the DICOM committee. He is closely involved with the Integrating the Healthcare Enterprise (IHE) initiative, where he is currently acting as the technical manager for IHE in Germany.

Farshad Fotouhi received his PhD in computer science from Michigan State University in 1988. He joined the Faculty of Computer Science at Wayne State University, USA, in August 1988 where he is currently professor and chair of the department. Dr. Fotouhi major area of research is databases, including object-relational databases, multimedia information systems, bioinformatics, medical image databases and web-enabled databases. He has published more than 80 papers in refereed journals and conference proceedings, served as a program committee member of various database related conferences.

Tim Furche holds a master's degree in computer science from the University of Munich (2002). He is currently employed as a research assistant at the Institute for Computer Science, University of Munich, assisting in the coordination of the RE-WERSE working group on "reasoning-aware querying". His research interests are in XML and semistructured data, in particular query evaluation and optimization, and advanced Web systems. He has (co-)authored publications on characterizing, optimizing, and evaluating the W3C query language XPath and, more recently, on the use of XML query languages, in particular Xcerpt, for querying Semantic Web data.

Asunción Gómez-Pérez is the director of the Ontological Engineering Group at UPM. She earned a BA in computer science (1990), an MSc in knowledge engineering (1991), and a PhD in computer science (1993) from the Universidad Politécnica de Madrid (UPM), Spain. She also has an MBA (1994) from the Universidad Pontificia de Comillas. From 1994 to 1995, she visited the Knowledge Systems Laboratory at Stanford University. She is an associate professor at the Computer Science School at UPM. From 1995 to 1998 she was executive director of the Artificial Intelligence Laboratory at the school. She is currently a research advisor of the same lab. Her current research activities include, among others: interoperability between different kinds of ontology development tools; methodologies and tools for building and merging ontologies; ontological reengineering; ontology evaluation; and ontology evolution, as well as uses of ontologies in applications related with Semantic Web, e-commerce and knowledge management. She has published more than 100 papers on the above issues. She has led several national and international projects related to ontologies funded by various institutions and/or companies. She is the author of one book on ontological engineering and is co-author of a book on knowledge engineering. She was the co-director and local organiser of the first and second European summer schools on ontologies and the Semantic Web, and chair of the 13th International Conference on Knowledge Acquisition and Management (EKAW-02). She has been co-organizer of the workshops and conferences on ontologies at ECAI-04, IJCAI-03, ECAI-02, IJCAI-01, ECAI-00, IJCAI-99, ECAI-98, SSS-97 and ECAI-96. She has taught tutorials on ontological engineering at ECAI-04, ECAI-98, SEKE-97 and CAEPIA-97. She acts as reviewer in many conferences and journals.

James Hendler is a professor at the University of Maryland, USA, and director of Semantic Web and agent technology at the Maryland Information and Network Dynamics Laboratory. He has joint appointments in the Department of Computer

Science, the Institute for Advanced Computer Studies and is affiliated with the Institute for Systems Research. One of the inventors of the "Semantic Web," Hendler was the recipient of a 1995 Fulbright Foundation Fellowship and is a fellow of the American Association for Artificial Intelligence.

Kevin Hughes is a member of the Department of Surgical Oncology at the Massachusetts General Hospital, USA, where he is the surgical director of the Breast Screening Program, surgical director of the Breast and Ovarian Cancer Genetics and Risk Assessment Program, and co-director of the Avon Comprehensive Breast Evaluation Center. He is a graduate of Dartmouth College and Medical School, and trained at Mercy Hospital of Pittsburgh for general surgery. He did a fellowship in surgical oncology at the National Cancer Institute. Dr. Hughes is an assistant professor of surgery at Harvard Medical School and was formerly on the faculty of Tufts University, the University of California, Davis and Brown University. Dr. Hughes has served on numerous national and regional committees and is actively involved in research regarding the genetics, screening, and diagnosis and treatment of breast cancer. He is the author of numerous papers and book chapters on the subjects of breast cancer, screening, diagnosis and treatment, and risk assessment.

Lakshmi Iyer is a faculty member in the Information Systems and Operations Management Department at The University of North Carolina at Greensboro, USA. She obtained her PhD from the University of Georgia, Athens. Her research interests are in the area of electronic commerce, global issues in IS, intelligent agents, decision support systems, knowledge management, and cluster analysis. Her research work has been published or accepted for publication in *CACM*, *eService Journal*, *Annals of OR*, *DSS*, *Journal of Global Information Technology Management*, *Journal of Scientific & Industrial Research*, *Encyclopedia of ORMS*, *Journal of Information Technology Management*, *Journal of Data Warehousing*, and *Industrial Management and Data Systems*.

Aditya Kalyanpur is a PhD student at the University of Maryland, USA, and a GRA at MINDSWAP. His research interests broadly lie in ontology engineering for the Semantic Web with a focus on tool support for editing, refactoring, annotating, searching, and debugging ontology data. He is also the principal author of SWOOP.

Olena Kaykova, 1960, received her engineer-system-analytic degree on automatic control systems from Kharkov State Technical University of Radioelectronics (Kh-NURE) (1982). She became a candidate of technical sciences in 1989 on technical cybernetics and information theory. She was acting as docent of the Software Department (1992), docent of the Department of Artificial Intelligence and Information Systems (1997), and docent of the Artificial Intelligence Department (1999). She was acting as deputy vice-rector on international research co-operation since 1996 and since 1999 has been co-ordinator of international and European affairs in Kh-NURE. Her area of research interests include: artificial intelligence: logic, temporal reasoning, AI and statistics. She is the director of the Metaintelligence Laboratory in KhNURE, the co-ordinator of the co-operation and exchange program with the University of Jyväskylä (Finland). Until recently, she had been acting as a study advisor on mobile computing in the MSc program at the University of Jyväskylä (October 2000). Since January 2003 she has been a member of the 'Industrial Ontologies Group' research group. She has nearly 40 scientific publications — 10 of which are in internationally recognised magazines and conferences.

Oleksiy Khriyenko obtained his engineer's degree in computer sciences (a study line is intelligent decision support systems) in June 2003 from the Kharkov National University of Radioelectronics (KhNURE), Ukraine. He is also involved with the Master of Science, Department of Mathematical Information Technology (a study line is mobile computing). He obtained this degree in December 2003 from the University of Jyväskylä, Finland. Now he is a postgraduate student with the Department of Mathematical Information Technology (University of Jyväskylä). He has been a member of the 'Industrial Ontologies Group' research group (http://www.cs.jyu.fi/ai/OntoGroup/) since January 2003 and a researcher with the Agora Center (research center in Jyväskylä). His research interests include: artificial intelligence, Semantic Web, agent technology, Web-services, distributed resource integration, context aware adaptive environments and the industrial application of these and new mobile technologies.

Ozgur Kilic recevied a BS in computer engineering in 1998 from the Bilkent University. He recevied an MS in computer engineering in 2001 from the Middle East Technical University (METU), Turkey. He is currently a PhD student in computer engineering at the Middle East Technical University.

Christoph Koch is an assistant professor at Vienna University of Technology, Austria. His research mainly focuses on databases theory and systems.

Dmytro Kovtun graduated from the National Mining Academy of Ukraine (mine surveying line) in 1995. In 2003 he graduated from Kharkov National University of Radioelectronics, Ukraine (intelligent decision support systems line). In 2004 he graduated from the University of Jyväskylä, Finland (mobile computing line). His career is in the area of information technologies and was started in 1999 with the

IT Department, PJSC "Ordzhonikidzevsky GOK", Ukraine. His current activities belong to domain of mobile computing, wireless sensor networks and are related to issues of positioning and localization of mobile nodes.

Gokce B. Laleci is a PhD candidate at Middle East Technical University (METU), Computer Engineering Department, Turkey, and a senior researcher at SRDC. Her research interests include Semantic Web, Web service technology, and health care informatics.

Shiyong Lu received his PhD in computer science from the State University of New York at Stony Brook (2002). He is currently an assistant professor of the Department of Computer Science, Wayne State University (USA). His research interests include databases, the Semantic Web and bioinformatics. He has published more than 30 papers in top international conferences and journals in the above areas. He is a member of the IEEE.

Ambjörn Naeve (www.nada.kth.se/~amb) has a background in mathematics and computer science and earned his PhD in computer science from KTH in 1993. He is presently the coordinator of research on interactive learning environments and the Semantic Web at the School of Computer Science and Communication (Nada) at the Royal Institute of Technology (KTH) in Stockholm, Sweden, where he heads the Knowledge Management Research group (KMR: http://kmr.nada.kth.se). He has been involved with research and development of interactive learning environments since he initiated the Garden of Knowledge project at Nada in 1996. He has also taught mathematics at KTH since 1967 and in the last two decades he has headed the development of several tools for ICT-enhanced mathematics education (http://kmr.nada.kth.se/math). Ambjörn Naeve is also a well-known industry consultant with extensive experience in various forms of modeling for software engineering and business applications. He has invented the concept browser Conzilla (www.conzilla.org) and has developed a modeling technique called Unified Language Modeling (http://kmr.nada.kth.se/cm), based on UML, which has been designed to "draw how we talk about things," (i.e., to depict conceptual relationships in a linguistically coherent way). Over the last decade the KMR group has developed an information architecture (the Knowledge Manifold), an infrastructure (Edutella), two frameworks (SCAM and SHAME) and a number of tools (Formulator, Meditor, VWE, Confolio and Conzilla). These items should be considered as contributions towards a publicly accessible Knowledge and Learning Management Environment, based on open source and open international ICT standards as well as on Semantic Web technology. The KMR group is active within several international networks for technology-enhanced learning and Semantic Web, notably WGLN, Prolearn, SIGSEMIS, and Sakai.

Anton Naumenko is currently working as a researcher at the Agora Center, University of Jyväskylä (JYU), Finland. He has a Master of Science in IT from JYU and in computer science from Kharkov National University of Radioelectronics (KhNURE). He also earned a Bachelor of Economics from KhNURE. In 2004, he started postgraduate education with the JYU Faculty of Information Technology. Anton's professional career started in KhNURE with a position of technician (2000) and he is currently a leader of a software development team and a researcher in SmartResource project. He recently participated in an adaptive services grid integrated project supported by the European Commission. His expertise and interests consist of Semantic Web, agent technologies, object-oriented software design, information management systems, system analysis, and access control models.

Bijan Parsia is a research philosopher at the University of Maryland, USA, specializing in the Semantic Web, description logics, epistemology, oppression theory, AI planning, and the philosophy of mathematics and computer science.

Cartic Ramakrishnan is a PhD student in computer science at the University of Georgia, USA. He graduated from the Univeristy of Pune, India, with a BE in computer engineering. He is currently working at the Large Scale Distributed Information Systems (LSDIS) Lab, University of Georgia. He leads the research efforts in ontology learning and semantic association discovery with other members at the LSDIS lab.

A. F. Salam is a faculty member in the Information Systems and Operations Management Department at The University of North Carolina at Greensboro, USA. He earned both his MBA and PhD degrees from the State University of New York at Buffalo. His research interests include e-business and emerging technologies, intelligent systems in e-business, and information technology management. His research has been published or accepted for publication in *CACM*, *Information & Management*, *eService Journal*, *CAIS*, *Information Systems Journal*, and *Journal of Information Technology Cases and Applications*. He has served as co-guest editor of a special issue of the *JECR* and a special section on Internet and marketing in the *CACM*.

Sebastian Schaffert holds a PhD in computer science from the University of Munich, Germany (2004). He is currently employed as a teaching and research assistant at the Institute for Computer Science, University of Munich. His research interests are in XML and semistructured data, as well as functional and logic programming. He has several publications on the language Xcerpt and related topics. Besides this, Sebastian is interested in Linu and Open Source software.

Amnon Shabo (Shvo), PhD, works at IBM Research Lab in Haifa as a research staff member and is involved in various health care and life sciences projects. He is a co-chair and the modeling facilitator of the Clinical Genomics Special Interest Group in HL7 (an ANSI-accredited Standards Development Organization in health care), and a co-editor of the HL7 CDA Release 2 standard for clinical documents. In addition, Amnon specializes in longitudinal and cross-institutional Electronic Health Records (EHR). Amnon was the visionary and a co-author of the mEHR proposal made by a consortium of nineteen partners to the European Commission's Sixth Framework Program, based on his vision of Independent Health Records Banks for addressing the lifetime EHR sustainability challenge. In his academic studies he has built on his BSc degrees in biology, mathematics, and computer sciences to conduct research at the Hebrew University of Jerusalem in the areas of educational technology for biology and medicine, as well cognitive sciences and case-based reasoning through his postdoc research at the College of Computing of Georgia Institute of Technology in the USA. Amnon has extensive experience in education through 20 years of teaching basic programming to life sciences university students.

Rahul Singh is a faculty member in the Information Systems and Operations Management Department at The University of North Carolina at Greensboro, USA. He obtained his PhD in business administration from Virginia Commonwealth University. His research interests are in the area of the design of systems that apply intelligent technologies to business decision systems. Specific interests include intelligent agents, knowledge management systems, data mining and machine learning systems. His research work has been published, or accepted for publication in *CACM, eService Journal, Information Resources Management Journal, Journal of Decision Systems, International Journal of Production Engineering Socio-Economic Planning Sciences* and *The Encyclopedia of Information Systems*.

Vagan Terziyan received his engineer-mathematician degree in applied mathematics from Kharkov National University of Radioelectronics (1981). He became a Candidate of Technical Sciences (DrTech equivalent) in 1985 and a Doctor of Technical Sciences in 1993 (Dr Habil Tech equivalent) with the Software Engineering Department. He is acting as professor on software engineering (1994) and as head of the Department of Artificial Intelligence (1997). His area of research interests and teaching includes but are not limited by the following: intelligent Web applications, distributed AI, agents, multiagent systems and agent-oriented software engineering, Semantic Web and Web services, peer-to-peer, knowledge management, knowledge discovery and machine learning, and mobile electronic commerce. Recently he has been working as an associate professor with the MIT Department, University of Jyväskylä, Finland, and as a senior researcher and team leader at the SmartResource (Proactive Self-Maintained Resources in Semantic Web) TEKES Project in Agora

Centre and head of "Industrial Ontologies Group." He has more than 100 scientific publications, more than half of them in internationally recognised magazines and conferences.

Wilfried Thoben is the director of the Healthcare Information and Communication Systems R & D division at the OFFIS research institute in Oldenburg, Germany. He is a graduate of Friedrich-Alexander-University Erlangen-Nürnberg where he received his MS in computer science in 1993. Dr. Thoben received his PhD in computer science from the Carl von Ossietzky University of Oldenburg, Germany in 1999. His research topics include security of workflow based applications and epidemiological cancer registration. Since 2001 he is also CEO of the OFFIS CARE GmbH, a spin-off of OFFIS that is responsible for the cancer registry Lower-Saxony.

Christopher Thomas is a PhD student in the LSDIS lab, University of Georgia, USA. His academic background is computer science and artificial intelligence. His main research focus is semantics, knowledge representation and reasoning. Recently he has been working in the field of computational biochemistry to develop ontologies and reasoning mechanisms suitable for the complex carbohydrate domain. His research in representation of uncertain, incomplete and partially inconsistent knowledge is geared towards developing formalism that can be applied beyond the life sciences domain in all Semantic Web areas.

Andriy Zharko graduated from the Kharkov National University of Radielectronics in June 2003 with a Diploma of Engineer in intelligent decision support systems. In December 2003 he successfully finished the Master's program at the University of Jyvaskyla, Finland, Department of Mathematical Information Technology, where he obtained a degree of Master of Science in mobile computing study line with the highest grade. Additionally, he obtained Excellent Master's Thesis Award in 2004. He has also been a member of the "Industrial Ontologies Group" research group since January 2003 and a researcher at the Agora Research Center, University of Jyväskylä, Finland. In the beginning of 2004, he started his postgraduate studies with the MIT Department with a topic "Active Resources in Semantic Web." His research is concerned with peer-to-peer Semantic Web based large-scale systems combined with agent-oriented analysis. The main research activities are carried out within the SmartResource Tekes project.

Index